In
Search
of
God

—— A Quest for Truth

Warren Henderson

In Search of God – A Quest for Truth
By Warren Henderson
Copyright © 2007

Published by Warren Henderson
P.O. Box 416
Colfax, WI 54730

Cover Design by John Nicholson

ISBN 978-0-9795387-0-4

ORDERING INFORMATION:
Case quantities of *In Search of God* may
be purchased for $4.00/book through
Grace and Truth, Inc. Individual copies
may be obtained from Gospel Folio Press
or various on-line book retailers.

Gospel Folio Press
Phone: 1-800-952-2382
Website: order@gospelfolio.com

Grace and Truth, Inc.
Phone: 217-442-1120
Website: www.gtpress.org
(Case quantities only)

Printed in the United States of America

Table of Contents

Preface

At the writing of this book, I have a son, a daughter, and several friends attending institutions of higher learning. Judging from their reports and from what I read in various publications, it would seem that many secular universities outwardly uphold multicultural policies, free speech, and religious equality, yet allow guerrilla warfare to be waged against Christianity in the classroom. The attack is not focused on religion per se, for accommodations are made for many religious groups, but on the essence of biblical Christianity – the work, the word, and the person of Jesus Christ.

Some instructors seem more focused on divesting students of their Christian faith than on teaching the assigned curriculum. One professor flatly declared to my daughter's English class that Christianity was "an oppressive religion," and then proceeded to mock the doctrine of the Trinity by asking the class why there wasn't "God the Mother" since Christians believe in God the Father and God the Son. How these statements fit within a college English course is dumbfounding. Another professor, teaching Ethics, quoted a verse from the Old Testament, compared it to one verse in the New Testament which seemed to be contradictory, and concluded that the entire Bible was inconsistent and, therefore, could not be trusted as a standard for morality. He completely ignored the truth of all Scripture and proper rules of interpreting Scripture, such as understanding context, the setting, the audience, etc.

I am deeply concerned that those attending government-controlled educational institutions are being adversely affected by a steady diet of atheistic propaganda without an opportunity to consider a wider range of evidence for supernatural cause. Charles Darwin noted that objectivity is critical to a "fair" investigation of the facts, "A fair result can be obtained only by *fully* stating and balancing the facts and arguments on both sides of the question."[1] Have you sought a "fair result" by thoroughly considering all the evidence for the supernatural realm, or are you simply content to live out your life clutching a one-sided argument?

If you presently hold to a supernatural-denying worldview, please know that I value you greatly as a fellow human being and would ask you to objectively ponder the information contained in this book. There is no room for derogatory language, browbeating, or the like when people are sharing ideas, discussing facts and reasoning out conclusions. I am a Christian; I am not hiding that fact, my bias, or my concern for you. From the start you know where I stand. In the pursuit of balance, the following pages contain far more quotations from materialists and naturalists holding atheistic or agnostic positions than from those favoring some form of creationism (Theistic, Deistic, Christian, etc.). If you are a Christian attending a secular university or are in frequent company with skeptics, you will find this book helpful for graciously and respectfully dialoguing with others concerning your faith.

Is there legitimate evidence for the supernatural realm? If so, who originated such influences? If there is a God, how can we be sure that the Bible is His message to mankind? Is the Bible we have today authentic, and can we trust what it says? What advantage does Christianity have over the religions of the world? These questions and others will be posed and rationally addressed.

Dear reader, please examine the evidence and determine for yourself if *biblical* Christianity is a logical choice. If the Christian message is true, eternity is a very long time to suffer for ignorance. Why not invest a few moments now to think about your eternal destiny? Do you know where you will spend eternity?

— Warren Henderson

Within Reason

John Drummond once wrote, "He who will not reason is a bigot; he who cannot is a fool; and he who dares not, is a slave."[1] Man possesses five senses to observe the rudiments of time and space, and an intellect to reason out sensible conclusions about his physical surroundings. But how does one rightly scrutinize that which is, naturally speaking, indiscernible? Is it possible for man, through natural observation, to explore a supernatural realm?

Human history has shown that reasoning from few observations yields fanciful variations of perceived truth, while more information allows man to better converge on actual reality. While visiting a remote village in central China, an impoverished man once expressed to me his astonishment to learn that all people worldwide did not eat with chopsticks. Because his information was limited, his conclusion was misguided. More information does allow for more accurate determinations; but perfect conclusions require absolute information and the flawless understanding of it.

Consequently, science will *almost* be able to explain the physical realm through empirical reasoning but will be unable to afford any explanation for the supernatural realm; for this domain, if it does exist, would defy sensory validation. The scientific viewpoint of reality is, "you can't know what you cannot measure." With this understanding the following question is posed for the reader to consider: Though science cannot *validate* the supernatural realm, is it possible for science to *identify* supernatural phenomenon? If the answer to this question is "yes," how would man logically determine supernatural influence within natural order, and what ideologies would hinder man from understanding such evidence? The remainder of this chapter pursues a reasonable answer to these important questions. If your answer to the initial question is "no," have you not closed your mind to any and all possible expressions of supernatural cause? Please consider the evidence before concluding the matter.

What is Truth?

What is real? What is knowable? What is truth? Perhaps silly questions to some, but at the heart of these inquires is the basis for human philosophy. Those who consider nature to be all there is are referred to as *naturalists*, while those who believe that something else exists besides nature are called *supernaturalists*.

The naturalist believes only nature itself is real; it is everything and the cause of everything. The supernaturalist believes that there was an initial personal cause to create nature and an ongoing influence to sustain it (the deist may disagree) – creation order then refers to man's discernable reality. For the naturalist, random accidents and predictable (but not necessarily understood) natural causes delineate natural law – the constitution of reality by which all things exist. However, the supernaturalist generally believes that though nature operates according to foundational laws, there is a supreme consciousness which transcends and intervenes in nature with wisdom and power beyond natural understanding. Yet, how may such a metaphysical understanding of the universe be empirically verified through naturalistic means? This is quite a difficult task given that these two ontological worldviews conceptually oppose one another.

It behooves us then, before embarking on the academic journey of searching for the supernatural, to first contemplate a logical approach for detecting and identifying it; otherwise, we will have no means of determining success. By definition, *philosophy* is a study which processes known information in an attempt to quantify truth. But what is truth? Normally, we speak of truth as that which conforms to fact or reality; however, some use truth to more freely infer a sincere statement. Reality exists independently of our understanding of it. Because man is neither omniscient nor omnipresent he cannot completely understand what reality is through *natural* logical means. Consequently, no amount of human effort and mental exercise can enable man to fully and accurately know everything there is to know. With this limitation stated, the difficulty of posing a viable, logical and scientific approach for searching out God and the supernatural is self-evident. Whatever is naturally developed will be imperfect, meaning we need supernatural help to understand what truth really is.

Science and Reasonable Proof

As science is the study of the natural world, it stands to reason that science will not be able to prove what is not natural – the existence of God for example. God is not nature; though He supernaturally dwells within and beyond nature. We turn to science to learn about nature, not to determine if there is anything else but nature. This limitation constrains the extent that science should be used. On this subject, Mike Pool of King's College, University of London, poses this essay question, "Is Science the Ultimate Test?" This is his answer:

> In the early 20th century, some scientists and philosophers thought so. But, curiously, science itself turned out to be the first victim of this way of thinking. This is because, in order to get started, science has to make certain assumptions that cannot be proved scientifically. They are:

Rationality – that our thinking processes are basically reliable. (This assumption is needed in every area of life – even to discuss rationality!)

Orderliness – that there is an order to be discovered in nature – otherwise why do science at all?

Intelligibility – that our minds are able to discover this order.

Uniformity – that doing exactly the same experiment twice gives the same results. The scientific enterprise would be impossible without the assumption that there is a general uniformity in nature.

These basic beliefs, necessary for science, can't be proved scientifically, so any idea that science is the final court of appeal for everything we believe shoots itself in the foot![2]

With this understanding it should be equally evident that science cannot prove atheism. Even dogmatic atheistic-evolutionist Richard Dawkins admits that atheism cannot be proved to be true, "Of course we can't prove that there isn't a God."[3] Not only can science not prove or disprove God's existence, many scientists are content not to see supernatural cause in nature no matter how much proof is available. A professor in the Department of Biology at Kansas State University admitted, "Even if all the data point to an intelligent designer, such a hypothesis is excluded from science because it is not naturalistic."[4] Although science will be unable to *validate* supernatural cause, I do believe science can be effectively used to *identify* supernatural cause within natural order; I will explain later.

Human Reasoning

Man has developed systems of logic, namely *induction*, *deduction*, *abduction*, and various integral forms of these to explore absolute truth to the degree feasible. Reason, statistical analysis, observation, demonstration, mathematical modeling, etc. all have their part in man's quest for determining the truth about himself and his surroundings. The limitation with each of these synthetic logic systems is that each originates with man and is thus governed by imperfect reasoning. As man cannot naturally know absolute truth, it stands to reason that man's devices to pursue truth will be imperfect also. The conclusion of a deductive argument is only true if the premises are perfect; but how does one validate perfection? If a divine being who truly transcends natural order does exist, any imperfect reasoning system constrained by natural law would then be inconclusive in validating His existence. *Appendix I – Imperfect Logic* contains a detailed discussion of this subject matter.

In summary, humanistic science narrows in on absolute truth to the degree that methodical naturalism will allow observation and verification. Though some form of induction seems neces-sary to advance the cause of science, and is indeed necessary for man to progress through day-to-day life, accurate induction or abduction does not exist because man cannot discover absolute reality by himself. Even if one piece of the natural order puzzle is unknown, there will be varying degrees of error as to what the full picture actually is. Falsification is not absolute either and, therefore, can only predict with a certain degree of correctness what the whole picture is not. Consequently, no form of *human-derived* methodology can either prove or disprove supernatural existence with 100 percent certainty, or completely prove or dis-prove laws governing natural existence for that matter.

Comprehensive reasoning of true premises usually will yield sound, but imperfect conclusions. Consequently, it is illogical for the skeptic to demand 100 percent proof of supernatural cause, when no such humanized system of validation exists for natural cause. What evidence for supernatural cause should be considered realistic? Sound arguments and good reasoning.

Logic and Naturalism

A more technical definition of supernaturalism is: the conviction of a transcendent, non-natural dimension of reality (i.e. a spiritual domain) from where a transcendent, non-natural consciousness influences natural order. How does the lack of precise validation then pertain to the various forms of naturalistic and supernaturalistic study?

Metaphysical Naturalism, sometimes called *Philosophical Naturalism,* assumes an ontological approach to natural order (i.e. what is real in nature) where the existence of supernatural influence is logically denied; by definition, strong atheism is a binding (some say blinding) mindset. *Methodological Naturalism* assumes that science must look to natural cause and effect (including random dynamics) in lieu of supernatural cause and effect for naturalized science to be successful. Steven D. Schafersman clarifies the meaning of methodological naturalism:

> [Methodological Naturalism is] the adoption or assumption of philosophical naturalism within scientific method with or without fully accepting or believing it … science is not metaphysical and does not depend on the ultimate truth of any metaphysics for its success (although science does have metaphysical implications), but methodological naturalism must be adopted as a strategy or working hypothesis for science to succeed. We may therefore be agnostic about the ultimate truth of naturalism, but must nevertheless adopt it and investigate nature as if nature is all that there is.[5]

Methodological Naturalism says nothing about the existence or nonexistence of the supernatural, as the supernatural would be beyond natural verification. Robert T. Pennock explains why, from a humanistic standpoint, science must logically rule out supernatural recourse:

[Supernatural agents] are above and beyond the natural world...[and] are not constrained by natural laws.... If we could apply natural knowledge to understand supernatural powers, then, by definition, they would not be supernatural .... Experimentation requires observation and control of the variables .... But by definition we have no control over supernatural entities or forces.[6]

Rationally speaking, what is the result of methodological naturalistic science? What is the logical result of a scientific method which insists that the natural world is a closed system composed of permanent and unalterable laws? First, a wealth of developing information with varying degrees of imperfections is realized. Second, its internalized epistemology precludes the recognition of supernatural influence, which may or may not be present as a stimulus within natural order.

Man, from his limited vantage point, cannot perceive all available evidence which might validate supernatural cause in natural order or falsify (discredit) phenomena as being supernatural in origin. Even if one adopts Methodological Naturalism as a framework for science, it is irrational to close one's mind to the possibility of supernaturalism. Additionally, God being supernatural would transcend the physical realm; consequently, validation or falsification through a time and space dependent means would be insufficient to detect the supernatural realm, *unless God chose to reveal Himself within natural law*.

Just because an observable irregularity can be scientifically identified and perhaps explained by known natural law, it does not exclude it from being supernatural in origin. If God does exist, this would be His primary means of communicating with mankind, and the only means by which man, in the physical world, could discover God. Can science logically presuppose what is discoverable before it has been discovered? The crux of naturalism is this: We do not want to discover the supernatural; we do not need the supernatural; we can do a sufficient job of defining ourselves and our environment without any outside help. We don't need God. Thus, man's knowledge becomes superficial, enslaved by materialistic paradigms, a mere abstract of absolute truth! Through exclusive naturalism, man locks himself into a diminished reality with no practical reason to live, nor to stride out with confidence of a better future; man has no reason to hope.

David Hume promoted practical skepticism based on common sense where the inevitability of induction is accepted but could not be emphatically trusted. Einstein and Topper affirmed that no logical path leads to the discovery of the universal laws of nature. These conclusions are the predictable fallout of naturalistic science. The random chance development of natural order produces random chance reasoning which, therefore, cannot be fully trusted. Additionally, until naturalism defines an initial natural cause, its reasoning remains suspect. How can rational reasoning be based upon an unknown or non-rational or random cause? Even if such perchance reasoning could hypothetically render a valid conclusion, there would be no means to prove it valid without complete knowledge. Consequently, even if naturalism were factual, *perchance* reasoning derived from it, could never be trusted to validate it as such. Therefore, reasoning from a naturalistic standpoint, for all of the above reasons, can neither emphatically prove nor disprove naturalism.

If this conclusion is true, how much more preventive would human methodology be in proving God's existence through an empirical procedure? How is it possible to validate or disprove the validity of what cannot be known through scientific investigation alone? It is impossible. Yet this conclusion does not mean that supernaturalism is illogical. On this point, Barbara Forrest writes:

The fact that there is no successful *procedure* for knowing the supernatural does not logically preclude its being known *at all*, i.e., through intuition or revelation. The problem is that there is no *procedure* for determining the legitimacy of intuition and revelation as ways of knowing, and no *procedure* for either confirming or disconfirming the supernatural content of intuitions or revelations.[7]

It seems plausible to assume that a mysterious invisible realm of influence exists in human relativity, which man may at times detect, but cannot validate. If these unique influences do exist and are indeed beyond human comprehension, all logical arguments for or against their origin would be insufficient to prove anything categorically. Consequently, human reasoning will be prone to error in the explanation of observable phenomenon resulting from supernatural stimulus, if indeed it does exist. This is not to say man is not to think, but that he should not copiously trust what he thinks. Aristotle understood this point when he said, "It is the mark of an instructed mind to rest satisfied with the degree of precision which the nature of the subject admits and not to seek exactness when only an approximation of the truth is possible."[8]

On this point, philosophy and the Bible agree: Absolute truth is something to behold; it cannot fully be grasped through human reckoning alone. Consequently, if there is a God, man is going to need divine help to search Him out; in doing so man learns that truth is indeed unchanging and knowable. Without divine illumination, man's search for God would be similar to playing the children's game *hide and seek* in absolute darkness, with someone you don't know, who resides on the other side of the planet, and who does not want to be found. God will only be found by those who sincerely seek Him through avenues of truth He has revealed to man.

Identifying Supernatural Cause

The Bible does not set forth a proof for God's existence. Genesis 1:1 states, *"In the beginning God created the heavens and the earth."* The Bible declares that God exists, the consequences of which flows from deduction. If God chose not to supply a metaphysical proof of Himself in Scripture, why should man attempt to prove His existence? Accordingly, the focus of this book is not to prove God's existence (scientifically speaking, this is an impossible task), but rather, through systematic means, to attempt to *identify, evaluate,* and *explain* irregularities (unexplainable observations) within natural order by supernatural cause.

The following approach for accomplishing this goal is proposed:

(1) The application of science in the *identification* of certain anomalies within natural order for which there is no known natural explanation.

(2) The *evaluation* of such irregularities to ascertain the likelihood that such anomalies could be explained in the future by natural cause.

(3) Anomalies determined to have a very low likelihood of being naturally caused will be viewed as having *potential* supernatural cause, and a biblical *explanation* of the irregularity will be sought.

The approach has abductive form in that I am inferring various natural or supernatural causes from observed irregularities in order to determine the best explanation of such observations. In the same way that a physician must apply reason to diagnose a patient's illness from various symptoms, the reader is encouraged to diagnose the irregularity based on available information.

During the course of our search, I will provide evidence as to why I believe the Bible and not other self-proclaimed divine revelation should be used to investigate potential supernatural cause. It is noted that many naturally occurring phenomenon may have supernatural cause, but because these are readily explained by natural law, nothing is gained towards accomplishing the stated goal through their evaluation. The above uncomplicated approach seems to be a fair means of legitimately identifying *potential* supernatural intervention within the natural realm and of identifying *potential* reasons why such events did occur.

For those anomalies where natural law offers no explanation and is not likely to ever do so, I *believe* that an adequate supernatural explanation *may* be supplied by the Bible. If the Bible, which claims to be God's revelation to man, can supply a supernatural explanation for such irregularities within natural order, the reader must then decide by the agent of *faith* whether to trust in a feasible supernatural explanation (as derived from the Bible) or in an undefinable natural solution. In some cases yet to be determined, natural law is the right answer for observed irregularities within natural order, but not likely so for those which have been shown to have astronomically improbable natural cause. In other words, understood natural law indicates the proposition of natural cause for such baffling events is preventative. I readily concede that this is not a perfect approach for identifying supernatural cause in natural order, but I believe it is a reasonable one.

The Limitations of Philosophy

Modern philosophy considers reason and faith to be disassociated, but the Bible teaches that both must be exercised to know God and to understand truth. Philosophy teaches that these are conflicting agents – the former intellectual and the latter emotional. But is this true? Is there no common ground in which both faith and reason might labor together for a greater benefit than either could accomplish alone? What is the consequence of determining reality solely through a philosophical means?

Aristotle defined philosophy as a science that considers truth. Voltaire, an eighteenth century French philosopher and atheist alleged, "The truths of religion are never so well understood as by those who have lost the power of reasoning."[9] Twentieth century British mathematician and philosopher Bertrand Russell once proclaimed, "What is wanted is not the will to believe, but the will to find out, which is the exact opposite."[10] On another occasion he said:

> We may define 'faith' as the firm belief in something for which there is no evidence. Where there is evidence, no one speaks of 'faith.' We do not speak of faith that two and two are four or that the Earth is round. We only speak of faith when we wish to substitute emotion for evidence.[11]

In the pursuit of truth, much of modern philosophy, like modern science, shuns any supernatural cause as a workable explanation for disturbances within natural order. We live in a day when people do not know God and don't care to know Him. It is thought that to believe in the supernatural cripples the mind's ability to properly reason; *faith* of this sort is just an emotional crutch for the human psyche. Sigmund Freud viewed the existence of a Creator as desirable fabrication of man's deepest longings:

> It would be very nice if there were a God who created the world and was a benevolent providence, and if there were a moral order in the universe and an after-life; but it is a very striking fact that all this is exactly as we are bound to wish it to be.[12]

Like most skeptics, Freud believed that humans invented God out of necessity – as a means of fabricating a sense of comfort, hope, and security in a world full of suffering, uncertainties and disappointments. Logic does not favor this conclusion on at least two points. First, if the God of the Bible was invented to provide human comfort and hope, why would man fabricate such a demanding holy God who condemns those who sin. The God of the Bible demands a standing of perfection to merit heaven and to have fellowship with Him, yet no one's nature exhibits God's moral perfection as stated in the Bible. Behaving more morally upright than others is not sufficient to escape the punishment of a holy God. A holy God does not grade on a curve or forget unforgiven offenses; everyone is measured against His own perfect character. Why would man create such a demanding God which would inevitably condemn him? Where is the comfort and hope aspects of Freudian religion?

Secondly, experience counters Freud's supposition, for indeed a host of *make believe* characters instill feelings of joy and happiness within us as children, but later in life these figments of imagination lose their grip on our hearts. Why? Because we realize that Santa Claus, the Easter Bunny, and the tooth fairy do not exist. Mentally competent adults do not continue believing in fictitious characters, even if those characters once aroused sentimental or jubilant feelings within us. Obviously, if people believed in whatever would pump up their blissful emotions, many adults would still be looking for a fat man in a red suit each Christmas morning. By Freud's logic, the educated person should naturally outgrow God, yet many of the brightest scientists this world has ever known emphatically believed in God, and their belief motivated their scientific exploration.[13]

Rather than simply brushing God aside as a figment of man's deepest longings, as Freud does, it behooves man to answer the question, "From where do such longings originate?" The answer must either be evolutionary development or sophisticated design. Russell's philosophical position was that it was a complete waste of time to consider the existence of God. In fact, he wrote a book entitled *Why I Am Not a Christian* in which he postulated:

> I do not pretend to be able to prove that there is no God. I
> equally cannot prove that Satan is a fiction. The Christian god

may exist; so may the gods of Olympus, or of ancient Egypt, or of Babylon. But no one of these hypotheses is more probable than any other: they lie outside the region of even probable knowledge, and therefore there is no reason to consider any of them.[14]

Russell also said, "I would never die for my beliefs because I might be wrong."[15] Russell's philosophy is typical of humanism: Don't declare as fact what cannot be absolutely proven, and don't absolutely conclude anything because you may be wrong. Where does that leave man, but in the gray twilight between the dread of night and the illumination of day. "It is often supposed," said Christian apologist G. K. Chesterton, "that when people stop believing in God, they believe in nothing. Alas, it is worse than that. When they stop believing in God, they believe in anything."[16]

Warped Reasoning

Because philosophy, sociology, psychology, and the human sciences approach the notion of God from man's viewpoint, where man, not God, is at the center of considerations, humanism will derive an inferior and warped concept of God. Consequently, humanism will conclude that exercising faith in supernatural fantasy is merely an emotional crutch. Skeptic Richard Dawkins puts the matter this way:

> Faith is the great cop-out, the great excuse to evade the need to think and evaluate evidence. Faith is belief in spite of, even perhaps because of, the lack of evidence.[17]

As the five senses and reason constrain modern philosophy as a science, intellectualism will never see an almighty God, or have any need for Him. But is this type of naturalistic worldview consistent? The following two observations would suggest that it is not.

First, science has shown that we can enjoy many things without fully understanding them. Whether light is particle or wave energy doesn't affect our appreciation for the flashlight which illuminates our way during a nighttime stroll. On a sultry day, we welcome the air stream of an electric fan regardless of how valence holes and electrons flow at the atomic level to create the electric current. We can exist in space and time without understanding invisible subatomic mysteries. We harness nuclear energy through fusion and fission reactions without actually knowing exactly what connective matter was converted to energy. We can appreciate heavenly constellations without comprehending the invisible dark and exotic matter which some believe composes much of their mass. Many aspects of our existence are beyond the realm of our senses and comprehension, yet these aspects can be characterized by their influences; thus, their existence is validated. Could not the same logical process be applied to identify potential supernatural influence?

Since man does not intellectually fathom much of the universe, it seems absurd to close one's mind from considering a supernatural possibility for our existence. Is it not possible that there is a Creator and that He has intentionally allowed us to perceive only a portion of absolute reality in order to prompt us to ponder the vast void beyond? Is it possible that a Supreme Being has constructed a cosmic stage, has put something bigger in motion than we can comprehend, and at the same time, administers an unavoidable test for every conscious individual? Is it plausible then that all such human quandaries may be duly satisfied by a divine Creator? Former atheist C. S. Lewis came to just this realization: "I believe in God as I believe that the Sun has risen, not only because I see it, but because by it I see everything else."[18]

Secondly, science has shown that we can comprehend much without truly appreciating it. I believe this is true of God also. When considering the universe and the origin of all things, man should not switch his mind off from all possible explanations. Man should use technology and his reasoning skills to contemplate what is unexplored and mysterious. The great physicist Albert Einstein once said, "The most incomprehensible thing about the universe is that it is comprehensible."[19] The laws which seem to govern the universe are largely understandable; man has been bestowed with an opportunity to explore, ponder, and discover the origin of life, to the extent that he is able.

It doesn't seem scientific or rational to say, "Because I cannot validate the supernatural, I conclude that there is no knowable God." All possible explanations of natural order – including supernatural influence should be considered. A philosophy that precludes the possibility of supernatural cause by nature will be a *doubting science*. The words of German philosopher Nietzsche illustrates this point well, "If you could prove God to me, I would believe Him all the less."[20]

For you have trusted in your wickedness;
You have said, 'No one sees me';
Your wisdom and your knowledge have warped you (Isa. 47:10).

Reasoning With Help

It is understood that some readers will not acknowledge the Bible as being supernatural in origin. I have yet to offer any evidence to suggest otherwise, as that will come later. If the reader is not familiar with Bible reference notation, one of the sixty-six books is identified first, the chapter reference next, and lastly the appropriate verses (Bible quotes) are italicized.

If the Bible is supernatural in origin, as I believe it is, the method that the Bible presents to successfully search out God would be an important consideration. Biblically speaking, God challenges man, *"Come now, and let us **reason together**"* (Isa. 1:18). *"You will seek Me and find Me, when you search for Me with all your heart"* (Jer. 29:13). *"Now set your heart and your soul to seek the Lord your God"* (1 Chron. 22:19). *"The Lord is near to all who call upon Him, to all who call upon Him in truth"* (Ps. 145:18). God is reason-able, and He invites man to search Him out.

King Solomon wisely instructed, *"Consider the work of God"* (Eccl. 7:13). Man is to ponder God's nature, character, Word, and works, but not without including Him in the exercise, or else humanly derived conclusions will be lacking. We must reason together with God. Why? Because without God's help man cannot understand or reason out what God has purposely concealed: *"The secret things belong to the Lord our God, but those things which are revealed belong to us and to our children"* (Deut. 29:29). Because God alone holds absolute truth, He will always transcend human reasoning. Solomon once surmised:

> *I saw all the work of God, that a man cannot find out the work that is done under the sun. For though a man labors to discover it, yet he will not find it; moreover, though a wise man attempts to know it, he will not be able to find it* (Eccl. 8:17).

The words of Louis Cassels to the intellectual sound true: "You can save yourself a lot of time and mental agony by recognizing at the outset that you cannot reason your way to a belief in God."[21] God spiritually calls and pleads with people to trust Him, but He does not force them heavenward against their will. Because reason and free choice are required to approach God, man is required to weigh out the evidence, wrangle over the possibilities, consider God's Word, and come to a logical conclusion which will cause him to act in good faith. God assists a true seeker every step of the way.

Summary Points

1. Science is progressively converging upon an accurate understanding of natural order, but perfect understanding of absolute truth cannot be attained through empirical means alone.
2. *Metaphysical Naturalism* assumes an ontological approach to natural order where the existence of supernatural influence is denied.
3. *Methodological Naturalism* says nothing about the existence or non-existence of the supernatural, as the supernatural would be beyond natural verification.
4. Humanly devised logic systems are imperfect and cannot emphatically prove or disprove the existence of God.
5. Because human sciences approach the notion of God from man's viewpoint these disciplines will naturally derive an inferior and warped concept of God.
6. Though science cannot *validate* the supernatural realm, science may *identify* supernatural cause within natural order.
7. According to the Bible, God invites individuals to reason with Him in order to understand and know truth; without God's assistance, we will not understand the supernatural realm.

"Have You Lost Your Mind?"

Some skeptics view Christians as being brainless zombies who simply believe whatever their religious authorities tell them. This observation may characterize Christendom as a humanized religious form, but the Bible encourages people to diligently seek understanding and commends those who do. Man is not to remain destitute of understanding, but is diligently to seek for it: *"The heart of the prudent acquires knowledge, and the ear of the wise seeks knowledge"* (Prov. 18:15).

As there is much confusion today about what Christianity actually is, we begin by defining the term. *Biblical Christianity* is not an earthly institution, or a human-conspired organization, or a set of systematized teachings per se, but rather it is the opportunity to experience spiritual union with Jesus Christ. Oneness with Christ secures eternal life and affords the believer an opportunity to enjoy a life that is meaningful and pleasing to God (Luke 9:23-26). Bible commentator Josiah Strong put it this way, "Christianity is neither a creed nor a ceremony, but a life vitally connected with a loving Christ."[1] Oswald Chambers, a Christian author, echoes this thought, "Christianity is not devotion to work, or to a cause, or a doctrine, but devotion to a person, the Lord Jesus Christ."[2]

The main distinction between biblical Christianity and all the religions of the world is that it teaches a vital need to be saved from spiritual death by trusting in a Savior alone, whereas the world's religions present a system of *doings* to merit salvation or to obtain an improved afterlife. Religion equips man with a "do it yourself" manual and workbook through which he may impress himself as to how well he is *doing* by completing religious exercises and checklists. Christianity, however, is not a *religion*; it is a *relationship* with Jesus Christ. Apart from Christ, there is no forgiveness of sins, no life, and no hope. This is the Christian message as revealed in the Bible.

Biblical *faith* is not blind belief as some skeptics claim. On the contrary, the Bible challenges its readers to test and reason out Scripture. *"Test all things; hold fast what is good"* (1 Thess. 5:21). This testing is not to prove that Scripture is true, but to personally affirm that it is true. Paul complimented the Bereans because *"they received the word with all readiness of mind, and searched the Scriptures daily, whether those things were so"* (Acts 17:11; KJV). Biblical Christianity has this distinction over the religious movements of the world – the seeker is challenged to test the Scripture to validate its truthfulness. Religion imposes propaganda without permitting an opportunity to validate truthfulness against itself and available evidence. God knows man will only live out faithfully that which he has first proven to be true. The fear and scare tactics of the world's religions effectively strangle the heart from ever exercising love that is anchored in truth.

So, despite what some skeptics think, Bible-believing Christians have not "kissed their brains good-bye;" they have not been hoodwinked by religious nonsense. If an individual will put aside his or her preconceived notions and intellectual bias to examine the evidence, there is more than sufficient cause *to believe* that biblical Christianity is a rational choice. This conclusion can only be realized, however, if three critical assertions are affirmed:

1. There is a knowable divine (supernatural) presence. Atheistic and agnostic philosophies, therefore would be rejected. Theism, deism, polytheism, panentheism (i.e. "all in God"), or pantheism (i.e. "all is God," which includes

those in awe of nature and/or the practice of animism – all things possess an innate soul) would generally be in agreement with this statement.

2. There is only one holy and righteous God, not many gods or a god-consciousness which consists of all creation. This monotheistic view is held by Islam, Judaism, many cults, diminished Christianity (works-based salvation) and biblical Christianity (salvation based solely in Christ).

3. The Bible is God's exclusive written revelation to humanity; therefore, it is without error, infallible, and must be believed to enter into a right relationship with the one true God. Thus, the field of monotheism is reduced to biblical Christianity. Religiosity, "churchianity," and the like don't make it past the second assertion.

If these three assertions are determined to be valid, *then* every individual is understood to have an inherited fallen nature which ensures that no one can continue in well-doing (behaving perfectly, as God requires). The only solution the Bible offers man for falling short of God's standard of righteousness is to recognize his or her need for salvation and accept God's solution – Jesus Christ as Savior. Salvation through the Lord Jesus Christ is possible, because He substitutionally and willingly bore the judicial penalty for all human sin some 2000 years ago (1 Tim. 2:5; Heb. 2:9; 1 Jn. 2:2).

How is it possible *to believe* that these three assertions are true? The remainder of this book will address all three points. We begin by showing that atheism and agnosticism are irrational as *absolute* positions.

Is Atheism Logical?

The atheist is *generally* governed by two fundamental principles: All beliefs must be supported by observational evidence;

and beliefs that contradict this evidence cannot be accepted as fact. Atheism, however, states that there is no god, even though observational evidence indicates that the universe had a cause at its conception, although that cause cannot be detected observationally. Despite the lack of observational evidence for a naturalistic cause for the universe, the atheist *believes* that the universe has a naturalistic cause and also that there is no god. This conclusion contradicts the tenet that all beliefs should be based upon observational evidence, and this position violates the atheistic worldview – it is an unreconcilable dichotomy.

Practically speaking, how much does an educated atheist really know? In 1950, science and technology doubled the total sum of all human knowledge accumulated before 1900. By 1980, knowledge was doubling every five to eight years; today it is doubling every two to four.[3] Obviously, even if you are an expert in a particular field of science, you are likely to be ignorant of the technical ramifications of other fields of science, medicine, engineering, architecture, art, music, etc. Even if you were an expert in all these disciplines, your total knowledge would represent only a minute fraction of a percent of all available knowledge in a decade or two. Is it not possible then that you don't understand all that is revealed concerning God in nature also? The Christian understands that absolute truth is revealed in the Bible, and that it reveals only what God wants man to understand about Him.

The atheist says, "There is no God." Is this a scientifically rational statement? From a biblical perspective it is foolish (Ps. 53:1). Some scientists now believe that the universe is between 78 and 93 billion light years across,[4] which means if one could travel at the speed of light (186,000 miles per second), a trans-universe journey would require 78 to 93 billion years. How is it possible for a minuscule speck of dust on one of several planets circling one of 200 billion stars in the Milky Way, which is one of 100 billion galaxies in the known universe, say, "There is no God anywhere at any time.'"?

Though the atheist may present arguments for not believing in a Creator, he or she cannot offer a single irrefutable proof that He does not exist. The only undeniable means by which the atheist may emphatically say that there is no God is if the atheist is omniscient (all-knowing), or omnipresent (all-present), and eternal. His omniscient or omnipresent qualities would ensure that God was not hiding behind some constellation in the far reaches of the universe, whereas the atheist's eternal conscious- ness would verify that God had not merely appeared and disap- peared into unquantifiable dimensions beyond space and time. The only way to say, with surety, that there is no God is if the atheist has the wherewithal to exist eternally everywhere simul- taneously or to have an eternal consciousness that permeates the universe.

The logic of atheism collapses on two fronts. First, no rea- sonable human being would claim to be omnipresent, omniscient or self-existing independent of time. Every tombstone provides ample proof to the foolishness of such a statement. Secondly, if an individual did claim to possess these attributes, would not he or she be god? In fact, when the atheist asserts that there is no God, what he is really implying is that he is god. In either case, the claim of atheism is not logical. He can't say for sure that there is no God, and if he does, he can only do so if he is god – meaning that in truth he is not an atheist but merely a humanist.

The first Russian Cosmonaut, Yuri Gagarin, blasted into space on April 12, 1961. After returning to the Earth, he promptly noted that he didn't see God. Shortly after this, another Russian astronaut, Gherman Titoy, returned from space and said, "Some people say there is a God out there. ... but in my travels around the earth all day long, I looked around and didn't see Him. ... I saw no God, nor angels. The rocket was made by our own people. I don't believe in God. I believe in man, his strength, his possibilities, his reason."[5] God was present in outer space, just as He is here on Earth. The astronauts' difficulty was not in seeing God; it was in not wanting to see God.

Self-exalted man will never see an undervalued God. It is a bit like a child closing his or her eyes and saying, "I don't see you, so you're not there." The Lord stated that only those that seek after God with a pure heart will see God (Matt. 5:8). Through the prophet Jeremiah, God exhorted Israel, *"You will seek Me and find Me, when you search for Me with all your heart"* (Jer. 29:13). Those who do not humble themselves and open their minds to legitimately contemplate God's existence will never know Him.

Concerning the term "atheist," G. K. Chesterton concludes, "If there were no God, there would be no atheists."[6] If there were no Christ, we would not speak of anti-Christ – a term used in the Bible to speak of anyone who denies that the divine Son of God came to the Earth as Christ in the flesh (1 Jn. 2:22, 4:3). None of the above arguments prove that God exists, but rather show that it is illogical for the atheist to assert that there is no God.

Is Agnosticism Logical?

The term "agnostic" was invented by "Darwin's bulldog," Henry Huxley. Suffering from poor health and depression for the last 40 years of his life, Darwin did not have the strength to defend his own theories of naturalism. But the energetic Henry Huxley emerged, to take up the atheistic mantle and rose to fame by defending Darwin. Huxley coined the term *agnostic* to describe a person who professed "not to know" about God or religious beliefs in general.

The *agnostic* being more sensible than the *atheist*, would conclude "I don't know whether there is a God or not, but if there is a God, you cannot know Him." In the agnostic's mind, God is a concept or an entity which cannot be readily observed and verified. *If* God exists, He completed His work long ago and departed, or He now chooses not to be known. Agnostics by definition are "ignorant" and many are content to remain that way because they feel it is impossible to know more.

The opposite of the religious fanatic is not the fanatical atheist but the gentle cynic, who cares not whether there is a God or not.

— Eric Hoffer

Since neither the atheist nor the agnostic understands all natural law, neither can logically say that "God has affected no influences within viewable natural order – He has given no knowable revelation of Himself." Unfortunately, many who say, "You cannot know God" have abandoned all hope of ever knowing Him. Such a biased conclusion is contrary to the very spirit of science which ever challenges man to plumb beyond the fathomable and to continue evaluating new evidence and new information.

The *theist* and *atheist* are similar in that they hold a position that is partially based on *faith*. As there is no known means of substantiating life having arisen from dead chemicals, the *atheist* requires a great deal of faith to believe a cell could be randomly formed from primordial soup. The *agnostic* is different from the *atheist* in that he requires little or no faith to operate comfortably within a worldview of not knowing – ignorance being the acceptable status quo. In reality, both the atheist and the agnostic, for various reasons, have chosen to ignore observable revelation of God and the possibility that future evidence may prove that God has uniquely influenced natural law and, therefore, indeed may be knowable.

What evidence is being ignored? The following ten evidences for divine influence within natural order are submitted for the reader's contemplation. The first two evidences pertain to nature, the next three relate to the Bible, and the last five are associated with humanity.

- The Uniqueness of the Earth
- The Testimony of Nature
- The Authenticity of the Bible
- The Uniformity of the Bible
- The Prophecy of the Bible
- The Human Conscience
- The Human Spirit's Need
- The Inflammatory Name of Jesus
- Miracles
- Changed Lives

Think of these evidences as ten *open portals* of truth, open doors of divine revelation, leading from the physical domain into the supernatural realm. No doubt there are additional evidences of supernatural influence, but these will be the key portals explored in this book. Each stimulates man to peer beyond his physical surroundings and ponder the possibility of what lies beyond. Though reason is present, one cannot enter these portals (spiritual corridors leading to God) without exercising faith. Thus man is presented with a divine test.

Faith compels a soul to stretch beyond what is verifiable through the five senses to actively trust God. Faith that is not tested by God will not be trusted by man. It is impossible to please God without exercising genuine faith (Heb. 11:6). Consequently, a purely intellectual acknowledgment of God is only a hypothetical possibility, for science cannot validate God's existence and intellectualism can be easily swayed by philosophy, deceit, and traditions (Col. 2:8).

In conclusion, it is illogical to state that there is no God. It is premature to say a person cannot know Him; and, it is impossible to know God without reasoning out what is revealed and exercising faith for that which cannot be verified apart from God's help. With this awareness let us consider the scientific evidence for supernatural influence within natural order.

#1 The Uniqueness of the Earth

Have you ever wondered how many planets like the Earth might exist in the universe? I am not speaking of how many planets might have life similar to what we observe on Earth, but how many planets, like Earth, have a hospitable environment to support complex life. In recent years, science fiction novels and movies have conveyed the idea that there are numerous planets on which mankind could comfortably live. But what has scientific discovery shown to be the truth on this matter?

The fact is that there is something *extremely* unique about the Earth and life on the Earth. From a probability standpoint, the existence of planets in the universe capable of sustaining complex life, as we understand it, is exceedingly improbable. From an observational standpoint, none of the dozens of planets and moons in our own solar system has an environment which can sustain complex life. Furthermore, the dozens of planets which have been observed orbiting neighboring stars (with the possible exception of one newly discovered non-rotating earth-size planet) appear to be gaseous giants, similar to Jupiter. Although this sampling is limited, direct observation of nearly 200 heavenly bodies provides some indication of the Earth's uniqueness in supporting life.

Nearly 500 years ago, astronomer Nicolaus Copernicus discovered that the Earth rotated on its axis and, with the other planets in the solar system, revolved around the Sun. What motivated Copernicus' study of the heavenly realms? He wanted to understand "the mechanism of the universe brought to us by a supremely good and ordered Creator."[1] He understood that such sophistication of design was only possible through the intricate work of a divine Architect.

Since the days of Copernicus, humanism has sought to discredit the existence of a Creator by opting for such philosophical principles as the *Principle of Mediocrity*. This principle states that the Earth occupies no preferred place in the universe and that man's status and location are mediocre; they are unexceptional; man has no privileged position in the universe. Does scientific observation indicate that there truly is nothing spectacular about the Earth?

The complex factors needed to support life on Earth are really the best parameters for considering whether life could be sustained on other planets throughout the universe. So what parameters make Earth so incredibility unique? Guillermo Gonzalez and Jay Richards co-authored a well-researched book entitled *The Privileged Planet* to answer this very question. The following is a sampling of some of the key factors which have been identified.

1. An abundance of liquid water

Large amounts of liquid water are necessary to sustain an inhabitable planet with carbon-based life forms. Liquid water is the basis of all of the vital chemical and physical activities on which life depends. Consequently, most organisms are composed of more than 50 percent water; the human body is approximately 70 percent water.

If the Earth's water was found primarily in either its gaseous form (vapor) or its solid form (ice) life's processes would greatly be impeded. One of the unique physical dynamics which ensures that the Earth's oceans, seas, and lakes do not freeze solid is the density aspects of liquid water molecules. At atmospheric pressure, the spacing between water molecules expands when heated and contracts when cooled until the temperature of 39.2 degrees

Fahrenheit is reached. Below this temperature, water molecules begin to expand again until they change state at 32 degrees to become ice. If water continued to contract below 39.2 degrees Fahrenheit until the freezing point of water, the Earth's bodies of water would slowly freeze solid from the bottom up. Very little of the Sun's energy ever makes it to the bottom of these bodies of water to thaw any ice which would have been formed – the cascading result would be eventual freeze out – killing the life in our oceans, seas, lakes and ponds. This characteristic of liquid water ensures that the coldest water rises to the surface and that freezing occurs on the surface. Furthermore, because water continues to expand when it freezes, ice will float above the water beneath it. This unique physical property of water allows liquid water to exist on our planet, and life to continue living in the water.

2. Within the galactic inhabitability zone

The outer region of the Milky Way does not contain the heavy metals which are needed to support life. If the Earth were closer to the center of the galaxy, it would be exposed to much higher levels of hazardous x-rays, gamma-rays and particle radiation ensuring that life would not be possible. It also would need to be away from the galaxy's spiral arms in order to avoid stellar collisions, supernovas and dust extensions over a long duration of time. The Earth just happens to be in a region of space where these catastrophes are avoided.[2]

It is also noted that only spiral galaxies (those having extended spiral arms of matter rotating about the center) support the formation of rocky planets, as opposed to gaseous planets. Small galaxies do not support the formation of planets. A recent survey, published by the *Space Telescope Science Institute,* of the small galaxy globular cluster 47 Tucanae indicated that scientists had found no extrasolar planets out of 37,000 stars searched.[3] It is generally understood among scientists that galaxies must undergo multiple generations of star formation in order to *naturally* produce the heavy elements needed to create rocky planets. Globular clusters and irregular galaxies (which make up more than 90 percent of all known galaxies) do not support continued star formation.[4] Thankfully, we live in a significantly sized spiral galaxy!

3. Orbiting a main sequence G2 draft star

The Morgan-Keenan stellar classification organizes classes of stars from hottest to coldest with mass, radius and luminosity correlated to the Sun, which is used as a reference point. The letters O, B, A, F, G, K, M are used to identify the hottest stars (blue) to the coldest stars (red); the Sun is designated a G class star (light yellow in color with a 5,000 to 6,000 degree Kelvin operating temperature).

Orbiting a smaller star would require a planet to have a much closer course in order to maintain an inhabitable zone for liquid water; however, the gravitational pull of the star would be much greater and cause the planet's rotation to synchronize with its orbital rotation about the Sun. If this were the case, one side of the planet would be constantly facing the Sun and be baked, while the dark side of the planet would remain frozen. This situation would cause extreme temperature variations on the planet and prevent the development of complex life. The Earth's gravitational force creates this same dynamic upon the Moon.[5] If the Earth orbited a larger star, the steady luminosity increase before it became a red giant (its time in main sequence is much shorter) would lead to surging climate changes, preventing a long-existing habitat for complex life.

4. Large gaseous planets in same solar system

These large gaseous planets protect the Earth from catastrophic impact as threatening comets are pulled in by the strong gravitation forces of these immense planets.[6] The solar system seems uniquely designed to preclude the collision of huge aster-oids and comets with the smaller interior planets. Of the nearly 200,000 asteroids in our solar system, only a few dozen orbit within the Earth's proximity to the Sun. Of the some 400 comets which infrequently visit our solar system, approximately 50 make brief excursions within the Earth's orbital domain.[7]

5. Within the circumstellar habitational zone

If the Earth were five percent closer to the Sun, the Earth's oceans would boil, and the same greenhouse effect that creates 900 degree Fahrenheit temperatures on Venus would be realized on the Earth. If the Earth were ten percent further away from the Sun, the oceans would freeze. So not only must a planet have an abundance of water to sustain life, but that same planet must orbit a star at just the right distance to maintain water in a liquid state. Also, as the Earth is moved further away from the Sun, more carbon is needed in the atmosphere to create a greenhouse effect to keep the planet warm enough to sustain life; however, too much carbon shields visible light from penetrating the atmosphere, which then diminishes plant photosynthesis.[8]

6. Nearly circular orbit about the Sun

An elliptic orbit lasting for months would cause extreme temperature variations on the Earth. It is also noted that in our galaxy about 60 percent of all stars are grouped in closely spaced pairs called *binaries*. Fortunately for us, our Sun does not have a binary partner. If it did, temperatures on Earth would vary too much to support life.

7. An oxygen rich atmosphere to support life

Though the Earth's atmosphere is composed of about twenty gases, the main gases are nitrogen and oxygen (78 percent nitrogen and 21 percent oxygen). Almost all life must have the element oxygen. Ozone, a special form of oxygen, assists in shielding the Earth from harmful radiation (such as in the ultraviolet frequency range).

8. Atmospheric transparency and shielding

The nitrogen/oxygen mixture in the atmosphere shields the Earth from cosmic radiation while allowing radiation in the visible light frequency range to penetrate through – the exact electromagnetic wavelength that is needed to sustain life on Earth (such as plant photosynthesis). Astonishingly, the frequency band of visible light comprises only a minute slice of the entire observable electromagnetic spectrum (i.e. a frequency bandwidth about 1/12 trillionth of a 1/12 trillionth of the entire known electromagnetic spectrum). The only radiation allowed to penetrate the atmosphere is that which is beneficial – the near-ultraviolet rays, visible light, and near-infrared light. The remainder of the electromagnetic spectrum is harmful or lethal to life on Earth, but virtually all gamma, X-ray, microwave, or dangerous portions of ultraviolet and infrared radiation are filtered out before reaching us.[9]

Thus, our atmosphere has been specifically designed to keep out what is harmful and allow through an exceptionally thin bandwidth of radiation which is essential for life on earth. If the atmosphere were composed of more carbon, the transparent nature of the atmosphere would be diminished (less visible light would penetrate), and a greenhouse effect resulting in global warming would be realized.

9. Correct mass

A smaller planet would not generate enough surface gravity to prevent the atmosphere from dissipating into space, while the higher surface gravity of a larger planet would prevent the planet's organisms from growing very large and would also tend to keep the planet's terrain more flat, thus, allowing surface water to cover more of the planet, perhaps the entire planet.[10]

If the Earth were twice its size, the intense pressure would compress materials so much that our planet would have a mass fourteen times greater than it originally had and consequently 3.5 times the original surface gravity.[11] Personally, the thought of weighing 700 pounds is a bit overwhelming. Such an increase in gravitational pull would force more gases like water vapor, methane, and carbon dioxide into the atmosphere but would reduce the rate in which these gases would dissipate into space. The bottom line: a slightly bigger Earth would be transformed into a gaseous planet similar in appearance to the outer planets in our solar system, and complex life could not exist on such a planet.

10. Orbited by a large moon

In respect to planet-moon arrangements in our solar system, the size of the Earth's moon is uniquely large – approximately one fourth the size of the Earth. What does this accomplish? A large moon stabilizes the axial rotation of the Earth at 23.5 degrees, which ensures temperate seasonal changes worldwide and allows the growth of vegetation over a vast portion of the planet in lieu of a narrow band centered at the equator. The size of the Moon also causes significant tidal mixing of the oceans' cold and warm water masses which provides temperate control of the planet and prevents thermal stagnation of various bodies of water.[12]

11. Magnetic field

The magnetic field circulating the Earth from pole to pole is strong enough to protect the atmosphere from being stripped away by solar wind.[13] Mercury is the only other planet to have a magnetic field in our solar system, but its strength is over 100 times less than that of the Earth's Van-Allen radiation shield.

12. Plate tectonics

The tectonic plate structure of the Earth is thin enough to allow tectonic mixing, which circulates carbon and other elements essential to support life, but it is also thick enough (some 4 to 30 miles) to prevent the Earth's molten iron core from cooling off too fast. This fluid movement of the Earth's core produces the Earth's magnetic field. The number of surface plates and the liquid water-to-continent ratio of the Earth's surface are optimized to maintain these geometric dynamics.[14] Constant erosion wears down mountains and even the continents over time, but plate tectonics rebuilds land masses above the oceans, otherwise over an extended time period the Earth would tend to become a "water-world."

Scientists now know that planets like the Earth, with large amounts of both water and land, are virtually impossible to form spontaneously. Large planets would not form continents because the increased surface gravity precludes significant mountain and continent formation. Earth-sized planets would eventually become covered with water as any land formed would be eroded by the oceans. Smaller planets lack tectonic activity, so no land masses would be developed – a virtual waterworld.[15]

13. Variety of carbon based biomechanisms

The Earth is a terrestrial planet with a diversity of biomechanisms to support a variety of complex life. It is not designed just for single types of life but a broad spectrum. Complex life requires more raw elements than simple life. For example, a human being needs twenty-seven elements, while a single-cell bacteria requires only seventeen.[16] The Earth contains a large supply of carbon, which has metastable properties making it ideal for interacting with other elements to create the building blocks of life (amino acids, proteins, etc.). Dr. Edward Boudreaux provides this synopsis of how carbon (somewhat of a miracle element) reflects creative design:

Consider the element carbon (C). This is the most unique of all the chemical elements in the periodic table. It is a nonmetal, having unlimited capacity to participate in every known type of covalent chemical bonding (i.e., pairs of electrons shared between atoms), which unites atoms of the same kind to each other and to other kinds of atoms as well. This feature, called *catenation*, is virtually unlimited for the element carbon alone.

Other elements, such as silicon (Si), nitrogen (N), sulphur (S), phosphorus (P), etc., display some very limited capacities for catenation, which do not even come close to rivalling the catenation ability of C. Without this unique feature, the formation of such essential biomolecules as proteins, DNA, RNA, cellulose, etc., would be impossible. Ironically, in spite of its crucial importance, carbon comprises only 9 to 10 percent by weight of the composition of all living things and only 0.017 percent of the earth's composition. Nonetheless, there is no other element that can replace even one or two C atoms in biomolecules, without destroying the biological integrity of these systems.[17]

No other element even comes close to the unique properties of carbon. Our planet possesses a wide variety of both elements and biomechanism to sustain a broad range of living organisms.

14. Orbiting a stable star

The Sun is a highly stable star. Its light output varies by only 0.1 percent over a full sunspot cycle (about eleven years). Among Sun-like stars, a wider variation of light intensity has been observed. A consistent star is needed to prevent wide climate swings on Earth.[18]

15. Moderate rate of rotation

A moderate rate of rotation keeps the days from getting too hot and nights from becoming too cool.

Researchers have calculated that the probability of other planets randomly possessing the critical parameters needed to sustain complex life would be exceedingly remote, about one planet out of every 10^{15} planets in the universe.[19] Therefore, one out of every 1,000,000,000,000,000 planets would have an inhabitable environment to support life. It is thought that there are about 200,000,000,000 stars in the Milky Way. If each of these stars had ten orbiting planets (this is a generous assumption as many stars are known to have no planets) it would mean that there would be an Earth-like planet in about every 500 Milky Way-type galaxies. On the galaxy scale, the Milky Way is a giant with nearly a trillion solar masses and a diameter of 100,000 light years.[20]

Most scientists, including a few creationists, accept the Big Bang explanation of the origin of the universe (these creationists would see God as the cause of the Big Bang and the designer behind all the aftermath). The Big Bang theory is not being endorsed by its mention here; I speak only of a theory which most scientists view as the most rational explanation of how everything came about for the purpose of extending a logical argument. To begin with, the probability of the Big Bang event as theorized by physical analysis is incomprehensibly improbable. Stephen W. Hawking has calculated that if the rate of the universe's expansion one second after the Big Bang had been less by even one part in 10^{17}, the universe would have re-collapsed into a fireball.[21] Physicists Paul Davies has determined that the odds against the initial conditions being suitable for later star formation to be at least 1.0×10^{21}.[22] He has also calculated that a change in strength of gravity or of the weak force by only one part in 10^{100} would have prevented a life-permitting universe.[23] If the Big Bang did occur, dozens of such improbable physical factors had to be intricately tuned to achieve the life-permitting universe we now witness.

Assuming for the moment that the Big Bang model were correct, what would be the likelihood of a planet with Earth's qualities for sustaining life to arise out of the explosion by chance? Hugh Ross, in his work *Big Bang Refined by Fire,* addresses this question. He found that the combined probability of 75 needed physical parameters to fall in the range which would permit a planet like Earth to develop was 10^{-99}. He then estimates that the maximum possible number of planets in the universe, assuming ten planets for each star, is equal to 10^{23}. The conclusion of this analysis is that there should not be any planets in the universe capable of supporting life as a result of the Big Bang.[24]

The scientific evidence is so overwhelming that many cosmologists are acknowledging that intelligent design is the only logical answer for the Earth's existence. J. Glanz writes in *Science* magazine: "This type of universe, however, seems to require a degree of fine tuning of the initial conditions that is in apparent conflict with 'common wisdom.'"[25]

S. W. Hawking and R. Penrose, writing in the *Astrophysical Journal,* similarly concluded:

> In all of these worlds statistically miraculous (but not impossible) events would be necessary to assemble and preserve the fragile nuclei that would ordinarily be destroyed by the higher temperatures. However, although each of the corresponding histories is extremely unlikely, there are so many more of them than those that evolve without 'miracles,' that they would vastly dominate the livable universes that would be created by Poincare recurrences. We are forced to conclude that in a recurrent world like de Sitter space our universe would be extraordinarily unlikely.[26]

Scientifically speaking, the Earth is an extremely unique planet. Its exceeding uniqueness speaks of masterful design, not the aftermath of some astronomically improbably random accident. Even more evidence exists, however, which suggests the

Earth was designed with purpose in mind. Besides the unique qualities that the Earth possesses to support complex life, it also has very unusual features for its most intelligent inhabitant, man, to understand just how unique the Earth really is.

Discovering Our Uniqueness

Many of us have used a road atlas to navigate to some unfamiliar destination. In the same way, I believe the Creator has provided a creation atlas to guide scientific discovery to its proper conclusion – that man might be in awe of nature and thus be compelled to consider its Creator. Some will close their eyes to the atlas and not stop for directions (especially men). These individuals will resolutely find their own way to an alternative destination of their choosing; blind pride, not systematic discovery of truth, will determine their end.

Consequently, some will not deeply contemplate the information and analyses just presented; rather they will resort to the familiar, the programmed, the status quo of philosophy – that all resulted from random accident. They would say, "We are here by freak chance; there is no God." Our human tendency is to choose the effortless path over the mysterious and unknown one.

It is an unmistakable fact that we all tend to bias the facts we are evaluating with preconceived conclusions; we really want to be true what we prefer to be true. Sometimes these biases are quite humorous as in the case of Rule 46 of the Oxford Union Society in London which reads: "Any [one] introducing a dog into the Society's premises shall be liable to a fine of £1. Any animal leading a blind person shall be deemed to be a cat" (*The Times*, London). At other times, prejudices, such as India's caste system, are destructive. Of India's total population, almost 100 million are ranked as untouchables. The untouchables compose the lowest rung on the Hindu caste ladder and are mainly restricted to despised jobs like scavenging, cleaning, cremating, etc.[27]

Putting aside preconceived biases for a moment, let us consider an observation even more astonishing than the rare life-sustaining aspects of the Earth, namely, that the Earth's unique orientation with the Sun and the Moon enables man to discover just how unique his planet really is. Beneath the vast canopy of majestic obscurity, lunar and solar eclipses have prompted man for millennia to ponder the significance of his planet. Many religious myths and folk legends have been spawned from these brief and infrequent celestial events. Aristotle was one of the first to surmise that the earth was circular after observing the circular shadow of the earth passing over the surface of the moon during a lunar eclipse.

Not until recently, however, has man become aware of the extraordinary information available during perfect solar eclipses. Benjamin Wiker explains both the tremendously unique features of a perfect solar eclipse and some of the unique scientific gleanings made available through such events:

> Without the sense of light, and in particular our ability to distinguish colors, it would have been next to impossible to crack the code of the periodic table. Without the spectral lines occurring in the narrow slice of the electromagnetic spectrum where light is visible to the human eye, the elements discovered through spectroscopy may have remained beyond our reach, as would have the underlying pattern of the periodic table. It bears repeating just how thin this slice is … it's a mere one part in 10^{25} of the full electromagnetic spectrum … the equivalent to one second in 100 quadrillion (100,000,000,000,
> 000,000) years.

> A more tangible but no less amazing instance may help us sense the extraordinary convergence of factors. Our planet experiences not merely total eclipses, but perfect eclipses – where the Moon

almost precisely covers the Sun, enough to block its dazzling direct light, allowing astronomers to observe its chromosphere. This oddly perfect "fit" of Moon over Sun is only possible because of the particular sizes, sphericity and distances of the Sun and Moon. The Sun is four hundred times larger than the Moon. But it's also four hundred times farther away, meaning it has the same apparent size on the face of the sky as does the Moon, and so the Moon just covers it during a perfect eclipse.[28]

The unique convergence factor of the Sun and Moon during a perfect solar eclipse has played a key role in unlocking the science of spectroscopy, the chemical makeup of the stars, and in turn, the order of all the elements.[29] The human eye responds to wavelengths from 400 to 700 nm, which constitutes a very narrow frequency band within the entire electromagnetic spectrum. Yet this exceedingly thin frequency band of light is what the sun generates with the greatest intensity, and is also the range of frequencies most transparent in our atmosphere. Is it by chance that this critical spectral information is within this narrow electromagnetic frequency band which is highly sourced by the Sun, is nominally filtered by our atmosphere, and is within man's limited visual ability of observation? The probability is astronomically impossible to be a coincidence.

Besides the spectral density information, another important benefit of a perfect eclipse is that when the blinding light of the Sun is obscured, the light of the stars on the opposite side of the Sun becomes visible. From the Earth, the light from these distant stars was observed to be originating from a different location than where the stars were known to be; the Sun's gravitational pull actually bent the light of the stars. These observations were used to unquestionably affirm Einstein's theory of relativity.[30]

Another very unique feature of a perfect eclipse is that the optical spectrum of the Sun is optimized to provide density of absorption information (used to identify isotope ratios), but still maintains a spectral continuum for referencing such information.

A hotter star would have less absorption information (perhaps immeasurable), while a cooler star would have a wider varying reference; in fact continuum integrity may be lost althogether.[31] Observationally, our G2 main sequence star is an optimal compromise – not too hot and not too cold.

The Earth is not only a unique planet for supporting complex life, but it also has been exceptionally oriented to provide earthlings with the opportunity to understand the Earth's rareness and sophistication of ordered design. Consider these unique properties:

1. Only one creature (man) on the planet has the cognitive capacity to understand Earth's uniqueness.
2. The Sun and Moon's shape, size and distance from the Earth are such to produce a perfect solar eclipse – no other planet we know of has that configuration.
3. The Sun's spectral density information during a perfect eclipse conveys precise chemical element information in a very narrow frequency range of the electromagnetic spectrum.
4. This narrow frequency band corresponds to the actual electromagnetic frequency range that man can see (visible light). Remember the frequency band that we can actually see is the equivalent to one second in 100 quadrillion years!
5. This narrow frequency band is not filtered out by the earth's atmosphere, as is nearly all the electromagnetic spectrum.
6. The Sun's size, sequence, and intensity are optimal for gaining absorption data.
7. Stars on the opposite side of the Sun are positioned in such a way that during a perfect solar eclipse Einstein's theory of relativity was demonstrated to be accurate.

These are only a few of the unique physical parameters of our solar system which afford man a special opportunity to understand the Earth's uniqueness and order. Such overwhelming evidence of order caused Sir James Hopwood Jeans to conclude, "The universe seems to have been designed by a pure mathematician."[32] The rational conclusion of Earth's origin is purposeful design rather than an accident of nature. No other planet that we know of enjoys the same opportunity nor has the intelligent life to appreciate these distinct features.

Why is the earthly dynamic of supporting life so rare in the universe? The Earth's rareness must suggest a specific unique purpose and design, otherwise many planets like our own would exist. The skeptic inquires, "O.K., if there is a God, why would He go to so much trouble to create a colossal size universe if the Earth is His central focus?" Good question. If the Creator had only put one star and one planet in the heavens, we would wonder about how they came to exist, but we would not be afforded an opportunity to understand His greatness. If there was a Creator, would not the universe from man's perspective need to be infinite to best manifest His awesome presence? If we could determine the boundaries of all we know, would we not think God was limited and somewhat mediocre? The answer is yes, for some have already come to this conclusion despite a vast universe staring them in the face. A miniature physical realm then would be contrary to the revelation God would want us to know of Himself – it would not display the full extent of His attributes.

Both the immensity of and the uniqueness of what we observe in creation provide evidence of a single Designer, a Mastermind, the Creator. In this matter, man has an advantage over the entire universe, for the universe has no will, no power to choose, no opportunity to know the Creator, but man has been bestowed a special privilege to view His handiwork and ponder His presence. Given the astronomical odds of winning the cosmic lottery the uniqueness of the Earth is valid evidence for supernatural influence.

#2 The Testimony of Nature

Since man first began to walk upon the Earth the testimony of nature has mainly fostered two opposing world views – exaltation of the Creator, or of a creature. In ancient Babylon, Nimrod led his people to rebel (the literal meaning of his name) against the Creator and to pursue a state of divinity through human effort. Consequently, paganism can be traced back to Babylon, specifically to Nimrod. During the glory days of the Greek empire, those who believed in universal law in accordance with divine will, the brotherhood of humanity and an afterlife, were called *Stoics*. Those believing that the universe and all life itself happened by chance, and that the avoidance of pain and pursuit of pleasure constituted the good life, and that the human soul ceased to exist at death, were called *Epicureans*. That was over two thousand years ago, and the testimony of creation still has the same effect on mankind; either a Creator who controls our existence and rules man, or a chance existence where man rules but denies a Creator.

Abraham Lincoln once said, "I can see how it might be possible for a man to look down upon the Earth and be an atheist, but I cannot conceive how he could look up into the heavens and say there is no God."[1] Though the celestial bodies are more impressive than the terrestrial aspects of our habitation, they are no less mysterious in origin. In fact, we affirm conscious design in everything that we see.

When we look at a rocking chair, the family automobile, or a towering skyscraper no one questions the fact that engineers and architects worked to develop a functional design, while craftsmen, mechanics, and construction workers labored to create the finished product. A beautiful oil painting demands an artist, an engagement ring requires the skill of a jeweler, and a computer depends on the know-how of hardware and software engineers – and the list goes on. How is it, then, that some can observe the sophistication of design in every aspect of nature and conclude, "No Designer – it happened by random processes over time."?

If you were hiking along some secluded trail deep in a national forest and suddenly came upon a three-foot high stack of walnuts in the shape of a perfect cube, what would be your explanation for the occurrence? Would it be logical to assume that the walnuts randomly fell from the trees to form the cube, that an earthquake arbitrarily tossed the nuts into such a configuration, that a strong wind blew the nuts together, or that some conscious design is present here – probably human, but perhaps a hyperactive squirrel. The logical conclusion would be conscious design. Why? Because every ordered pattern or functional system that we observe was created by precise engineering and construction. Complex order does not occur by random accident. Some four hundred years ago, before sophisticated technology existed, Edward Herbert, contemplating the complexity of the human body surmised, "Whoever considers the study of anatomy, I believe will never be an atheist."[2]

Based on what we observe around us, it seems logical that creation demands a Creator in the same way that an automobile requires a team of engineers to develop it and the skill of those in manufacturing to build it. Furthermore, the complexity, order, and uniform nature of creation boast of one Mastermind, one Master-designer, one Master-builder instead of many smaller gods somehow hashing it all out.

Historically speaking, many of the scientists who discovered and developed the foundational physical, chemical, biological, astronomical, and mathematical laws by which nature is observed to abide were both Christians and creationists. Scientists such as Newton, Faraday, Maxwell, Kelvin, Boyle, Pascal, Leibnitz, Euler, Galileo, Kepler, Herschel, Ray, Mendel, Dalton, Ramsay, Copernicus – the list is quite long. If atheistic evolution were true (that all is by accident and chance), how is it, then, that these scientists were able to reason out what has been shown not to be random and accidental. C. S. Lewis, who turned from atheism to Christianity explains:

> If the solar system was brought about by an accidental collision, then the appearance of organic life on this planet was also an accident, the whole evolution of Man was an accident too. If so, then all our thought processes are mere accidents – the accidental by-product of the movement of atoms. And this holds for the materialists' and astronomers' as well as for anyone else's. But if their thoughts – i.e., of Materialism and Astronomy – are merely accidental by-products, why should we believe them to be true? I see no reason for believing that one accident should be able to give a correct account of all the other accidents.[3]

The above scientists believed in a Creator because it was a logical conclusion of design and order, in lieu of theories based and developed on random processes, chance happenings and so-called accidents. The more we study about life, the more complexity of order is discovered.

General Theory of Evolution

Perhaps man's greatest attempt at discrediting God's creative handiwork is the teaching of *naturalism,* often referred to as the *General Theory of Evolution (GTE).* Evolutionist G. A. Kerhut defines GTE to be "the theory that all the living forms in the world have arisen from a single source which itself came from an inorganic form." He then adds, "the evidence which supports this is not sufficiently strong to allow us to consider it as anything more than a working hypothesis."[4] Evolution teaches that particles will eventually turn into people given enough time for natural selection and random processes to work out the details; divine assistance is neither needed nor wanted.

Macroevolution refers to evolutionary change in the biological category of species and higher classifications. *Microevolution* refers to less prominent changes within a species or population such as cause and effect mechanisms or genetic diversity. As an example, *macroevolution* would include the appearance of feathers on birds as they evolve from a distinct dinosaur group. *Microevolution* would include the slow progressive change in the beak of a particular species of bird in order to effectively crack hard shell nuts indigenous to an environment that the birds were introduced into. Many creationists refer to *macroevolution* to describe the type of evolutionary change which they reject. Creationists generally accept naturalistic change within a species, but deny that one species can evolve into another; dogs remain dogs even after intense breeding. This is consistent with the biblical account of creation which states that God created creatures (species if you will), each designed to procreate "after its kind" (Gen. 1:20-25).

Public Opinion

"People in the United States," writes James Owen, "are much less likely to accept Darwin's idea that humans and apes share a common ancestor than adults in other Western nations, a number of surveys show." That was the conclusion of extensive study conducted by *National Geographic News* (August 10, 2006). The survey went on to state, "In the U.S., only 14 percent of adults thought that evolution was 'definitely true,' while about a third firmly rejected the idea. ... The investigation also showed that the percentage of U.S. adults who are uncertain about evolution has risen from 7 percent to 21 percent in the past 20 years." The study also found that in some countries, including

Denmark, Sweden, and France, more than 80 percent of adults surveyed said they accepted the concept of evolution.[5]

BBC News (January 26, 2006) posted the results of a recent survey of Britons: "Just under half of Britons accept the theory of evolution as the best description for the development of life, according to an opinion poll. ... Furthermore, more than 40% of those questioned believe that creationism or intelligent design (ID) should be taught in school science lessons."[6]

These opinion polls highlight the struggle that many have in concluding that man is simply a random product of nature when a viable supernatural explanation declares otherwise. Decades of aggressive naturalistic programming have yet to convince the masses that man is no more significant in nature than an amoeba.

Baffling Complexity

Our bodies consist of approximately 30 trillion cells, and each cell's nucleus has twenty-three pairs of chromosomes. The amount of genetic information in these chromosomes if decoded into text would fill 4000 volumes of information. The human brain weighs roughly three pounds and is made up of 100 billion cells providing a memory storage capacity of a million megabits. Each neuron in the brain averages a thousand junctions with other neurons. Some scientists have spent years studying the encoding and translation of our DNA and the interactions of RNA, amino acids and enzymes which ultimately produce proteins that enable life to exist. Is it possible for such complexity to occur by accident given enough time for natural development from base elements? Even British evolutionist J. B. S. Haldane claimed in 1949 that evolution could never produce "various mechanisms, such as the wheel and magnet, which would be useless till fairly perfect."[7] How much more complex is the human DNA than a wheel or a magnet?

Over the last hundred years, evolutionists have repeatedly increased the age of the Earth as they gain further understanding of the complexity of life (i.e. more time for random development is needed). As technology increases, scientists continue to learn just how sophisticated life really is, meaning more time is required for natural processes to cause the evolved state we observe today. Many evolutionists, of late, find their backs against the wall – 4.5 billion years is just not enough time for the Earth to develop and for life to originate and evolve into the complexity we witness today. Some evolutionists are now looking outside the solar system for answers – perhaps an implantation of primitive living structures occurred on the Earth several billion years ago and all that we see has evolved from those. In other words, they are looking beyond our cosmos for the answer to life but will not consider that all life originated with a Creator. Saying that life originated elsewhere doesn't answer the question, "How did life originate from non-living materials?"

A basic definition of *science* is, "the theoretical explanation of observed natural phenomena." Observation of or demonstration of that which requires hundreds of millions of years to accomplish is an impossible task – evolution, or creationism for that matter, will never be emphatically *proven* by science (i.e. science may produce well-established theory, but not absolute fact). Often scientists supporting naturalism or creationism use the same observations to arrive at completely different and often opposite conclusions. Obviously, something other than scientific reasoning is affecting the judgment of men.

The next three chapters highlight discoveries in various fields of science in respect to the origin of life. Many of the various scientists quoted in the next three chapters are atheists, and most hold some type of evolutionary thinking. The scientific information pertaining to the origin of life is immense and often quite technical, which means most of us will be exercising prudence in considering the conclusions of those who are more highly trained in various fields of science. It is good to keep in mind that fallible men spawn fallible theories. What is the scientific testimony of nature for the origin of life?

The Testimony of Physics and Chemistry

The theory of naturalism suggests that the Earth is some 4.5 billion years old or older – this time span is needed for the Earth to cool and geologically develop, for life to be spontaneously generated from raw elements, and for simple life to evolve into complex life. Many scientists believe that evolution is a well-substantiated explanation of observable data. Is there, however, scientific evidence that batters against the wake of popular opinion? I believe the answer is "yes;" scientific evidence indicates that naturalism is still an unsubstantiated *theory*.

In this chapter, we will explore some of the evidences *against* naturalism as exposed in Physics and Chemistry. This exercise utilizes science to scrutinize the accuracy of naturalism as a workable theory to explain nature. If naturalism is shown by science to be doubtful, should not man consider other viable alternatives to explain nature?

Physics

The First Law of Thermodynamics

Former evolutionist, now creation scientist, Walter Brown explains why the first law of thermodynamics and natural processes are not compatible:

> The first law of thermodynamics states that the total energy in the universe, or in any isolated part of it, remains constant. In other words, energy (or its mass equivalent) is not now being

51

created or destroyed; it simply changes form. Countless experiments have verified this. A corollary of the first law is that natural processes cannot create energy. Consequently, energy must have been created in the past by some agency or power outside and independent of the natural universe. Furthermore, if natural processes cannot produce mass and energy—the relatively simple inorganic portion of the universe—then it is even less likely that natural processes can produce the much more complex organic (or living) portion of the universe.[1]

The relative question is "From where did all the original energy and matter come, if God did not create it? Any naturalistic answer devised ultimately will violate the first law of thermodynamics. There is also a law of *Cause and Effect* which we demonstrate in every aspect of physical science, but if the Big Bang were true, what caused the explosion? The Bible states, *"By the word of the Lord the heavens were made"* (Ps. 33:6). God was the original cause of creation! Even the famous skeptic David Hume understood that nature must have a cause, "I never asserted so absurd a proposition as that anything might arise without a cause."[2] The universe is something; it does exist, therefore it had an initial cause.

Bertrand Russell argued, "If everything must have a cause, then God must have a cause."[3] To be candid, this argument is silly; by definition "cause" pertains to the physical realm of mass and energy, but God is Spirit (John 4:24), eternal (Gen. 21:33; Heb. 9:14), immutable (Num. 23:19; Mal. 3:6) and self-existing – the very meaning of His name, *Jehovah* (Ex. 3:13-15). His attributes cannot be explained by physical laws because He is not constrained by them. Thomas Aquinas used Aristotelian logic to prove the existence of God as the logical "uncaused cause."[4]

God creates and controls the law of cause and effect, but these do not control Him. Would it be logical for a lump of clay affixed on a spinning wheel to protest to the potter, "You are not real unless you are spinning"? The concept that God is eternal is difficult to grasp because we had a beginning, and everything else we observe is time dependent.

The Second Law of Thermodynamics

Rationally speaking, evolution does not make sense: how does that which is less ordered become more ordered by natural processes? Nearly everything we observe at a common level wears out, rusts out, rots away, ages, or functionally degrades over time. The Second Law of Thermodynamics states, "The entropy (a measurement of system disorder) of the universe must always either increase or remain the same. It can never decrease."[5] Although this law does not directly disprove evolution, it does make it extraordinarily unlikely, in that for evolution to occur, a corresponding disordering must be observed in our overall surroundings. Dr. Jay Wile explains:

> The Second Law says that *if* evolution were to occur, then each step of that evolution must be accompanied by an immediate increase in the entropy of the surroundings. If anyone ever comes up with a mechanism by which this might happen, then evolution could at least be made consistent with the Second Law. Currently, however, no one can come up with even a vague notion as to how this might happen. As a result, the plausibility of evolution (from a thermodynamic standpoint) is very, very, very low.[6]

Whether an open or closed system is assumed for man's environment, the ultimate difficulty is the encoding of information to produce proteins necessary to advance chemical order into life. Neil Broom, a Ph.D. in Chemical and Materials Engineering, explains:

A fundamental problem that science has never been able to solve is how to produce energy flow through the system to do this work of coding in order to produce, for example, a functioning protein. Living systems do, of course, harness energy for this purpose, but only because the required, purposefully assembled metabolic machinery is already in place and functioning.[7]

Concerning the origin of the universe in relationship to the second law of thermodynamics, Rich Deem writes:

Now consider the entire universe as one giant closed system. Stars are hot, just like the cup of coffee, and are cooling down, losing energy into space. The hot stars in cooler space represent a state of available energy, just like the hot coffee in the room. However, the second law of thermodynamics requires that this available energy is constantly changing to unavailable energy. In another analogy, the entire universe is winding down like a giant wind-up clock, ticking down and losing available energy. Since energy is continually changing from available to unavailable energy, someone had to give it available energy in the beginning! (i.e. someone had to wind up the clock of the universe at the beginning.) Who or what could have produced energy in an available state in the first place? Only someone or something not bound by the second law of thermodynamics. Only the creator of the second law of thermodynamics could violate the second law of thermodynamics, and create energy in a state of availability in the first place.[8]

The Bible teaches that God originated life with the metabolic machinery to both harness energy to sustain life (Gen. 1:29-30) and to propagate His order in life by procreation (Gen. 1:28). These functions adhere to the Second Law of Thermodynamics. The Bible also teaches that the universe had a distinct beginning and is now winding down or "wearing out" (Ps. 102:25-26). This fact agrees with the second law of thermodynamics which ensures that the universe will "wind down" and experience "heat death" or maximum entropy.

Chemistry

Practically speaking, there are only two possible explanations of the existence of life: the chance development of life from chemicals, or a Creator who assembled life from chemicals. It is my opinion that the Achilles' heel of naturalism is not its explanation of the supposed evolution of life to a higher order through random processes, but the origin of life itself. Consequently, creationism is the only major scientific theory to provide a feasible explanation for the origin of life. Evolutionists speculate that we somehow randomly happened, perhaps coming from clay, or ocean vents, or a cup of primeval soup zapped by lightning, or possibly from space seeding. The latter explanation ignores the issue of how life started. Dr. Walter Brown explains why the chemical evolution of life is ridiculously improbable:

What could improve the odds [of life developing from lifeless chemicals]? One should begin with an earth having high concentrations of the key elements comprising life, such as carbon, oxygen, and nitrogen. However, as one more closely examines these elements, the more unlikely evolution appears.

Carbon. Rocks that supposedly preceded life have very little carbon. One must imagine a toxic, carbon-rich atmosphere to supply the needed carbon if life evolved. For comparison, today's atmosphere holds only 1/80,000th of the carbon that has been on the earth's surface since the first fossils formed.

Oxygen. No theory has been able to explain why earth's atmosphere has so much oxygen. Too many chemical processes should have absorbed oxygen on an evolving earth. Besides, if the early earth had oxygen in its atmosphere, the compounds (called *amino acids*) needed for life to evolve would have been destroyed by oxidation. But if there had been no oxygen, there would have been no ozone (a form of oxygen) in the upper atmosphere. Without ozone to shield the earth, the sun's ultraviolet radiation would quickly destroy life. The only known way for both ozone and life to be here is for both to come into existence simultaneously—in other words, by creation.

Nitrogen. Clays and various rocks absorb nitrogen. Had millions of years passed before life evolved, the sediments that preceded life should be filled with nitrogen. Searches have never found such sediments.

Basic chemistry does not support the evolution of life. DNA cannot function without at least 75 preexisting proteins, but proteins are produced only at the direction of DNA. Because each needs the other, a satisfactory explanation for the origin of one must also explain the origin of the other. The components of these manufacturing systems must have come into existence simultaneously. This implies creation.

When a cell divides, its DNA is copied, sometimes with errors. Each animal and plant has machinery that identifies and corrects most errors; if it did not, the organism would deteriorate and become extinct. If evolution happened, which evolved first, DNA or its repair mechanism? Each requires the other. To claim life evolved is to demand a miracle. The simplest conceivable form of single-celled life should have at least 600 different protein molecules. The mathematical probability that only one typical protein could form by chance arrangements of amino acid sequences is essentially zero —far less than 1 in 10^{450}. To appreciate the magnitude of 10^{450}, realize that the visible universe is about 10^{28} inches in diameter.[9]

Meaningful Molecules – Not by Chance!

If you enjoy mathematics, you will find the following analysis performed by John P. Marcus, a Ph. D. in biochemistry, illuminating. He calculates the mathematical probability of base chemicals assembling into the correct amino acids to produce the needed proteins to create a single simple living cell. The possibility of this happening by random chance is simply absurd.

Now let us consider the probability of just one of the above 75 proteins coming about by chance. Consider a smaller than average protein of just 100 amino acid residues. *If* all the necessary left-handed amino acids were actually available, and *if* the interfering compounds, including right-handed amino acids, were somehow eliminated, and *if* our pool of amino acids were somehow able to join individual amino acids together into protein chains faster than the proteins normally fall apart, then the chances of this random 100 amino-acid protein having the correct sequence would be 1 in 20^{100} possible sequence combinations; 20 available amino acids raised to the power of the number of residues in the protein, i.e., 1 in 1.268×10^{130}. ....

To put this number in some perspective, we must do some calculations. ... Let us take a more-than-generous scenario and see how desolate the theory of evolution becomes in view of the probabilities. The earth has a mass of around 5.97×10^{27} grams. If the entire mass of the earth were converted to amino acids, there would be in the order of 3.27×10^{49} amino acid molecules available. If all of these molecules were converted into 100-residue proteins, there would be 3.27×10^{47} proteins. Since there are 1.27×10^{130} possible combinations of amino acids in a 100-mer protein, a division of the number of possibilities by the number of proteins present on our hypothetical globe shows that the chances of having just *one* correct sequence in that entire globe of 100-mer proteins is 1 in 3.88×10^{82}.

Even if each of these 3.27×10^{47} 100-mer proteins could be re-arranged many times over into different sequences during the timespan of the earth, the chances that one correct sequence would be produced are still not close to being realistic. Consider that there are "only" 1.45×10^{17} seconds in the mythical evolutionary age of the earth. It can be calculated that each and every 100-mer protein in that hypothetical earth would need to rearrange itself an average of 2.67×10^{65} times per second in order to try all possible combinations! The 100-amino-acid molecules could not even come close to assembling and disassembling that quickly. It is physically impossible.

An age of 4.6 billion years is an extremely long time, to be sure, but I suspect evolutionists wish they had picked a much larger number for the age of the earth and of the universe. It becomes obvious why evolutionists are never quick to point out the actual numbers associated with the probabilities of life coming about by chance. Remember, we have only examined a small protein of 100 amino acids. The very same calculations could be performed considering that we need at least the 75 proteins mentioned above in order to have a self-replicating system. For 75 proteins of the same size, the probability of obtaining the correct sequences for all of them comes to 20^{7500} or 3.7779×10^{9700}!!! (That is correct, almost 9,700 zeros.)

Even if there were oceans full of amino acids just trying all kinds of different combinations, a correctly formed molecule in the Indian Ocean is not going to be able to cooperate very easily with another correctly formed molecule in the Atlantic Ocean. Nor would a correct sequence of amino acids be able to interact with another functional protein which happened to occur in the same physical location but a mere one year later. Truly, the thought of even one single functional protein arising by chance requires blind faith that will not or cannot grasp the numbers! Such thoughts are pure fantasy and have nothing to do with science.[10]

Dr. Chandra Wickramasinghe, professor and chairman of the Department of Applied Mathematics and Astronomy, University College, Cardiff, Wales calculates an even more pessimistic probability for human life by chance:

> Precious little in the way of biochemical evolution could have happened on the earth. If one counts the number of trial assemblies of amino acids that are needed to give rise to the enzymes, the probability of their discovery by random shufflings turns out to be less than one in ten to the 40 thousand.[11]

Is the Chemical Origin of Life Realistic?

If you're still not convinced that life could not develop by chance, just consider the number of understood physical laws that would have to be violated in order for chemicals to naturally produce life. Rich Deem provides the following analysis of chemical science applied to known biological facts in order to scientifically assert the impossibility of any other explanation of life than a Creator:

1. Homochirality somehow arose in the sugars and amino acids of prebiotic soups, although there is no mechanism by which this can occur[12] and is, in fact, prohibited by the second law of thermodynamics (law of entropy).[13]

2. In the absence of enzymes, there is no chemical reaction that produces the sugar ribose, the "backbone" of RNA and DNA.[14]

3. Chemical reactions in prebiotic soups produce other sugars that prevent RNA and DNA replication.[15]

4. Pyrimidine nucleosides (cytosine and uracil) do not form under prebiotic conditions and only purine (adenine and guanine) nucleosides are found in carbonaceous meteorites

(i.e., pyrimidine nucleosides don't form in outer space either).[16]

5. Even if a method for formation of pyrimidine nucleosides could be found, the combination of nucleosides with phosphate under prebiotic conditions produces not only nucleotides, but other products which interfere with RNA polymerization and replication.[17]

6. Purine and pyrimidine nucleotides (nucleosides combined with phosphate groups) do not form under prebiotic conditions.[18]

7. Neither RNA nor DNA can be synthesized in the absence of enzymes.

8. Enzymes cannot be synthesized in the absence of RNA and ribosomes.

9. Nucleosides and amino acids cannot form in the presence of oxygen [Geologists have overwhelming evidence that the Earth has always had oxygen present in the atmosphere].[19]

10. Adenine synthesis requires unreasonable HCN concentrations. Adenine deaminates with a half-life of 80 years (at 37°C, pH 7). Therefore, adenine would never accumulate in any kind of "prebiotic soup." The adenine-uracil interaction is weak and nonspecific, and, therefore, would never be expected to function in any specific recognition scheme under the chaotic conditions of a "prebiotic soup."[20]

11. Cytosine has never been found in any meteorites nor is it produced in electric spark discharge experiments using simulated "early earth atmosphere." All possible intermediates suffer severe problems.[21] Cytosine deaminates with an estimated half-life of 340 years, so would not be expected

to accumulate over time. Ultraviolet light on the early earth would quickly convert cytosine to its photohydrate and cyclobutane photodimers (which rapidly deaminate).[22]

12. Mixtures of amino acids in the Murchison meteorite show that there are many classes of prebiotic substances that would disrupt the necessary structural regularity of any RNA-like replicator.[23] Metabolic replicators suffer from a lack of an ability to evolve, since they do not mutate.[24]

13. The most common abiogenesis theories claim that life arose at hydrothermal vents in the ocean. However, recent studies show that polymerization of the molecules necessary for cell membrane assembly cannot occur in salt water.[25] C. Shyba and C. Sagan published a report indicating that the early oceans were at least twice as salty as they are now.[26] If this is true, the likelihood of life originating from hydrothermal vents in the ocean would be next to impossible.

At the conclusion of his compilation of chemical anomalies required to generate life spontaneously, Rich Deem notes:

New theories, such as assembly of biomolecules on mineral surfaces, are constantly being proposed to attempt to get around the problems associated with the spontaneous origin of life. However, even if you put purified chemicals together (which can't be synthesized prebiotically), you can get polymers only up to 50 mer (obviously not enough for life). Therefore, none of these theories has been able to get around the fundamental chemical problems required for life to have begun on the Earth.[27]

What have evolutionists concluded from their own analyses concerning the plausibility of life being spontaneously produced from mere chemicals?

It's a very long leap from [mineral] surface chemistry to a living cell.[28]

> — Norman Pace (Evolutionary Biologist, UC Berkeley; 1998).

There is now overwhelmingly strong evidence, both statistical and paleontological, that life could not have been started on Earth by a series of random chemical reactions.... There simply was not enough time ... to get life going.[29]

> — Niles Eldridge (paleontologist, American Museum of Natural History; 1992).

There is no agreement on the extent to which metabolism could develop independently of a genetic material. In my opinion, there is no basis in known chemistry for the belief that long sequences of reactions can organize spontaneously and every reason to believe that they cannot. The problem of achieving sufficient specificity, whether in aqueous solution or on the surface of a mineral, is so severe that the chance of closing a cycle of reactions as complex as the reverse citric acid cycle, for example, is negligible.[30]

> — Leslie Orgel, (The Salk Institute for Biological Studies; 1998).

Prebiotic chemistry would produce a wealth of biomolecules from non-living precursors. But the wealth soon became overwhelming, with the "prebiotic soups" having the chemical complexity of asphalt (useful, perhaps, for paving roads but not particularly promising as a wellspring for life). Classical prebiotic chemistry not only failed to constrain the contents of the prebiotic soup, but also raised a new paradox: How could life (or any organized chemical process) emerge from such a mess?

Searches of quadrillions of randomly generated RNA sequences have failed to yield a spontaneous RNA replicator.[31]

> — Steven A. Benner, (professor of Chemistry, University of Florida; 1999).

Summary

What does the testimony of Physics and Chemistry convey to man concerning his planetary environment? British cosmologist Sir Fred Hoyle colorfully summarizes the matter for us:

> A common sense interpretation of the facts suggests that a superintellect has monkeyed with physics, as well as with chemistry and biology, and that there are no blind forces worth speaking about in nature. The numbers one calculates from the facts seem to me so overwhelming as to put this conclusion almost beyond question.[32]

Most scientists are trained in classic evolution while gaining their accreditation for a specific field of expertise. Yet, with credentials in hand, a good number of scientists are reaching conclusions quite contrary to their evolutionary training. Frank Tipler, Professor of Mathematics at Tulane University, is one such scientist:

> When I began my career as a cosmologist some twenty years ago, I was a convinced atheist. I never in my wildest dreams imagined that one day I would be writing a book purporting to show that the central claims of Judeo-Christian theology are in fact true, that these claims are straightforward deductions of the laws of physics as we now understand them. I have been forced into these conclusions by the inexorable logic of my own special branch of physics.[33]

When one ponders the sophistication and complexities of the human body what is the rational conclusion concerning man's origin? Scott Huse answers this question.

> In the human body, DNA 'programs' all characteristics such as hair, skin, eyes, and height. DNA determines the arrangement for 206 bones, 600 muscles, 10,000 auditory nerve fibers, two million optic nerve fibers, 100 billion nerve cells, 400 billion feet of blood vessels and capillaries and so on. Such extraordinary sophistication can only reflect intelligent design.[34]

It is generally agreed that anything less probable than one chance in 10^{50} will statistically never happen. Because of the astronomically impossible odds of life developing through chance chemical operations, many evolutionists are bewildered, yet they will not consider the only workable alternative – a Creator God. During one particular conference in which evolutionists were discussing different theories of how life started, Dr. J. D. Bernal, who chaired the conference, made an astounding statement, "It would be much easier to discuss how life didn't originate than how it did."[35] After years of study, evolutionist Johnjoe McFadden (Professor of Molecular Biology and Quantum Physics) concluded, "The simplest living cell could not have arisen by chance."[36] May more naturalists come to this scientific conclusion! Life itself is a timeless testimony of an ever-living God – there is no explanation for life apart from Him. In fact, life would have no meaning apart from Him.

The Testimony of Fossils

Paleontology and Geology have provided man some of the most concrete evidence of what has and has not happened on Earth in the past. By assessing these facts together, we can contemplate the various possibilities for the origin of life. Do the observations of Paleontology and Geology verify evolutionary theory or another cause of life? You be the judge.

Charles Darwin alleged that if evolution were true, the evidence would be contained in the fossil record. He predicted that the geological strata would reveal gradual upward evolutionary development in the complexity of species, and if these were not found, the validity of his theory of evolution should be brought into question:

> The abrupt manner in which whole groups of species suddenly appear in certain formations has been urged by several paleontologists ... as a fatal objection to the belief in the transmutation of species. There is another and allied difficulty, which is much more serious. I allude to the manner in which species belonging to several of the main divisions of the animal kingdom suddenly appear in the lowest known fossiliferous rocks. ... To the question why we do not find rich fossiliferous deposits belonging to these assumed earliest periods prior to the Cambrian system I can give no satisfactory answer. ... The case at present must remain inexplicable; and may be truly urged as a valid argument against the [evolutionary] views here entertained.[1]

In fairness to the theory of evolution it is understood that much of the fossil record has yet to be determined. Keith Miller suggests, "Our knowledge of history of life can be put into perspective by a comparison with our knowledge of living organisms. About 1.5 million living species have been described by biologists, while paleontologists have cataloged only about 250,000 fossil species...."[2] It is likely that a number of extinct species will not be found in the fossil record and it is also likely that some species not previously cataloged will be found. However, if evolution were true, the fossil record should be packed full of transitional forms – these forms should be very evident. A leading evolutionist, Jeffrey Schwartz, professor of anthropology at the University of Pittsburgh, acknowledges this point: "Given that evolution, according to Darwin, was in a continual state of motion ... it followed logically that the fossil record should be rife with examples of transitional forms leading from the less to the more evolved."[3]

So the pertinent question to be answered is not what we do not know concerning the fossil record, but rather what evidence has been found after 150 years of digging to support Darwin's evolutionary theory. Appendix II, organized by various biological classifications, contains the conclusions of dozens of experts in the fields of archeology, paleontology and biology, most of which hold an evolutionary mindset. It is recognized that there are some debatable findings which may support evolutionary development of life, but the overwhelming testimony of these experts is that the fossil record does not support the theory of evolution. The quotes, which range over decades of scientific study, indicate that not much has changed verification-wise since the theory was first introduced.

The Fossil Record Summarized

Vance Ferrell's *The Evolution Handbook* (2006) is an excellent compilation of information on evolution. He draws from the testimonies of hundreds of experts in the various scientific fields of study and summarizes several of the key problems with evolutionary theory in conjunction with fossil evidence in various strata. He states, "These problems are serious enough that any one of them is enough to overthrow the evolutionary theory in regard to paleontology and stratigraphy." Why does the fossil record not support evolution?

1. Life suddenly appears in the bottom fossil-strata level, the Cambrian, with no precursors.
2. When these lowest life forms appear (they are small slow-moving, shallow-sea creatures), they are outstandingly abundant, numbered in the billions of specimens, and quite complex.
3. No transitional species are to be found at the bottom of the strata, the Cambrian.
4. Just below the Cambrian, in the Precambrian, there are no fossil specimens. [This statement may be slightly overstated – I will clarify in the next section].
5. No transitional species are to be found below the lowest stratum, in the Precambrian.
6. No transitional species are to be found above the bottom stratum, from the Ordovician on up.
7. Higher taxa (forms of life) appear just as suddenly in the strata farther up. These higher types (such as beavers, giraffes, etc.) suddenly appear with no hint of transitional life forms leading up to them.
8. When they appear, vast numbers of these life forms are to be found.[4]

Most of us, from early grammar school upwards, were taught that evolution was the best scientific explanation of life. Was this explanation, however, based on true scientific findings or conjecture? Does the fossil record uphold evolution as a valid theory? What is the consensus of leading evolutionists concerning the fossil record?

This regular absence of transitional forms is not confined to mammals, but is an almost universal phenomenon, as has long been noted by paleontologists. It is true of almost all classes of animals, both vertebrate and invertebrate ... it is true of the losses, and of the major animal phyla, and it is apparently also true of analogous categories of plants.

> — G. G. Simpson, *Tempo and Mode in Evolution* (1944), p. 107.

The history of most fossil species includes two [only one is quoted here] features particularly inconsistent with gradualism: 1. Stasis. Most species exhibit no directional change during their tenure on earth. They appear in the fossil record looking much the same as when they disappear; morphological change is usually limited and directionless.

> — Steven J. Gould, "Evolution's Erratic Pace," *Natural History*, May 1977, p. 14 [The late Steven Jay Gould was a leading proponent of evolution].

The absence of fossil evidence for intermediary stages between major transitions in organic design, indeed our inability, even in our imagination, to construct functional intermediates in many cases, has been a persistent and nagging problem for gradualistic accounts of evolution.

> — Steven J. Gould, "Is a new and general theory of evolution emerging?", Paleobiology 6:119–130, 1980, p.127.

The fact is that subsequently no new phyla have appeared, and no new classes and orders. This fact, which has been long ignored, is perhaps the most powerful of all arguments against Darwin's generalization.

> — G. R. Taylor, in *The Great Evolution Mystery* (1983), p. 138.

Paleontology is now looking at what it actually finds, not what it is told that it is supposed to find. As is now well known, most fossil species appear instantaneously in the record, persist for some millions of years virtually unchanged, only to disappear abruptly.

> — T. Kemp, "A Fresh Look at the Fossil Record," *New Scientist*, December 5, 1985, p. 66.

Evolutionary biology's deepest paradox concerns this strange discontinuity. Why haven't new animal body plans continued to crawl out of the evolutionary cauldron during the past hundreds of millions of years? Why are the ancient body plans so stable?

> — Jeffrey S. Levington, "The Big Bang of Animal Evolution," *Scientific American*, Vol. 267, Nov. 1992, p. 84.

It is a simple ineluctable truth that virtually all members of a biota [plant and animal life in a particular region] remain basically stable, with minor fluctuations, throughout their durations [speaking of the fossil record].

> — Niles Eldredge, *The Pattern of Evolution* (W. H. Freeman and Co., New York; 1998), p. 157.

... it was and still is the case that, with the exception of Dobzhansky's claim about a new species of fruit fly, the formation of a new species, by any mechanism, has never been observed.

> — Jeffrey H. Schwartz, *Sudden Origins* (John Wiley, New York; 1999), p. 300.

We cannot identify ancestors or "missing links," and we cannot devise testable theories to explain how particular episodes of evolution came about. Gee is adamant that all the popular stories about how the first amphibians conquered the dry land, how the birds developed wings and feathers for flying, how the dinosaurs went extinct, and how humans evolved from apes are just products of our imagination, driven by prejudices and preconceptions.

> — Bowler, Peter J., Review of *In Search of Deep Time* by Henry Gee (Free Press, 1999), *American Scientist* (vol. 88, March/April 2000), p. 169 [both men are evolutionists].

Wherever we look at the living biota ... discontinuities are overwhelmingly frequent.... The discontinuities are even more striking in the fossil record. New species usually appear in the fossil record suddenly, not connected with their ancestors by a series of intermediates.

> — Ernst Mayr, *What is Evolution*; 2001, p. 189.

The Field Museum of Natural History in Chicago, Illinois contains one of the largest collections of fossils in the world. The former Dean of the Museum, Dr. David Raup, summarizes what transitions of life are observed or not observed in the fossil record.

Well, we are now about 120 years after Darwin and the knowledge of the fossil record has been greatly expanded. We now have a quarter of a million fossil species but the situation hasn't changed much. The record of evolution is still surprisingly jerky and, ironically, we have even fewer examples of evolutionary transition than we had in Darwin's time. By this I mean that some of the classic cases of darwinian change in the fossil record, such as the evolution of the horse in North America, have had to be discarded or modified as a result of more detailed information—what appeared to be a nice simple progression when relatively few data were available now appears to be much more complex and much less gradualistic. So Darwin's problem has not been alleviated in the last 120 years and we still have a record which does show change but one that can hardly be looked upon as the most reasonable consequence of natural selection. [5]

Although many of the experts in the field of paleontology still hold to some form of evolutionary thinking, their keen evaluations of the fossil record indicate serious problems with the theory. The general consensus of paleontologists has not changed much since Darwin first published *The Origin of Species* – the testimony of fossils does not favor the theory of evolution.

Fossil Dating

Various scientific means of dating fossils have been developed, though some are more accurate than others, none have proven reliably accurate. Whether one refers to the exponential decay properties of carbon-14 or other radioactive isotopes, or the magnetic field strength of the igneous layer in which fossils are imbedded, the extrapolation of huge periods of time from limited data will be prone to error.

What is generally agreed is that the lowest rock strata containing fossils is the Cambrian. Below the Cambrian system is

71

the Precambrian, which has no fossils, other than occasional al-
gae on its surface and a few debatable protists and bacteria.
Some have claimed that sponges, cnidarians, ctenophores, and
mollusks can also be found in the upper Precambrian strata, but
this is not the general consensus of paleontologists.

One of the difficulties in fossil dating for the evolutionists is
the fact that fossils of all major branches of the animal kingdom
(each type and species, without blending) have been found in the
Cambrian system of rocks, allegedly the second oldest system.
Staunch evolutionist Steven J. Gould admits, "The Cambrian
explosion was the most remarkable and puzzling event in the
history of life."[6] It seems odd, if evolution were true, that fossilized examples of complex life should be found in layers beneath
those containing simpler organisms and that no transitional species are found beneath the Cambrian system. Unless, of course,
the layers were originated at nearly the same time and while a
wide range of living organisms inhabited the Earth. This would
be the case in Noah's day, but is it possible for all these fossils to
have formed in less than 5000 years?

Actually, it is quite feasible that living creatures destroyed
and buried by the biblical deluge could be fossilized already. But
doesn't it require millions of years to create fossils? Scientific
evidence has proven that petrifaction can happen quickly. A petrified bowler hat is on display in 'The Buried Village,' an open
air museum dedicated to the Mt. Tarawera eruption in New Zealand. Petrified wood can form quickly under the right conditions
– one process has even been patented.[7]

Thousands of fossil formations all over the world provide
evidence of quick sedimentary capture and fossilization. For example, soft parts (jellyfish, animal feces, scales and fins of fish)
or whole, large, fully-articulated skeletons (e.g., whales or large
dinosaurs such as T-Rex) are preserved. We also find many creatures' bodies contorted. This evidence shows that these creatures
were buried rapidly (in many cases even buried alive) and fossil-

ized before scavengers, micro-decay organisms and erosional processes could erase the evidence. These are found all over the world and all through the various strata.[8]

A petrified shark was found to have the cross-sectional width of only one half inch indicating that it had been expediently compressed shortly after its death by an enormous amount of sediment. Fossilized trees have been found with oval cross-sectional areas indicating that they were water logged and quickly compressed by sediment.

Billions of well-preserved fossilized fish have been located in rock layers around the world. Frequently, these fossils include intact fins and scales, indicating that they were buried rapidly and that the encasing rock hardened quickly. In the real world, dead fish are scavenged within 24 hours. Even in some idealized cold, sterile, predator-free and oxygen-free water, they will become soggy and fall apart within weeks. A fish buried quickly in sediment that did not harden within a few weeks would be subject to decay by oxygen and bacteria, such that the delicate features like fins, scales, etc. would not be preserved. Rapid burial in the many underwater landslides (turbidity currents) and other sedimentary processes accompanying the Genesis Flood would explain not only their excellent preservation, but their existence in huge deposits, often covering thousands of square kilometers. This rapid burial explains why many discovered fossils seem to provide a snapshot in time of special events. A fossilized mother ichthyosaur in the process of giving birth, and fossilized fish which are found either in the process of swallowing other fish or with undigested fish intact in their stomachs are but a few examples.[9]

Thousands of fossil formations all over the world provide evidence of quick sedimentary capture and also possess a general order. The fact that the Cambrian system contains many fossils of the larger slower moving creatures and that the rock formations above the Cambrian contain higher fossil concentrations of smaller (faster) creatures would also give evidence of rising water throughout the world. Some creatures would be able to seek higher ground more quickly than others during catastrophic flooding.

More Evidence of a Worldwide Flood

Some creationists have suggested that the Genesis account of the flood refers to a localized flood and not a worldwide deluge. This position undermines the weight of the biblical narrative which clearly states that God destroyed all non-aquatic life on the earth by the flood (Gen. 6:17, 7:21-23, 9:15), and that water first covered the tops of hills, then mountains (Gen. 7:18-21). If the flood was only a localized event how did the ark come to rest on Mt. Ararat, and why did Noah and his family have to remain in the ark for 377 days?

Researchers have generated volumes of evidence indicating that a worldwide flood occurred on the Earth a few thousand years ago. Besides the before mentioned, the following discoveries provide a few more examples of this evidence.

Unfossilized Dinosaur Bones

Red blood cells and hemoglobin have been found in some unfossilized dinosaur bones. These could not last more that a few thousand years, certainly not 65 million years ago, the time frame evolutionists think the last dinosaur lived.[10] This evidence would suggest that dinosaurs existed more recently than evolutionary theory indicates; perhaps the dinosaurs were widely wiped out by the flood.

Sea Shells on Mountains

Evolutionary theory cannot scientifically accommodate the devastation of a world wide flood. If there was no such flood, how then does one explain the fact that fossilized sea life has been found on every major mountain range on the planet? These fossils are well above sea level, and most were discovered far from any body of water.[11]

Polystrate Fossils

In Nova Scotia, the US, Germany and other parts of Europe, many polystrate fossils have been discovered; these testify of past catastrophic flooding. In Nova Scotia, fossilized trees protruding through twelve layers (straits) are affixed in limestone, and the only way to make limestone is with water. Similar polystrate fossils of trees have been found in Germany. The detail at the top of these fossils is as clear as at the bottom, and no budging marks are observed through the strata (the trees didn't grow up through the strata). In some cases, the trees are actually buried upside down with roots at the top. N. A. Rupke produced a photograph of "a lofty trunk, exposed in a sandstone quarry near Edinburgh, Scotland, which measured no less than 25 meters and, intersecting 10 or 12 different strata, leaned at an angle of about 40 degrees"[12] Through flooding dynamics, the tree was buried so fast that it neither had time to fall to the ground or to float upwards – massive amounts of sediments affixed the tree at an inclined angle.

This fossilized structure could not have been the result of twelve different localized floods; each one burying the same tree in additional feet of sediments, and only after the previous layer had hardened and before the tree rotted. The evolutionary geological time scale represented in this strata gradient would be hundreds of millions of years, but the short life of a tree confirms this assumption to be incorrect. Polystrate fossils are found throughout the world, confirming that immense flooding caused a number of sedimentary layers to quickly form all over the world.

The Bible speaks of such a flood in the days of Noah. Water rushed up from below the surface of the earth and water suspended in the atmosphere condensed to cover the entire surface of the planet (Gen. 7:10-19). This is the sobering consequence: *"So He [God] destroyed all living things which were on the face of the ground: both man and cattle, creeping thing and bird of the air. They were destroyed from the earth. Only Noah and those who were with him in the ark remained alive"* (Gen. 7:23). The fossil record supports the biblical account.

Some have suggested that the language of Genesis chapters 6 through 8 indicate that a localized flood wiped out mankind. If that were the case, why would Noah have needed to gather animals in the ark to preserve their posterity? If it were a local event, the water level could not have raised up over the tops of the tall hills and then the mountains (Gen. 6:19-20) without spreading out over all the Earth, as the region is well above sea level. The fact that Noah and his family didn't see land for approximately half a year and remained in the ark for over a year implies that it was not a localized flood, but a worldwide event. God did not spare the old world (*kosmos*); the only earth dwelling creatures not destroyed were Noah, his family, and the animals in the ark (Heb. 11:7; 2 Pet. 2:5).

Coal Deposits in Antarctica

Coal deposits are found along the coast of Antarctica and throughout the Transantarctic Mountains. Coal forms when plants are buried in water and sediment before decomposition can take place. Abundant vegetation once existed on Antarctica, even on its mountains, but this reality came to an end with a catastrophic flood, the aftermath of which buried the plant life in sediment (now coal deposits) and created the polar ice caps – all but three percent of Antarctica is ice bound to this day.[13]

The naturalist claims that it requires an enormous amount of time to turn vegetation into coal. Argonne National Laboratories has shown that heating wood (lignin, its major component), water and acidic clay at 150°C (rather cool geologically) for 4 to 36 weeks, in a sealed quartz tube with no added pressure, forms high-grade black coal.[14] The geological conditions immediately after Noah's flood would be a good explanation for the vast coal deposits found throughout the world – even in Antarctica.

Tightly Bent Strata

In many mountainous regions, strata thousands of feet thick are bent and folded into hairpin shapes. The conventional geologic time scale states that these formations were buried and solidified hundreds of millions of years before they were bent. Yet, the folding occurred without cracking, with radii so small that the entire formation would have had to have been wet and unsolidified when the bending occurred. This implies that the folding occurred within a relative short time, not hundreds of millions of years after deposition.[15]

Dr. Terry Mortenson writes:

> Thousands of feet of sedimentary rocks (of various layers) are bent (like a stack of thin pancakes over the edge of a plate), as we see at the mile-deep Kaibab Upwarp in the Grand Canyon. Clearly the whole, mile-deep deposit of various kinds of sediment was still relatively soft and probably wet (not like it is today) when the earthquake occurred that uplifted one part of the series of strata.[16]

Though some geologists have theorized that high pressure and extreme heat over time may account for this anomaly, the very thickness of the strata, which is not characterized by cracks but by fluid hairpin bends, seems better explained by vast sediments being deposited all at once and remaining soft during erratic shifting of the Earth's crust – this certainly would have been the case during Noah's flood.

Conclusion

The bottom line, Darwin predicted that the fossil record would show numerous transitional fossils, but a century and a half of digging has produced only a handful of disputable candidates; out of tens of millions of fossils unearthed, no conclusive transitional proof has been found. This fact baffled Charles

Darwin in his day and continues to confront the evolutionist today! H. Enoch writes:

> Charles Darwin, himself the father of evolution in his later days, gradually became aware of the lack of real evidence for his evolutionary speculation and wrote: 'As by this theory, innumerable transitional forms must have existed. Why do we not find them embedded in the crust of the earth? Why is not all nature in confusion instead of being, as we *see* them, well defined species?[17]

Darwin's question is answered in the book of Genesis. God created all the species of life, including man, at nearly the same time: *"And God made the beast of the earth according to its kind, cattle according to its kind, and everything that creeps on the earth according to its kind. And God saw that it was good"* (Gen. 1:25). Everything, including man, which is alive today or was alive yesterday, was originally created at nearly the same time. Man was the crowning act to God's grand creation (Heb. 2:9) – man was created on the sixth day: *"So God created man in His own image; in the image of God He created him; male and female He created them"* (Gen. 1:27).

Man was to represent God in His creation and have authority over it. When man rebelled against His Creator, however, God could not allow a fallen head to rule over a perfect creation; thus, God cursed man's domain, the Earth (Gen. 3:15-19; Rom. 8:22). Before man sinned he did not experience death and the Earth was not cursed (Rom. 5:12). Therefore, sin initiated the fossil record – a registry of death continued unabated unto this day. This explains why there is a sudden appearance of distinct species in the fossil records, as the above experts acknowledge, and why the supposed transitional links are widely missing. The fossil record and unique geological formations provide evidence of a Creator and of a catastrophic worldwide flood which actually occurred, just as recorded in the book of Genesis.

The Testimony of Astronomy, Biology and Anthropology

In this chapter, some of the findings in the fields of Astronomy, Biology, and Anthropology will be investigated, which may provide a testimony of supernatural influence within the physical realm rather than affirming naturalistic processes.

Astronomy

Early evolutionists following in Darwin's footsteps pinned all their hopes on the steady state theory of the universe, which indeed did blow up in their faces with a *Big Bang* at the turn of the twentieth century. The progeny of Darwin and a number of atheistic scientists believed that the universe had always been here and was unchanging, but discoveries in astronomy and mathematical models during the WW1 era by Vesto Melvin Slipher, Albert Einstein, Willem de Sitter, and Alexander Friedmann provided astounding evidence that the universe had a distinct beginning and was expanding. Some creationists were delighted with this development, while others voice concerned that a literal creation week was being compromised. Consequently, the *Big Bang* simply refocused an ongoing scientific debate from "Did the universe have a beginning?" to "When did the universe begin?"

The actual age of the Earth is an ongoing scientific debate in which astronomical data is being used in various ways to support both *Young Earth* and *Old Earth* positions. The objective here is to highlight scientific evidence indicating that man should be exploring another possibility of our origin beyond nature itself (i.e. the possibility of a Creator).

The difficulty of analyzing astronomical data is that so much of space is yet uncharted and the *apparent* fact that light from the edge of the universe requires tens of billions of years to arrive at the Earth. Therefore, both Old Earth and Young Earth advocates are challenged to explain: (1) Why do we see what we see? (2) What is beyond what we see? Several theories pertaining to variations in the speed of light and to the displacement of relative time due to gravitational shifting in the universe are being considered presently.

Because so much of this field is prone to assumption, speculation, and developing theories, I am limiting astronomical observation to what *seems* to necessitate design rather than chance development or what *seems* to confound evolutionary models (either in timing or dynamics). By the nature of the field, then, the following items of interest would be the easiest for a naturalist to rebuff with theoretical solutions.

Dissimilar Planets and Moons

If the planets and their 156 known moons all evolved from the same material and in the same way (i.e. from a swirling dust cloud billions of years ago), would not there be many physical similarities? Yet, this is not the case. The magnetic fields of the planets are vastly different. The Earth's surface was shaped by plate tectonics, but Venus has none. Theoretically, all nine planets (counting Pluto) should spin in the same direction, but Venus, Uranus, and Pluto rotate in the opposite direction that the Earth does. Of the known 156 moons in the solar system, 30 have backward orbits. Furthermore, Jupiter, Saturn, Uranus, and Neptune have moons orbiting in both directions. The orbit of each of these 156 moons should lie in the equatorial plane of the planet it orbits, but many, including the Earth's moon, are in highly inclined orbits.[1]

Old Sun – Frozen Earth

If, as evolutionists teach, the solar system evolved from a spinning dust and gas cloud 4.5 billion years ago, the slowly condensing Sun would have radiated 25 to 30 percent less heat during its first 600 million years than it radiates today. Some estimates are as high as 40 percent less radiation from its origin until now. Consequently, four billion years ago the earth would have been seven to ten percent cooler than it is today, thus, causing the water on the earth's surface to freeze. The Earth would have been like a large icy mirror reflecting the Sun's radiation back into space, further lengthening the time the Earth remained in a deep freeze. Once the Sun's output increased and the Earth thawed out, not enough time would have been remaining for life to develop according to naturalism.[2]

Missing Matter

The physical laws associated with the big bang theory require a certain amount of matter in the universe to keep the rapidly expanding universe from flying apart; otherwise, matter could not come together to form stars and galaxies. Estimates of the universe's actual mass always fell far short of that minimum amount. But to maintain the big bang theory, the missing matter must be there, so scientists have developed a name for the missing matter which cannot be detected – dark matter. Dr. Walter Brown reports that "neither 'dark matter' (created to hold the universe together) nor 'dark energy' (created to push the universe apart) can be seen, measured or tested. We are told that most of the universe is composed of invisible dark matter and dark energy. Few realize that both mystical concepts were devised to preserve the big bang theory."[3] This is faith-based science not evidence-based conclusions.

Hot Planets

Jupiter and Neptune each radiate more than twice the heat energy they receive from the Sun, while Saturn – which radiates nearly three times the energy it receives from the sun back into space – is of special interest as it has far less mass than its neighbor Jupiter. From a thermodynamic standpoint, Saturn in no way could have retained its primeval heat if formed 4.5 billion years ago. Calculations show it is very unlikely that this energy comes from nuclear fusion, radioactive decay, gravitational contraction, or phase changes within those planets. This suggests that these planets have not existed long enough, per the evolutionary model, to cool off.[4]

Io's Volcanoes

The Voyager I probe was launched into space on September 5, 1977 and made its closest approach to the planet Jupiter on March 5, 1979, at which time it relayed back to Earth thousands of pictures and measurements of Jupiter and its moons. Amazingly, Io, the innermost of the four original "Galilean moons" was found to have over sixty active volcanoes! These volcanoes spew plumes of ejecta at some 2,000 miles per hour to heights of 60 to 160 miles above Io's surface. The usual evolutionary model portrays all the planets and moons as being molten 5 billion years ago. During the next billion years, they are said to have had active volcanoes. Then, 4 billion years ago, the volcanism stopped as they cooled. Io is quite small, yet it has many active volcanoes. Obviously, it has not cooled off, so perhaps it is not as old as evolutionist say it is.[5]

Mercury's High Density and Magnetic Field

Mercury has been found to have the highest density of all the known planets (other than Earth). Mercury is so dense that it is thought to have an iron core occupying 75 percent of its diameter. This extraordinary density contradicts evolutionary models of planetary formation. Some evolutionists theorize that a very dense object collided with Mercury to provide it with such a high density. However, common sense would suggest that any small planet hit with the equivalent of 75 percent of its present mass would be destroyed – most of the remnants would pile into the Sun.[6]

Secondly, for Mercury to be billions of years old and still have a magnetic field means fluid motion must still exist within the planet's core: therefore, the core itself must be molten. Mercury is so small that the general opinion is that the planet (i.e. its core) should have frozen solid eons ago.[7] Therefore, by evolutionary reckoning the core could not be molten; Mercury cannot have a magnetic field. But it does!

Comets

Comets are continually being lost as their materials dissipate, as they collide with planets and asteroids, or as they are ejected from the solar system. If the solar system were billions of years old, all comets would have long ago ceased to exist if they were not continually being replaced. All known comets dissipate their material with each orbit around the sun and should not survive more than 100,000 years. So if the universe is billions of years old, how are comets formed and put into high speed motion? As with many scientific fields of study, the evidence is still coming in; Danny R. Faulkner (Ph.D. Astronomy) summarizes what is presently known:

> While it was once thought that the Oort cloud could account for all comets, computer simulations have clearly shown that short-period comets cannot originate from the cloud, so the Kuiper belt has been revived to explain the origin of the short period comets. ... It is now clear that short period comets do not evolve from long period comets, and so the two groups of comets require different sources. In their original forms, the Kuiper belt was devised to explain the existence of short pe-

riod comets, and the Oort cloud was to explain the origin of long period comets. While the orbits of these two groups of comets are quite different, there does not appear to be any difference in composition between the two groups. ... Evolutionary astronomers have spent much time developing scenarios to explain the existence of comets in a 4.6 Ga Solar System. Despite this effort and apparent progress, there are still many questions and problems. At this time it is still quite doubtful that either the Kuiper belt or Oort cloud exist, as they must in an old Solar System. It is concluded that comets still offer a good argument for the recent creation of the Solar System.[8]

Some recent analytical models indicate collisions during the theoretical Oort cloud formation would have left too little mass (perhaps only the mass of one to three Earths) to produce the millions of comets necessary to replenish an old solar system model (i.e. billions of years old).[9] The existence of the Kuiper belt and the unobservable Oort cloud of comets, which evolutionists claim somehow manufacture and randomly hurl new comets into our solar system by the effect of passing stars, remain unverifiable theories. Evolutionist Carl Sagan agrees: Many scientific papers are written each year about the Oort Cloud, its properties, its origin, its evolution. Yet there is not yet a shred of direct observational evidence for its existence.[10]

Spiraling Galaxies

If the universe were billions of years old, the numerous spiral galaxies we observe should have long ago unspiraled, and the high concentrations of matter in the universe should have dispersed long ago. Russel Humphreys (Ph.D. Physics) writes:

"The stars of our own galaxy, the Milky Way, rotate about the galactic center with different speeds, the inner ones rotating faster than the outer ones. The observed rotation speeds are so fast that if our galaxy were more than a few hundred million years old, it would be a featureless disc of stars instead of its present spiral shape."[11]

Because both nearby and faraway galaxies show the same spiral structure, the evolutionist astronomer is, thus, 'caught' in two ways:
1. The nearby galaxies should not be spirals anymore, because in the time that is supposed to have elapsed, they should have wound themselves up long ago, blurring the spiral appearance.
2. These recently-observed galaxies are ultra-young (according to 'big bang' belief) because they are so far away. So they should not have had time to develop even the beginnings of a spiral. [12]

Peering out into the vast expanse of space, various phenomenon confound man's reason as to the timing of it all. If an expanding universe and visible light from great distances seem to indicate an ancient existence, then why do binary star combinations contain old and new stars? Why do giant and high energy stars still exist? Why do enormous fast moving star clusters still exist? Why do only a very few widely expanded supernova remnants exist? Science can speculate concerning these and other mysteries woven into the vast canopy of space, but ultimately our conclusion will rest upon what we believe the answer is. As a side note, Russ Humphrey's book *Starlight and Time* is an excellent resource of information on the subject of light propagation in time.

The Bible states that God *"stretched out the heavens"* (Isa. 48:13) in such a way that all the various galactic forms *"declare the glory of God"* (Ps. 19:1). If this is true, by design the heavenly realms will leave some awestruck and others baffled as to their intended purpose. In either case, God has been exalted, and He receives the glory! What is the consequence of peering into space and continually witnessing the glory of God? Hugh Ross notes in his book *The Creator and the Cosmos*, "Astronomers who do not draw theistic or deistic conclusions are becoming rare, and even the few dissenters hint that the tide is against them."[13]

Biology
Mutations

Mutations are the only known means by which new genetic information becomes available for evolution. Mutations can produce new traits and even a longer DNA log, but they do not generate new genetic information which benefits the organism. Almost all observable mutations are harmful; some are meaningless; many are lethal. Rarely is a mutation beneficial to an organism in its natural environment, and no known mutations have increased genetic information, even in such rare instances as where the mutation confers an advantage.[14]

Lee Spetner (Ph.D. Physics, MIT) writes, "But in all the reading I've done in the life-sciences literature, I've never found a mutation that added information.... All point mutations that have been studied on the molecular level turn out to reduce the genetic information and not increase it."[15] Ray Bohlin (Ph.D. Molecular and Cell Biology) echoes this conclusion, "We see the apparent inability of mutations truly to contribute to the origin of new structures. The theory of gene duplication in its present form is unable to account for the origin of new genetic information – a must for any theory of evolutionary mechanism."[16] If natural selection were true, by definition harmful mutations and disorders would be eliminated, but in fact, genetic disorders are increasing at an alarming rate. The reader will find John Sandord's book *Genetic Entropy and the Mystery of the Genome* a helpful resource on this subject matter.

Species

The fact that all true plant and animal species are distinct types is a crux in the entire evolutionary controversy. In *The Origin of Species,* Darwin focused mostly on the development of various species without ever addressing the origin of the universe, the origin of life, or the origin of species – the very title of his book. Eldredge Niles writes: "Darwin never really did discuss the origin of the species in his *The Origin of Species.*"[17] Though Darwin proposed possible mechanisms for how species could become distinct (e.g. reproductive isolation coupled with natural selection), he was confounded by the fossil record which showed no species developed; in fact, the evidence for species distinction was overwhelming. H. Enoch records Darwin's later frustration concerning known reality as compared to his evolutionary theory:

> Charles Darwin, himself the father of evolution in his later days, gradually became aware of the lack of real evidence for his evolutionary speculation and wrote: "As by this theory, innumerable transitional forms must have existed. Why do we not find them embedded in the crust of the earth? Why is not all nature in confusion instead of being, as we see them, well defined species?"[18]

What did Darwin conclude concerning evidence to support the theory that one species slowly evolves into another? He wrote: "Not one change of species into another is on record ... we cannot prove that a single species has been changed."[19] Because evolutionists cannot figure out where species came from, "More biologists would agree with Professor Hampton Carson of Washington University, St. Louis, when he says that speciation is 'a major unsolved problem of evolutionary biology.'"[20]

Consciousness

The consciousness of humans is a mystery that has baffled neurophysiologists for decades. How did naturalism produce consciousness? No one really knows, according to Jim Holt:

> When an organism's neural pathways grow sufficiently complex, materialists insist, their firings are somehow accompanied by consciousness. But despite decades of effort by philosophers and neurophysiologists, no one has been able to come up with a remotely plausible explanation of how this happens--how the hunk of gray meat in our skull gives rise to private Technicolor experience. One distinguished commentator on the mind-body problem, Daniel Dennett, author of *Consciousness Explained*, has been driven to declare that there is really no such thing as consciousness – we are all zombies, though we're unaware of it.[21]

Evolution cannot explain consciousness or free will. In investigating websites supporting naturalism, I found this response to the argument that human consciousness is evidence of a Creator: "Not knowing an explanation does not mean an explanation is impossible. And since we are barely beginning to understand what consciousness is, it is not surprising that we would not have its origin worked out yet."[22] The logic is sound, but by the same reasoning, the following statement would also be true: "Not knowing God does not mean that God does not exist." Those who do not want to know Him personally will not be afforded the opportunity.

How does chemical matter become living tissue which is able to learn, reason, remember, communicate, show emotion, choose, and exhibit individualized personality? The only reasonable answer is that man was specifically designed with certain faculties in which he would be enabled to willingly accomplish some intended purpose (Rev. 4:11).

What does God expect from a creature fashioned in His image and likeness, who has moral understanding, consciousness, reasoning skills and a will to choose? *"He [God] has shown you, O man, what is good; And what does the Lord require of you but to do justly, to love mercy, and to walk humbly with your God?"* (Mic. 6:8). God created man with the intent of fellowship, but He will not force anyone to have communion with Him. *"Let him who thirsts come. Whoever desires, let him take the water of life freely"* (Rev. 22:17). *"Come to Me, all you who labor and are heavy laden, and I will give you rest. Take My yoke upon you and learn from Me, for I am gentle and lowly in heart, and you will find rest for your souls"* (Matt. 11:28-29). If man was without consciousness, there would be no opportunity to come! God did not want a robotic manufactured creation which could not freely express love back to Him in response to the love received from Him. Love is impossible without the choice to be selfless!

Anthropology

Cultural Legends
From an anthropological point of view, over 250 cultural legends exist concerning a great flood worldwide. Most have similarities to the Genesis story.[23] Certainly some of these legends relate to localized floods, but the strong similarities of many stories indicate a common source of information, a common cataclysmic event.

Population Growth
Creation scientist Don Batten poses a thought-provoking question: If evolution were true, and man did develop from apes, "Where are all the people?" He, then, provides analytical models for various population predictions based on how long man has

actually been on the earth and a brief analysis of what archeological evidence indicates on the matter.

The current growth rate of the world population is about 1.7%
per year. Many assume that modern medicine accounts for the
world's population growth. However, 'third world' countries
contribute most of the population growth, suggesting that modern medicine is not as important as many think. Population
growth in a number of South American and African countries
exceeds 3% per year. In many industrialized countries with
modern medical facilities, the population growth is less than
0.5%. ...

What growth rate is needed to get six billion people since the
Flood? It is relatively easy to calculate the growth rate needed to
get today's population from Noah's three sons and their wives,
after the Flood. With the Flood at about 4,500 years ago, it
needs less than 0.5% per year growth. That's not very much. Of
course, population growth has not been constant. There is rea-
sonably good evidence that growth has been slow at times—
such as in the Middle Ages in Europe. However, data from the
Bible (Genesis 10, 11) shows that the population grew quite
quickly in the years immediately after the Flood. Shem had five
sons, Ham had four, and Japheth had seven. If we assume that
they had the same number of daughters, then they averaged 10.7
children per couple. In the next generation, Shem had 14 grand-
sons, Ham, 28 and Japheth, 23, or 130 children in total. That is
an average of 8.1 per couple. ...

Let us take the average of all births in the first two post-Flood
generations as 8.53 children per couple. The average age at
which the first son was born in the seven post-Flood generations
in Shem's line ranged from 35 to 29 years (Genesis 11:10–24),
with an average of 31 years, so a generation time of 40 years is
reasonable. Hence, just four generations after the Flood would
see a total population of over 3,000 people (remembering that
the longevity of people was such that Noah, Shem, Ham, Ja-

pheth, etc., were still alive at that time). This represents a population growth rate of 3.7% per year, or a doubling time of about 19 years.

The Jews are descendants of Jacob (also called Israel). The number of Jews in the world in 1930, before the Nazi Holocaust, was estimated at 18 million. This represents a doubling in population, on average, every 156 years, or 0.44% growth per year since Jacob. Since the Flood, the world population has doubled every 155 years, or grown at an average of 0.45% per year. There is agreement between the growth rates for the two populations. ...

What if people had been around for one million years?

Evolutionists claim that mankind evolved from apes about a million years ago. If the population had grown at just 0.01% per year since then (doubling only every 7,000 years), there could be 10^{43} people today. ... Those who adhere to the evolutionary story argue that disease, famine and war kept the numbers almost constant for most of this period, which means that mankind was on the brink of extinction for most of this supposed history. ... Where are all the bodies?

Evolutionists also claim there was a 'Stone Age' of about 100,000 years when between one million and 10 million people lived on Earth. Fossil evidence shows that people buried their dead, often with artifacts—cremation was not practiced until relatively recent times (in evolutionary thinking). If there were just one million people alive during that time, with an average generation time of 25 years, they should have buried 4 billion bodies, and many artifacts. If there were 10 million people, it would mean 40 billion bodies buried in the Earth. If the evolutionary timescale were correct, then we would expect the skeletons of the buried bodies to be largely still present after 100,000 years, because many ordinary bones claimed to be much older have been found. However, even if the bodies had disintegrated, lots of artifacts should still be found.[24]

The Testimony of Two Skulls

Associated Press science writer, Seth Borenstein, reports on the challenge that two fossilized skulls have presented to the evolution theory:

> Surprising research based on two African fossils suggests our family tree is more like a wayward bush with stubby branches, challenging what had been common thinking on how early humans evolved. The discovery by Meave Leakey, a member of a famous family of paleontologists, shows that two species of early human ancestors lived at the same time in Kenya. That pokes holes in the chief theory of man's early evolution - that one of those species evolved from the other. And it further discredits that iconic illustration of human evolution that begins with a knuckle-dragging ape and ends with a briefcase-carrying man.
>
> The old theory is that the first and oldest species in our family tree, Homo habilis, evolved into Homo erectus, which then became human, Homo sapiens. But Leakey's find suggests those two earlier species lived side-by-side about 1.5 million years ago in parts of Kenya for at least half a million years. She and her research colleagues report the discovery in a paper published in Thursday's journal Nature.
>
> The paper is based on fossilized bones found in 2000. The complete skull of Homo erectus was found within walking distance of an upper jaw of Homo habilis, and both dated from the same general time period. That makes it unlikely that Homo erectus evolved from Homo habilis, researchers said.[25]

Discovered Civilizations

It is also significant that there are no verifiable archaeological datings of civilizations before about 3000 B.C. When older dates are cited, they come not from specific archaeological findings, but rather from radiocarbon dating, from methods other than written human records, or from the suspect Manetho's Egyptian-king list.[26] Consequently, no validated archeology and anthropology evidence exists to disprove the Genesis account of man's sudden appearance upon the Earth a few thousand years ago or that a worldwide flood actually occurred a few centuries later.

Summary of Science's Testimony of Nature

Each of the last three chapters has presented information which either opposes or does not support evolutionary thinking. Most of the quotes in these chapters are from professing evolutionists. Paul Davies (Ph.D., Physics) identifies the real reason many evolutionists are not publicly honest about their scientific findings: "Many investigators feel uneasy about stating in public that the origin of life is a mystery, even though behind closed doors they freely admit they are baffled. ... they worry that a frank admission of ignorance will undermine funding...."[27]

Dr. Michael Denton – molecular biologist at the University of Otago, New Zealand – is a self-described 'evolutionist,' but a more open-minded one than most. His book, *Evolution: A Theory in Crisis* has exposed a number of scientific problems with Darwin's theories. His scientific studies have led him to believe that the design of living things probably implies creative intelligence. Denton provides this concise summary of evolutionary theory: "[Evolutionary theory] is still, as it was in Darwin's time, a highly speculative hypothesis entirely without direct factual support and very far from that self-evident axiom some of its more aggressive advocates would have us believe."[28]

Even though no complete fossil or archaeological evidence developmentally links man and ape together, humanism asserts this to be one important connection to our random and perchance development. In my opinion, this mindset ignores the real message of nature – creation demands a Creator. Doesn't it require more *faith* to believe the following – that some short-lived *something* developed out of nothing, had the necessary encoding to maintain life and reproduce into two *somethings*, and in time develop gender and then evolved into every species of life that we observe today – than to believe in a Master Designer? Every cell in our body depends upon another living cell to form it. The complex attributes of each living cell, like the double-helix DNA strand (which contains genetic code) and the metabolic motor (which extracts and converts energy from the environment to accomplish specific functions) cannot be constructed without similar living cells. What is not living will not, and cannot, ever produce life. Life may be observed in the laboratory, but it cannot be created there.

So why, despite this fact, does the evolutionist deny creationism? Because, if embraced, he or she then becomes immediately accountable to his or her Creator. Evolution is man's attempt to explain away God, so that he has no divine accountability. The outcome then allows man to do what he pleases without restraint, and to create gods of his choosing which will certainly condone his behavior. Man resolves to live in a pseudo reality – a self-concocted realm of humanism protected by ignorance and sustained by the outright denial of creation's testimony for a Creator. In this self-imposed world, man will never understand the purpose of life, or personally know the long-suffering God who desires to have fellowship with him. Bertrand Russell confirms the forlorn position of the atheist, "I do not think that life in general has any purpose. It just happened."[29]

Dr. Francis Collins, lived in this realm of ignorance until he was 27 years old. He had completed his doctorate in physics and was working on his medical degree, when he was brought face to face with a woman dying of heart disease. Collins recalls, "She was very clear about her faith and she looked me square in the eye and she said, 'What do you believe?' I sort of stammered out, 'I am not sure.'" That sincere and simple question by a dying woman was used to awaken Collins out of spiritual slumber and cause him to search out the truth. He found it, and offers this counsel to the naturalist: "You will never understand what it means to be a human being through naturalistic observation. You won't understand why you are here and what the meaning is. Science has no power to address these questions – and are they not the most important questions we ask ourselves?"[30]

As a source of life, what does naturalism offer man? No vital meaning for life. No ultimate value of life. No absolute purpose in life. The universe is cooling off and winding down; from a naturalistic vantage point it is destined to be an ever-expanding dead oblivion – an eternal graveyard of drifting lifeless monuments that testify of past wonders, but where no one exists to know their meaning. So why does life matter? What significance does man really have in such a meaningless existence, where he is certain to die, and all that is apparent to him will cease to exist? Without God life is absolutely absurd and senseless. By contrast, life with God is *miraculous*; it has eternal consequence and immense blessing for those who ponder the testimony of creation and exercise faith in the Creator.

Paul Davies, physicist and evolutionist, writes in his book *The Edge of Infinity*: "[The big bang] represents the instantaneous suspension of physical laws, the sudden abrupt flash of lawlessness that allowed something to come out of nothing. It represents **a true miracle**...."[31] It seems that at the apex of both naturalism and creationism is the *belief* in a miracle – though miracles contradict the atheist's worldview.

The reader must decide whether to believe in a miracle of chance-which is void of meaning, logical purpose and ends in the death of all things – or in a miracle with sovereign purpose that offers man a meaningful life with value and purpose for eternity. Science will seek to prove both worldviews, but the weight of science and logic favors a Creator. Remember, most of the quotes in previous chapters were from atheists and/or naturalists. Ultimately, no logical middle ground exists – either one God created all, or one vast reality originated itself apart from God. There must be an original cause. Is it logical to think that what exists originated itself? No, there was an effectual cause, and it was God! Arbitrarily rationalizing God into obscurity is not intelligence; it is willful blindness.

Nature Demands a Creator

"In the beginning, God created the heavens and the Earth" (Gen. 1:1). The first sentence of the Bible affixes humanity in the presence of the infinite Creator. God is not creation, as some teach, for creation had a distinct beginning (Gen. 1:1, 2:4); it was subsequent to the eternal God (Ps. 102:27). However, God does permeate all His creation (Ps. 139:7; Acts 17:27-28) and maintains it in perfect order (Col. 1:17). The Bible does not put forth arguments to prove God's existence, for creation itself sufficiently testifies of a Creator: *"The heavens declare the glory of God"* (Ps. 19:1). *"The heavens declare His righteousness, and all the peoples see His glory"* (Ps. 97:6).

The Biblical Account of Creation

The Bible affirms that only God can create life. The Hebrew word *bara* is translated *created* in Genesis 1:1. Interestingly, this word is always used in connection with God's creative handiwork; it does not speak of human productivity. Only God can call into existence that which had no previous existence. This was Satan's limiting problem in mimicking the plagues God brought on Egypt through Moses. God caused lice to materialize from the dust of the Earth – life came from what was not living (Ex. 8:16-19). Satan cannot create life for the essence of all life is in God (John 1:4). Thus, Pharaoh's baffled magicians rightly spoke, *"This is the finger of God"* (Ex. 8:19).

Before Satan was lifted up in pride and rebelled against God, his name was Lucifer (meaning *light-bearer*). He was a cherub of great beauty who attempted to exalt himself to the throne of God and was immediately cast down – he lost his privileged position in God's presence (Isa. 14:12-16; Ezek. 28:12-17). Although Satan is perhaps the most powerful being ever created, God continues to limit Satan's authority, especially in relationship to man. Once God's purposes in time have been fulfilled, Satan and other fallen angels will be cast into the eternal lake of fire (Matt. 25:41; Rev. 20:10). The Bible states that Satan knows and understands his doom, a fact which causes him great rage towards God and wrath towards man, the creature fashioned in God's image who represents God on Earth (Rev. 12:12; Gen. 1:22).

From Genesis 1, we learn that God created life in discrete acts – from the simple to the more complex. He originally created something out of nothing (Gen. 1:1), then unconscious life – vegetation (Gen. 1:11), then conscious life – sea life, birds, land creatures (Gen. 1:20-21, 25), and lastly human life (Gen. 1:26-27).

Besides the creation account of Genesis 1, Scripture reveals many details concerning creation. God is a God of order, not confusion (1 Cor. 14:33); He creates with exact purpose. God created the world by His power, wisdom, and understanding (Jer. 10:12). All that is visible came from what was invisible (Heb. 11:3). The universe continues to expand (Job 9:8; Ps. 104:2; Isa. 44:24; 48:13) but is winding down and will eventually "wear out" (Ps. 102:25-26). The universe is said to have innumerable stars (Gen. 22:17; Jer. 33:22); the naked eye can confirm only about 2000. Every star is a unique creation of God (1 Cor. 15:41).

The Bible speaks of a definite beginning of the physical creation as it pertains to man (Eph. 1:4; 1 Pet. 1:20) and that before creation time did not exist (1 Cor. 2:7, NIV; 2 Tim. 1:9; Titus 1:2). God spoke, and what we see was fashioned from what we cannot see (Ps. 33:6; Heb. 11:3) – perhaps a reference to the conversion of invisible energy to visible matter. Apparently, spiritual beings were created just prior to physical creation that they might praise God and declare His glory for each successive creative feat (Job 38:6-7; Ps. 103:22). Though matter and energy are intimately tied to time by natural law, God is not. Scripture speaks of God as being *ad*, and *owlam*, Hebrew words for *everlasting*, *always*, and *forever*; these words only have relative significance in the presence of unfolding time. Before time, God was (John 1:1), but as far as Scripture reveals, there was nothing dependent upon God and nothing for Him to be sovereign over (Ps. 103:17). Time was not necessary until God created time-dependency. Consequently, from a relative perspective the universe has 'always' existed in that there was never *a time* in which it did not exist – in absolute reality it had a beginning. Creation was preceded by God, brought forth by an efficient cause with sovereign purpose. When did God create the universe? *"**In the beginning** God created the heavens and the earth"* – no sooner and no later. In the stillness and blackness before the dawning of time, there was only God.

Concerning the marking of time, the English word "day" in Genesis 1 is translated from the Hebrew word *yom* and may mean a 24-hour day, or a period of creative time. Seven *yoms* compose God's creative workweek, the seventh being a *yom* of rest which sets forth the example man would later be commanded to follow. Christians differ in their understanding of the word *yom* in Genesis 1; some favor long periods of time between creative acts (day-age, or progressive creationism), while others hold to a literal understanding of a day (young earth creationism). The literal interpretation is assumed because whenever *yom* occurs in Scripture proceeded by an ordinal (such as 1st, 2nd, etc.), it always means a literal 24-hour day. It is my opinion that *"God created the heaven and the earth"* (Gen. 1:1) refers to the creation of all matter, the building blocks of creation, and that what follows is an ordering of those elements into that which we see today. Sir Isaac Newton, in his work entitled *Optics,* put it this way: "God in the beginning formed matter in solid, massy, hard, impenetrable, movable particles, of such sizes and figures, and with such other properties, and in such proportion to space, as most conduced to the end for which he formed them."[1]

As a side note, it is beyond the purpose and scope of this book to enter into the age of the Earth debate. It is my opinion, after examining a number of scientific evidences and arguments supporting both *Young Earth* and *Old Earth* positions that the matter cannot be resolved through scientific observation, but solely through proper hermeneutics of Scripture.

God declares in Genesis 1:27 that He created man, not that man evolved. The Lord Jesus said God made male and female from the beginning (Matt. 19:4). Therefore, "theistic or God-guided evolution" is not sound. It is noted that the "beginning" spoken of by the Lord Jesus in Matthew 19:4 is the specific beginning of the world *as it pertains to man,* and not the beginning of all physical and spiritual assets of the universe for *all* the angels praised God when the original foundations of the Earth were created (Job 38:4-7). John uses the same terminology in 1 John 1:1 to speak of the beginning of the Lord's ministry on earth – it was the only beginning related to the life and sacrifice of Christ.

Living on a Cursed Planet

Before the creation described in Genesis 1, no life existed on Earth; after man sinned he began to experience death (Gen. 2:17), both physical (Rom. 5:12) and spiritual (Rom. 6:23). Because man was to reflect God's moral likeness and represent His authority by ruling over the Earth, he reflected God's glory in creation (Heb. 2:7; 1 Cor. 11:7). After man sinned, however, God could not have a fallen head ruling over a perfect creation, so God cursed the Earth and brought the whole thing crashing down (Gen. 3:16-19). Poetically speaking *"the whole creation groans"* (Rom. 8:22) for the day when the curse God levied upon the Earth will be lifted.

This is why bad things happen to *"good"* people today – we live on a cursed world. Sin was an intruder into humanity, and it exists today as a free agent in the world opposing God. We are responsible to God for our sin, but despite our depraved doings God works through the consequences of our sin to refine His people, to reveal Himself providentially and through Scripture, and to effect as much blessing as possible on man's behalf. Man was created a dependent being, but chose to be independent from God; this brought severe consequences. Man's world before sin was a glorious utopia, but not so afterwards. This understanding confronts the skeptic's argument against design:

> A universe with a God would look quite different from a universe without one. A physics, a biology where there is a God is bound to look different.[2]
>
> — Richard Dawkins

> When you come to look into this argument from design, it is a most astonishing thing that people can believe that this world, with all the things that are in it, with all its defects, should be the best that omnipotence and omniscience have been able to produce in millions of years. I really cannot believe it.[3]
>
> — Bertrand Russell

This world is not God's best, but it is the best He can bestow given man's rebellion. Some have used the presence of evil in the world as evidence that a righteous God does not exist; evil only has relevance if there is a holy God – what is not godlike is evil (Isa. 45:7; KJV). It is supposed that a Holy God would not allow evil into His creation if He is truly a good God. The Bible states that God is perfect, and therefore cannot tempt men to do wrong, but allows the sin within man and the evil about man to test man (Jas. 1:13). In this way, evil is constrained by God to work within His sovereign plan for humanity. Consequently, those *"who love the Lord, hate evil"* (Ps. 97:10). It is utter arrogance to blame God for not doing better, while all the time we are doing nearly our worst!

Religious Indoctrination

The preceding scientific observations and those of previous chapters are just a sampling of hundreds which indicate that design by a transcendent Being should be considered in the explanation of the physical realm. Naturalism has many philosophical and scientific problems. What caused the universe? What fixed the laws of nature? If evolution is pointless, why does it produce higher order species? Is man really no more impressive than an amoeba? Why does the fossil record not contain transitional forms and developing species? How can science endorse naturalism with such overwhelming biochemistry support which completely counters life occurring by accident? There is considerable scientific evidence which favors intelligent design instead of random chance development of life.

As no one was here to observe the creation of the world to document an evolutionary process, it is concluded that, from a scientific point of view, both creationism and naturalism are religiously based theories – one teaches of creation's dependence upon God and the latter that there is no scientific need for Him. Evolutionists often criticize creationists for being blinded by religious indoctrination because it is thought that faith cripples one's ability to reason, when actually Satan is the one who is doing the indoctrinating, leading men and women away from God and into deeper blindness. A conclusion that purposely obscures evidence from consideration is the essence of indoctrination – God never endorses such behavior!

Biologist G. A. Kerkut, an evolutionist, observed that candidates he examined for the Ph.D. in biological science were not aware that there are scientific arguments against evolution, and were equally unaware that in accepting naturalism one also accepts a number of far-reaching implications that cannot be proved but are of a philosophical or religious nature.[4] As Charles Singer acknowledges in his book, *A Short History of Science to the Nineteenth Century*, man rarely understands what he wants to avoid knowing: "Evolution is perhaps unique among major scientific theories in that the appeal for its acceptance is not that there is evidence of it, but that any other proposed interpretation of the data is wholly incredible."[5]

Sir Isaac Newton had a miniature replica of our solar system made with the sun in the center and its planets revolving around it. A fellow scientist entered Newton's study one day and exclaimed, "My! What an exquisite thing this is! Who made it?" "Nobody!" replied Newton to his atheist questioner. "You must think I am a fool. Of course somebody made it, and he is a genius." Newton arose, laid a hand on his friend's shoulder and said: "This thing is but a puny imitation of a much grander system whose laws you and I know, and I am not able to convince you that this mere toy is without a designer and maker; yet you profess to believe that the great original from which the design is taken has come into being without either designer or maker. Now tell me, by what sort of reasoning do you reach such incongruous conclusions?"[6] The answer is: muddled reasoning.

Rejecting the Testimony of Nature

Humanism is bent on denying any divine *cause and effect* explanation of nature and prefers to exalt the human intellect over the wisdom of God in His Word. Scripture confirms that the fear of the Lord is the beginning of knowledge and wisdom (Prov. 1:7; Ps. 111:10). Natural man, however, judges God by his own intellect, rather than submitting to the judgment of God's Word.

Evolutionist Mark Isaak wrote: "The goal of scientists is to explain the universe, period. If that could best be done by including God in the equations, it would be. However, God is inscrutable, even according to creationists, **so God is useless as an explanation**."[7] He also states, "Evolution does not require a God, but it does not rule one out either."[8] The former quote interprets the latter: Evolution has no need for God, as naturalized science excludes Him from the cause of the supposed Big Bang to the alleged development of man. For the evolutionist to say in one breath that "God is useless as an explanation of life," and in the next "God may exist" is humanistic double-talk! The truth of the matter is that naturalism, in its basic form, does not want and does not need God.

At the writing of this book, my oldest daughter is studying nursing at a major university in Wisconsin. She recently attended an arranged breakfast discussion between faculty and honors students; the advertised topic was "Evolution and the Myth of Creation Science." The pretentious implication is that creationism is some conjured-up mythology story with no scientific basis, while evolution is concrete science. Only five students attended the breakfast; one supported evolution, one was undecided, and three staunch creationists challenged the professor of Classical Evolution to substantiate his view. Given the evidence presented in previous chapters and volumes more not depicted, naturalism cannot be scientifically proven – in my opinion it is a humanistic myth of daunting proportion.

The Bible teaches that creation provides an adequate testimony of a Creator: *"For since the creation of the world His invisible attributes are clearly seen, being understood by the things that are made, even His eternal power and Godhead, so that they are without excuse"* (Rom. 1:20). The Bible also states that one will reject the revelation of creation without exercising faith: *"By faith we understand that the worlds were framed by the word of God, so that the things which are seen were not made of things which are visible"* (Heb. 11:3).

In the opening section of his epistle to the Romans, Paul explains that suppressing creation's evidence for God will result in four inescapable realities:

1. Rejecting the Creator leads to the worship of creation (including one's self).

   Professing to be wise, they became fools, and changed the glory of the incorruptible God into an image made like corruptible man – and birds and four-footed animals and creeping things (Rom. 1:22-23).

2. Worshipping creation results in immoral and vile behavior (rebellion against God's creation order results in homosexual behavior).

   Therefore God also gave them up to uncleanness, in the lusts of their hearts, to dishonor their bodies among themselves, who exchanged the truth of God for the lie, and worshiped and served the creature rather than the Creator, who is blessed forever. Amen. For this reason God gave them up to vile passions. For even their women exchanged the natural use for what is against nature. Likewise also the men, leaving the natural use of the woman, burned in their lust for one another, men with men committing what is shameful, and receiving in themselves the penalty of their error which was due (Rom. 1:24-27).

3. Those who do such things inherently know that they deserve God's judgment.

> *Who, knowing the righteous judgment of God, that those who practice such things are deserving of death, not only do the same but also approve of those who practice them* (Rom. 1:32).

4. Rejection of the Creator, as evidenced by immoral living and idolatry, leads to divine judgment.

> *For the wrath of God is revealed from heaven against all ungodliness and unrighteousness of men, who suppress the truth in unrighteousness, because what may be known of God is manifest in them, for God has shown it to them. For since the creation of the world His invisible attributes are clearly seen, being understood by the things that are made, even His eternal power and Godhead, so that they are without excuse, because, although they knew God, they did not glorify Him as God, nor were thankful, but became futile in their thoughts, and their foolish hearts were darkened.* (Rom. 1:18-21).

The first three of these realities may be observed presently in our western culture – the fourth reality is coming soon. The post-modern society of our day, in general, has departed from creation's witness of God; consequently, immorality is rampant: More and more couples are shunning the commitment of marriage and opting for sexual liberty and a lifestyle of fornication (sex outside of marriage).

Homosexuality, which defies both natural law and divine order (Rom. 1:21-32), is being touted as a legitimate and a respectable lifestyle. If man is at the pinnacle of evolutionary development, as naturalism teaches, where is the logic in promoting homosexuality: Why do less-advanced animals naturally mate (males and females) to propagate their genes while humans, the supposedly more superior life form, pursue a lifestyle that if unchecked would ensure extinction? Doesn't naturalism teach that the survival of the fittest mentality is necessary to both enhance a species and to avoid its extinction? Homosexuality, then, is a conscious choice to defy natural law and to rebel against God's ordained purpose for marriage; that one man and one women enter into a covenant of companionship for life with the goal of producing, not just children, but *godly* children (Gen. 2:22-24; Mal. 2:15).

Many of those engaging in immorality admit that deep down they know it is not right, yet they enjoy gratifying their own lusts too much to think too deeply about it. It is as if sexual satisfaction has become a narcotic to numb their conscience from the distressing reality of their conduct and the gravity of their forthcoming judgment.

The Four Horsemen of Atheism

The book of Revelation (chapter 6) speaks of four horsemen who bring widespread destruction and death to the Earth during the future Tribulation Period – a time in which God's wrath will be intensely focused upon the Earth just prior to Christ's return to establish His kingdom; the Bible foretells that most of the world's population will die. Biblically speaking, before God judges His people He mercifully sends prophets among them to call them to repentance and warn them of imminent judgment if they do not repent. Likewise, in the 19th century four prophets, but not from God, were used to prepare the way for the anti-Christ's agenda during the Tribulation Period. Consequently, atheism which had always existed in various forms became a systematized religion in the 19th century.

For the materialist and the atheist there are four champions of science, four heroes, four prophetic standouts for the anti-Christian agenda: Charles Darwin, Thomas Henry Huxley, Friedrich Nietzsche, and Sigmund Freud. In his book, *The Atheist Syndrome*, John P. Koster traces the lives of each of these men from the cradle to the grave. The similarities of family life, religious upbringing, vices, bents, and scientific ideology are profound. Each was reared in a strict home, where proper nurturing love was lacking and a fatherly connection was absent. Each sought to escape, and indeed did, his loathed home environment and the God who was reportedly revered there. Each experienced mental and physical degradation while promoting their anti-Christian theories and philosophies. In fact, hereditary insanity can be traced through the ancestry of Darwin, Huxley and Nietzsche.[9]

Darwin was an agile man, and quite physically fit during his five-year research trip in and about South America. Yet, after the HMS Beagle returned him to England in 1836, his health immediately declined. Darwin's countenance and demeanor had so significantly changed during his stint away from England that his family hardly recognized him at his homecoming. Although his health was waning, he married his cousin Emma in 1839. By 1842, Darwin was a semi-invalid at thirty years of age. The deeper he plunged into naturalism the worse his physical and mental health became; he soon admitted to no longer enjoying pleasant activities he once did, such as music, poetry, and reading Shakespeare. He spent the last forty years of his life in poor health, depressed and secluded.

Huxley's claim to fame was defending Darwin's naturalism, which he used to attack Christianity with a vengeance. His field of expertise was Physiology, which he used to devise a theory of human consciousness which eliminated the human soul.[10] Huxley disliked his hot-tempered father, an unsuccessful schoolmaster. His home was loveless, and he hated his harsh Victorian school days. He had a terrible fear of death; this was partly caused by psychological shock which almost killed him after witnessing his first autopsy. He later claimed that he had been poisoned by the vapors of the cadaver, the effects of which afflicted him his entire life. This is quite a strange mindset for a physician and physiology specialist to affirm. The death of his firstborn son, Noel, by scarlet fever in 1860 finished Huxley as an objective scientist. After this event, his rage vented through anti-religious propaganda and personal attacks on clergyman. In 1895, beset with influenza, kidney and heart problems, and constant vomiting, he wrote a friend that his native toughness would pull him through – he died three days later. He was survived by his long-suffering wife of forty years, Henrietta, a devout Christian.

Nietzsche understood more than Darwin and Huxley the ramifications of naturalism on society. With God, Jesus, and the human soul all being ruled "out of order," the basis of moral law would consequently be repealed also. It was Nietzsche who popularized the phrase "God is dead," and the idea that all men should become "supermen."[11] Nietzsche suffered from syphilitic paresis, whose symptoms include gradual paralysis, mental problems, depression, failing eyesight, and at the end, precocious drooling senility.[12] As a philosopher, Nietzsche was highly regarded and his influence on literature was enormous. His father, a pastor, died while Nietzsche was young and he was raised by his mother and grandmother. By his late teens, he dropped his plans for the clergy and chose instead to study philology. He vehemently degraded women and exhibited homosexual tendencies. In his latter years, Nietzsche was seized with attacks of internal pain, prolonged bouts of vomiting, and headaches so intense that he screamed out that he wished he could die.[13] After recovering from a collapse which rendered him unconscious for a time in January 1889, he continued to write between fits of insanity, but the final twelve years of his life he wandered about the upstairs rooms of his mother's house, completely psychotic and unable to speak coherently.[14]

Freud's hostility for his father probably stemmed from his hatred of his father's Jewish religion and heritage. Sigmund was obsessed with having sex with his mother, who was some twenty years younger than his father.[15] Freud was enthusiastic about the use of cocaine and claimed that it was not physically or psychologically addictive.[16] Freud, a lifelong smoker, and a self-proclaimed addict, who often smoked twenty cigars a day, contracted cancer of the jaw at the age of sixty-seven. The last sixteen years of his life were painful. Repeated surgical scrapings, iodine and x-ray treatments were a constant reminder of death, something he obsessively feared. In fact, Freud, on three different occasions predicted the date of his death. Freud continued his attack on Christianity until he died of cancer. His final years were quite painful; once he pleaded with his physician for a lethal dose of morphine.[17]

While many people suffer physical and emotional problems for a variety of organic and non-organic reasons, it is interesting that these four men, after using science to psychologically leverage God off His throne, began suffering from the same types of physical aliments, emotional problems, and as Koster's research notes, mental illness:

> [Darwin, Huxley, Nietzsche, Freud] had many of the hallmarks of mental illness stamped on their personality. In point of fact, a careful study of their biographies in the light of improved science knowledge may reveal not only that each man was mentally ill, but that each man suffered from the same form of mental illness. It was this mental illness that led each of them to pervert science into an attack on God. And it was this same illness that led each man to suffer from a nearly identical set of psychosomatic illnesses in his mature life and to share similar obsessions outside the sphere of science versus religion.[18]

The mid-nineteenth century saw a brutal assault against the Christian faith which had governed the morality of the western world for nearly two millennia (though the *professing* Church strayed from many biblical teachings during much of this era). The offensive was pioneered by these four would-be prophets of atheism. Each cleverly and willing overlooked much scientific evidence in nature to postulate and promote naturalistic propaganda. Closing their eyes to the testimony creation poses for a Creator led these men into a fanatical and fearful state of mind and into miserable physical conditions.

A Solemn Warning

During Jesus' sojourn on Earth, He served and blessed children; He was deeply concerned for their proper nurturing and care. On one occasion, after calling a child to Himself and sitting the child down in the midst of those who had gathered about Him, the Lord Jesus issued this stern warning:

> *Assuredly, I say to you, unless you are converted and become as little children, you will by no means enter the kingdom of heaven. Therefore whoever humbles himself as this little child is the greatest in the kingdom of heaven. Whoever receives one little child like this in My name receives Me.* **Whoever causes one of these little ones who believe in Me to sin, it would be better for him if a millstone were hung around his neck, and he were drowned in the depth of the sea** (Matt. 18:3-6).

What will be the social outcome of generations of children having been indoctrinated with the teachings of evolution, instead of being taught to be critical and objective thinkers? The four horsemen of the apocalypse of atheism have already led the way to that knowable and dreadful fate. Are spiritual despair, emotional anguish, mental illness, and physical ruin what we want our children to experience?

A ninth grade biology instructor recently reported that at the beginning of each school year he asks his students to indicate by a show of hands if they believe in creationism. He notes that year after year approximately ninety percent of his students affirmed that they believed in creationism. A ninth grade earth science teacher with thirty years of classroom experience in the

Twin Cities, MN metropolitan area asserts that by far the majority of his students claim to believe in creationism also. As both teachers are in the public school system, the obvious question is where are these children learning about a Creator? In my opinion, given our post-Christian society, a mere minority of children attending public schools these days are receiving Christian or religious training concerning creationism. If children believe in a Creator because of their home or church upbringing, why would parents send their children to public schools which teach naturalism, the exact opposite of what was taught in the home – it doesn't make sense. I believe there is a better reason to explain why the majority of these public school children believe in a Creator.

The message from creation seems to be more easily understood by children than adults. Then why are adults, who have no valid empirical rationale, endeavoring to distort a child's understanding of creation's testimony for its Creator? What is the social and emotional benefit to the child that warrants such a course of action? There is no logical justification for such conduct, only a religious one: To liberate the naive from a childish belief in God. But what is the child being liberated to? Evolution – a theory which many professing naturalists now claim is flawed. Evolution cannot be proven true by science any more than creationism can – either worldview requires an individual to exercise *faith*. Would it not be better, from a logical position, to favor a theory which offers the most benefit to a society as being the best ethical choice to *believe* in?

Humanism pushed God and His commandments out of the public school classroom some forty years ago; what have been the ethical reforms that evolution has accomplished since that time? Hostility and disrespect towards parents has risen, abortion became legalized, violent crime has escalated, the transmission rate of STDs has dramatically increased, educational performance has decreased, fornication, and now, the abduction and sexual abuse of children has become commonplace in our society. When you teach school children that they are the descendants of apes, that there is no divine standard of morality, that they cannot be expected to control their sexual urges, and that many need to be medicated to subdue feelings of anger, restlessness, and anxiety it only requires a few generations for a society to devolve into moral chaos.

With God's morality for man shoved aside, what has been the world's replacement ethical standard? Violent, explicit, and immoral programming. The American Academy of Pediatrics reports, "If your child watches 3 to 4 hours of noneducational TV per day [the average is 4 hours a day in the US], he will have seen about 8,000 murders on TV by the time he finishes grade school." They go on to say, "It is best not to let your child watch violent programs and cartoons."[19] How is a child benefited by watching 8,000 simulated murders? Violent programming and video games glamorize murder, and children simply act out what they have seen thousands of times; they become desensitized to the horridness of violence and confused between what is reality and fantasy. The consequence is school shootings, slaying of parents, and increased cases of suicide and murder.

The Bible teaches us to value life, and commands, *"Thou shall not murder."* Evolution devalues life – it is not a gift from God, but something that is random, accidental, and governed by the survival of the fittest mentality. Denying God's testimony of Himself in creation leads to the denial of His Word and ultimately to the rejection of Him altogether.

Scientific evidence will undoubtedly be used to support evolutionary theories or creationism thinking, but there is no way to *absolutely* validate either through science. Science is important, but not in verifying the origin of man; ultimately that will be a *faith-based* decision. Accordingly, science, politics, human agendas, and religious doctrines will sway men to and fro in their thinking about the origin of life. Consider for instance the complete turnabout in the state of Tennessee in just forty-two years:

> It shall be unlawful for any teacher in any of the universities, normals, and all other public schools of the State which are supported in whole or in part by the public school funds of the State, to teach any theory that denies the story of the divine creation of man as taught in the Bible, and to teach instead that man has descended from a lower order of animals.
>
> — Tennessee Legislature Act, March 21, 1925.
> **Repealed, May 17, 1967.**

Every parent, and each school board member, will ultimately stand before God and give an account of what message from nature he or she thought was best to teach children under their authority (Rom. 14:12). Will it be the unsubstantiated theory of evolution, or will it be a workable alternative that makes sense, benefits man, and honors God – design requires a designer; creation demands a Creator.

For thus says the Lord,
Who created the heavens,
Who is God,
Who formed the earth and made it,
Who has established it,
Who did not create it in vain,
Who formed it to be inhabited:
"I am the Lord, and there is no other" (Isa. 45:18).

The fool has said in his heart, "There is no God" (Ps. 53:1).

#3 The Authenticity of the Bible

We leave the testimony of nature for a Creator to ponder a new category of evidence of supernatural influence within natural order, namely three unique facets of the Bible: authenticity, uniformity, and prophecy – to be discussed in the next three chapters.

There simply is no ancient book on the planet that has the same authenticity as the Bible. Scientific analysis has verified that its original text has been almost perfectly preserved down through the centuries. When one considers how minute the Jewish nation was in comparison to surrounding nations and in respect to past world empires, it simply is amazing that it is the Old Testament writings entrusted to the Jews which have survived and not volumes of religious writings from the larger pagan populace. The Jews were a scattered people from 605 B.C. until 1948 A.D., yet the Old Testament was incredibly preserved, a testimony to their diligence to keep it.

If the Bible is God's word to mankind, would He not maintain an accurate record of it through the corridors of time? Without the record of Scripture we would not know Christ, the Savior, the divine solution for man's sin. Hence the preservation of an accurate record of God's revelation to humanity is critical for those generations following to understand God's attributes and character, and His plan for humanity.

French atheist Voltaire wrote, "If we would destroy the Christian religion, we must first of all destroy man's belief in the

Bible."[1] Voltaire understood that, without the Bible, there would be no basis for Christianity, as there would be no Savior, no Christ. This is true; the foundation of Christianity is the Bible – the Word of God. So why do university courses such as "Ethics," "Cultural Diversity," "Worldview," "Religion," etc. focus their attention on discrediting the Bible as a reliable and moral source of information instead of the Vedas, or Quran, or the sayings of Buddha? Because the Bible is the bedrock of Christianity, and the world hates Christ and His message! The psalmist writes, *"Your word is a lamp to my feet and a light to my path"* (Ps. 119:105). Without the revelation of Scripture, man would not know how to properly walk in life or what course to pursue with purpose – he would literally be stumbling over himself in spiritual darkness.

Some have said you cannot trust the integrity of the Bible. The Bible, however, is the most widely examined book on the planet; its textual integrity has been repeatedly validated. When copying worn out scrolls the Jews verified the integrity of each new scroll by counting each letter of the Hebrew alphabet and comparing it with the master's letter count; the original was destroyed only after an exact copy was verified. How can I know for sure that the Bible is God's message to humanity and that it is still trustworthy? Please carefully consider the evidence in this chapter and the two subsequent chapters.

When speaking of a book that is as much as 3,500 years old, it is understood that the original autographs would be unavailable, having perished over time. Today, the nearest fragment of Scripture to its autograph is dated within one generation. Scripture in its original form is God-inspired and perfect (2 Tim. 3:16). From a rational standpoint, this does not prove that the Bible is God's Word, for that would be circular logic that any religious book might self-proclaim – the book states it is revelation from God; therefore, it must be. The point here is only to substantiate the internal evidence – the Bible declares that it is God's word to mankind.

Over time, a few scribal errors were noticed (e.g. the copying of Hebrew numbers for example), but most of these can be identified and eliminated by comparing the various manuscripts with each other (thousands are available to accomplish this). As a result of such comparison, 99.5 percent of the New Testament has been determined to be authentic to the original autographs. Due to the finding of the Dead Sea scrolls in 1947, which produced some 900 separate documents and approximately 40,000 fragments dating between 300 B.C. and 70 A.D., 99.5 percent of the Old Testament has also been confirmed as accurate.[2]

As the truth of Scripture is in the whole, the 0.5 percent remaining is best tested by the integrity of Scripture itself – the result of which has shown that no new doctrines are imposed in the minute variations among the manuscripts.

Those who criticize the integrity of the Bible, such as those of the *Jesus Seminar*, toss about staggering figures claiming that there are over 200,000 variant readings in the existing manuscripts of the New Testament. What they don't tell you, however, is that if one single word is misspelled in 3,000 manuscripts, if is counted as 3,000 variants or readings! Most the variants (99.5 percent) are simple spelling mistakes, a lost letter or two words transposed. It doesn't take long to add up to 200,000 with this type of reckoning.[3]

Let us consider a scientifically proven example. How much difference was determined between the oldest known Old Testament Hebrew text (800 A.D.) prior to the Dead Sea scrolls discovery and the actual Dead Sea scrolls? Isaiah chapter 53 is perhaps the most astounding prophetic passage in the entire Old Testament in describing why Messiah must suffer, die and be raised up again. Examining the 166 words in Isaiah 53, we find only 17 letters in question. Ten of these are simply a matter of spelling variations; four pertain to minor stylistic changes, and the remaining 3 Hebrew letters compose one word, "light," apparently added in verse 11 to the Masoretic text – which does not affect the meaning of the passage at all.[4]

So, when Islam, or Mormonism, or any other religion of the world claims that the Bible is corrupt, cannot be trusted, and therefore, new revelation from God is needed, remember these facts and then evaluate the origin and historicity of their so-called holy books. Not to get too far sidetracked from the subject at hand, but a bit more clarification on this point is warranted.

Islam: The *Quran* did not exist at the time that Muhammad died. Based on Islamic traditions and legends, it is generally believed that Muhammad could neither read nor write (Quran 29:48) but that he recited what was revealed to him for his companions to write down and memorize. It is noted that, at first, Muhammad thought he was possessed by a demon (his epileptic seizures may have only heightened this fear), but his wife convinced him that the source of his revelations was divine. After Muhammad's death in 632 A.D., numerous versions of his teachings were in circulation. Some twenty years later, Uthman (the third Caliph of Islam according to Sunni Muslims) ordered that a collection be made of available writings and that these be put into some order. Imperfect men do not memorize or write perfectly, so one can only imagine the huge number of discrepancies between all the pieces of composition collected – a fact that Muslim scholars do not deny.

If Muhammad was truly the last prophet of God, then the vast differing assortment of Muhammad's teachings were pieced together by various non-prophets (non-inspired individuals) to create the Quran. After the collection was compiled, reduced and ordered in 656 A.D., all other versions were to be burned. The final version of the Quran had 114 "Surahs" or chapters, and this version has been remarkably preserved through the centuries. The fact that Muslims, themselves, have difficulty explaining how the Quran was actually assembled, and that there were many early forgeries cast doubt on the integrity of the book as representing exactly what Muhammad said. Sharon Morad Leeds summarizing the book *The Origins of the Quran: Classic Essays on Islam's Holy Book* writes: "Modern Muslims assert that the current Quran is identical to that recited by Muhammad. But earlier Muslims were more flexible. 'Uthman, A'isha, and Ibn Ka'b (among others) all insisted that much of the Quran had been lost"[5]

Mormonism: Concerning the *Book of Mormon*, leaders in the Mormon Church have added and deleted words and revised previously published revelations by introducing new material and/or falsely attributing it to an earlier date. The Book of Mormon is less than 200 years old, so why have all of these changes (over 3,900) been made, if in fact it is, as Joseph Smith declared, "the most correct of any book on Earth, and the keystone of our religion, and a man would get nearer to God by abiding by its precepts, than by any other book."[6] The book was first written in English by Joseph Smith, so we are not referring to refining translational accuracy, but wholesale change! Divine truth does not need to be corrected – it is timeless.

Having now situated the bar of credibility quite high, let us examine the authenticity of the Bible. The following are prominent Old Testament *manuscripts* and Greek *translations* of the Old Testament still in existence. It is noted that before the 15th century, Bibles were not printed but hand copied onto papyrus, parchment and later paper; these copies are called manuscripts.

Old Testament Manuscripts:

The Dead Sea Scrolls (300 B.C. to 70 A.D.)
>The entire book of Isaiah and portions of every other Old Testament book except Esther.

Geniza Fragments (400 A.D.)

Contains portions of the Old Testament, discovered in 1947 in an old synagogue in Cairo, Egypt.

Ben Asher Manuscripts (950 A.D.)

Several generations of the Ben Asher family made copies of the Old Testament using the Masoretic Hebrew text from 700-950 A.D. Examples of the Hebrew Masoretic text-type included the *Aleppo Codex* (950 A.D.), a complete Old Testament (one fourth of the Codex was destroyed during anti-Jewish riots in 1947) and the *Codex Leningradensis* (1008 A.D.).

Old Testament Translations

Chester Beatty Papyri (250 A.D.)

Contains nine Old Testament books from the Greek Septuagint.

Codex Vaticanus (350 A.D.)

Perhaps the oldest uncial on parchment or vellum (uncial is a majuscule script commonly used by Latin and Greek scribes during the 3rd to 8th centuries A.D.). This codex contains most of the Old Testament (Septuagint), some 617 leaves.

Codex Sinaiticus (350 to 400 A.D.)

Written on good vellum made from antelope skins, this Codex contains over half the Old Testament (Septuagint).

The entire New Testament was canonized by 165 A.D., except for 2 Peter. Over 5,300 Greek partial or complete New Testament manuscripts exist today which attest to the reliable and accurate transmission of Scripture.

New Testament Manuscripts

Of the 76 papyri manuscripts of the New Testament known today, the following two are given as important representatives:

John Rylands Fragment (Manchester, England; 117-138 A.D.)

This papyrus piece was found in Egypt and is written on both sides. It contains five verses from the Gospel of John (18:31-33, 37-38).

Chester Beatty Papyri (Beatty Museum near Dublin, Ireland; 250 AD)

It consists of three codices which contain most of the New Testament. The first portion is comprised of thirty leaves (the original had approximately 220) of a papyrus codex and contains the four gospel accounts and Acts. The second section is comprised of 86 slightly damaged leaves (104 in the original) and contains the book of Hebrews and the Pauline epistles (excluding portions of Romans, 1 and 2 Thessalonians, and Philemon). The third section is comprised of 10 slightly damaged leaves (the original had 32), containing Revelation 9:10-17:2.

Of the 297 uncial manuscripts of the New Testament known today, the following two are given as important representatives:

Codex Vaticanus (Vatican Library; 350 A.D.)

A complete New Testament (except for Hebrews 9:14 through Revelation, and Mark 16:9-20 and John 7:53-8:11). It has 142 New Testament leaves.

Codex Sinaiticus (British Museum; 350 A.D.)

Written on good vellum made from antelope skins, this codex contains all of the New Testament, with the exception of Mark 16:9-20 and John 7:53-8:11.

When you consider how few important Greek texts have survived 2000 years of history, one must conclude that God has preserved His Word – the Bible. To this fact, Norman Geisler concludes:

> It is sufficient to remember that while there are only 643 manuscripts by which the Iliad (a poem in which Homer re-accounts the siege at Troy) is reconstructed, nine or ten good ones for Caesar's Gallic Wars, twenty manuscripts of note for Livy's History of Rome, and only two by which Tacitus is known, yet there are about 5,000 Greek manuscripts to attest the New Testament.... Most of the New Testament is preserved in manuscripts less than two hundred years after the originals, portions of some New Testament books can be historically linked to documents of approximate one hundred years after their composition (e.g. the Bodmer Papyri), and one fragment of John comes within a generation of the first century (John Rylands Fragment).[7]

Ron Rhodes reports, "In addition to this [the Greek manuscripts] there are 86,000 quotations of the New Testament by the early church fathers. Because of this, all but 11 verses could be accurately reconstructed even if we had no manuscript copies."[8] In addition, over 10,000 copies of the Latin Vulgate and at least 9,300 copies of early versions of the Bible in various languages are in existence. The bottom line is that over 24,000 manuscripts attest to the accuracy of the New Testament. No other ancient book can boast the same level of authenticity as the Bible. It is distinct from all other books in message, unity, sophistication, and prophecy.

Religion and New Revelation

A common methodology among monotheistic religions developing after the divine issuance of the Bible, is to insist that new revelation from God is warranted because the message of the Bible is no longer authentic – they claim that the Bible has been corrupted and its message can no longer be trusted. The end goal is that biblical truth must be concealed, altered, or at least significantly deemphasized. Examples would be

Muhammad's Quran, Joseph Smith's Book of Mormon (with *Doctrines and Covenants*), the Jehovah's Witnesses' New World Translation, and the Roman Catholic Catechism.

The "holy books" of Islam and Mormonism lift various stories, teachings, verses, phrases, names, etc. from the Bible to confuse and blur the truth. Roman Catholicism is progressively replacing the Bible with Church Tradition, and the Jehovah's Witnesses distort the truth of Scripture through Watchtower interpretations of a tainted translation of the Bible. Deformation of the truth is a frequent tactic of Satan to lure men away from absolute truth. Normally, he introduces distortion in progressive degrees, rather than presenting an outright lie that would easily be recognized as such.

I will illustrate this point with the following example: "Despite what you might have thought previously, *black* really means *white*." You say, "No, black is the opposite of white." But then I pick up a reliable dictionary, say *The American Heritage Dictionary*,[9] and show you that the meaning of "black" is "dark," and then I confirm that one of the meanings of "dark" is "dim." Finding the entry for "dim" I prove to you that "dim" can mean "pale." And finally I look up the word "pale" and verify that one of the meanings of "pale" is "white." I have proven to you using a series of only four imprecise meanings, (variations of the best meaning, if you will) that *black* is equal to *white*, but black is not white – is it?

Absolute truth stands the test of time – it is immutable. There are no shades to divine righteousness or degrees of God's holiness; consequently man's religious endeavors color, flavor, change, or dilute truth in direct opposition to God's authority and Word. How have world religions and cults developed "new revelation" to promote their humanistic agendas and undermine absolute truth (i.e. God's revealed truth)? If the reader is interested in the answer to this question, please look for the sequel to this book *Hiding God*. There you will find an assessment of the authenticity and uniformity of important "holy books" from various world religions. I believe that the conclusion is self-evident – these books are not inspired and should not be trusted.

Summary of Bible Authenticity

Dr. Robert Dick Wilson, former professor of Semitic philology at Princeton Theological Seminary, states, "After forty-five years of scholarly research in biblical textual studies and in language study, I have come now to the conviction that no man knows enough to assail the truthfulness of the Old Testament. Where there is sufficient documentary evidence to make an investigation, the statements of the Bible, in the original text, have stood the test."[10] Dr. J. O. Kinnaman once said: "Of the hundreds of thousands of artifacts found by the archaeologists, not one has ever been discovered that contradicts or denies one word, phrase, clause, or sentence of the Bible, but always confirms and verifies the facts of the Biblical record."[11]

The internal and the external evidence prove the authenticity of the Bible. The Bible, the most ancient of preserved books, possesses many wonders. The thousands of existing manuscripts attest to God's preservation of its sacred content. Its unique formation, not by one religious founder, but by some forty men, most of which were uneducated, wrote as inspired by God over a 1600 year period. The full library composes sixty-six individual books which read as one. It is the best seller year after year, but also the most hated book. It is relished by the rich and the poor, by the scholar and the naive, by the believer and the non-believer.

> We account the Scriptures of God to be the most sublime philosophy. I find more sure marks of authenticity in the Bible than in any profane history whatsoever.
>
> — Sir Isaac Newton

#4 The Uniformity of the Bible

Besides authenticity, another unique facet of the Bible which gives evidence of supernatural origin is its uniform content. The Bible was written over a 1,600 year period by some forty different writers who were situated in various social backgrounds and geographical locations, yet uniform truth is displayed throughout. Often these prophets of old did not fully understand the meaning of the very words they uttered on God's behalf (1 Pet. 1:10-12). This fact puts the Bible in stark contrast with the religious books of the world, which are generally composed by one individual – a religious founder.

How did God accomplish such uniformity? He controlled the speech and pens of the prophets; the Bible was literally God-breathed (2 Tim. 3:16). Scripture, then, is a direct expression of both His truth and His love to mankind. Because God understands our natural limitations to comprehend spiritual and eternal matters, He utilized various literary forms in the Bible, including word-pictures, poetry, prophecies, shadows, types, allegories, symbols, plain language, historical narratives, the gospels, and epistles. All of these speak of His supreme gift of love – His own Son to the world. Thus, the uniform focus of the Bible centers in the progressive revealing of God's purposes in history that culminate in Jesus' life, death, and resurrection.

The main theme of the entire Bible is perhaps best expressed by John 3:16: *"For God so loved the world that He gave His only begotten Son, that whoever believes in Him should not per-*

ish but have everlasting life." Jesus Christ is the main theme of the Bible: *"For the testimony of Jesus is the spirit of prophecy"* (Rev. 19:10); *"For all the promises of God in Him [Christ] are Yes, and in Him Amen"* (2 Cor. 1:20).

To keep the plan of salvation in Christ a mystery until after His death and resurrection, for He would not have been crucified if the plan had been known (1 Cor. 2:7-8), the messianic prophecies concerning Christ are generally scattered, seemingly sporadically, throughout the Old Testament. The truth was declared, yet in such a way that full understanding of the events and benefits of Calvary would not be understood from just one text. Furthermore, most of the Old Testament pictures of Christ are concealed in abstract symbols, reclusive personal portraits and mysterious names. Though these Old Testament gems were once concealed from human comprehension, they accentuate Christ when illuminated by the light of New Testament revelation.

As one investigates the Old Testament with the light of the New Testament, these abundant pictures and types of Christ are understood. Truly, the New is in the Old contained, but the Old is by the New explained. Volumes of books have been written on these striking preludes of realities to come. It is no exaggeration to state that hundreds of pictures and shadows of Christ are contained in the Old Testament; here are just a few.

The Ark

Several wonderful prophetic pictures are seen in the ark (Genesis 6), for the ark itself is a type of Christ. In the broad sense, the ark pictures the safety that Christ offers all who will "enter in" His own body, the Church, by faith. Before the ark could be constructed, however, building materials were needed – gopher trees had to be cut down. The death of these trees pictured the humanity of Christ in that only through His sacrifice could spiritual life for man be secured. As trees don't have blood, God is careful to apply some to the ark that we not miss the "type." By the word *type*, we simply mean a picture, figure, or pattern that reflects something or someone in reality. The word *"pitch"* in Genesis 6:14 is most often translated "atonement" (nearly 75 times in the Old Testament). Prior to Calvary, man's sin could only be atoned (covered) by the blood of animals through sacrifices. The fact that the ark was pitched from within and without further shadows the future suffering and sacrifice of Christ. From His wounds, redemptive blood would rudely and profusely coat his outer skin, then drip and splatter upon the ground. The word usage and the typology of Genesis 6 both convey the image of a bleeding ark, thus, picturing the suffering Savior at Calvary.

There was only one door into the ark (Gen. 6:16), and only God could shut it (Gen. 7:16) once all those who entered by faith were within. It would be God who judged the Earth for man's wickedness (Gen. 6:7); thus, the very ark that Noah had built would know God's wrath. However, while the ark bore the judgment of Almighty God, all the souls that were in the ark were kept safe from judgment. The Lord Jesus said He was the only door (John 10:1) and the only way (John 14:6), and He bore the judgment of God for man's sin once and for all (Heb. 9:26-28, 10:9-18). The Lord said, *"whosoever liveth and believeth in Me shall never die"* (John 11:26). Our soul's security rests in the hand (John 10:28-29) and the sealing power of God (Eph. 1:13). We never read of water pouring through the door to despair Noah's family or of any family member being lost at sea. When God sealed the door shut, it was securely closed, and when God seals the believer in Christ, he or she is maintained secure.

Isaac

Isaac was the special son of promise and Abraham's only begotten son (Gen. 22:2; Heb. 11:17). Through Isaac and his descendants, all of the covenant blessings promised to Abraham would be fulfilled. At God's request Abraham and Isaac traveled to the land of Moriah and ascended the mount together to the place of sacrifice. The sacrificial offering was to be Isaac. One cannot survey this somber scene without contemplating the pattern it so clearly represents – Calvary. Even the very location would be that in which the Son of God would be crucified some two thousand years later. The two young men assisted Abraham and Isaac in their journey to the mount, but they were not permitted to ascend it – this was a private matter between the father and the son. Trespassing upon holy ground would not be tolerated. To ensure no intrusions at Calvary, the Father shrouded His suffering Son in a veil of darkness.

Abraham carried the fire and the knife up the mount, both symbols of judgment. Isaac, a strapping young man, bore the wood for the fire. Prior to being judged by the Father at Calvary, the Lord Jesus Christ had shouldered His cross until He was unable to carry it any longer. Then, after arriving at the place of public executions, He was nailed to it and lifted up for all to mock and jeer. *"He is despised and rejected by men, a Man of sorrows and acquainted with grief"* (Isa. 53:3). And there, while in physical agony, profusely bleeding, and struggling to breathe, He alone awaited the forthcoming cup of God's wrath to be poured out upon Him. Human sin must be punished! Isaac inquired about a missing lamb for sacrifice to which Abraham responded that *"God will provide for Himself the lamb"* – and He did some 2000 years later, in the Lord Jesus.

Isaac freely let himself be bound, and the Lord freely allowed Himself to be bound, abused, and crucified by mankind. John 10:17-18 reads, *"Therefore My Father loves Me, because I lay down My life that I may take it again. No one takes it from Me, but I lay it down of Myself. I have power to lay it down, and I have power to take it again. This command I have received from My Father."* It is significant to note that, in all the offerings, the victim was first killed then laid on the altar. With the offering of Isaac, however, a more striking type of Christ is presented; he was bound to the altar first before the knife was taken to slay him. Likewise, Christ was first nailed to a tree and then shed His blood. Abraham *"placed the wood in order"* and put Isaac upon it before drawing the knife to slay his son, but *"the Angel of the Lord"* called out to him not to harm his son and showed him a ram which had been prepared for sacrifice.

Isaac's death would have served no purpose. In the end, God had provided an offering for sacrifice – a ram caught by its horns. An animal uses its horns to protect itself or to substantiate its territory in the wild either through rubbings or fighting. Thus, throughout Scripture, the "horn" is used to symbolize power and strength. With the provision of the ram, the "type" of the Lord Jesus is transferred from Isaac to the ram for the suffering of death. Correspondingly, the Lord laid aside His glory and position in heaven to become a man in order to be a humble substitute for us at Calvary (Phil. 2:6-8). Meekness is "power in control" and is represented by the restrained ram – an innocent animal substitute caught by its horns. Perhaps another reason it was caught by its horns was to preserve it from being damaged (from being cut or torn by the thicket), thus, being an unblemished sacrifice. The Lord Jesus lived His entire life without sin – He was without blemish.

The Birth of Benjamin

The advents of Christ are wonderfully depicted in metaphoric form in this narrative (Gen. 35:16-20). Jacob departed Bethel to travel to Ephrath. During this journey, a very pregnant Rachel entered into hard labor to deliver her second son. This son was born at Bethlehem and was named "Ben-Oni" by Rachel just before her death, but Jacob renamed him "Benjamin." Jacob then buried Rachel at Bethlehem and set a pillar upon her grave. In this messianic portrait, Jacob represents God the Father, Benjamin the Lord Jesus, and Rachel, Benjamin's mother, the nation of Israel. Consequently, the names: Bethel means "house of God," Ephrath means "a place of fruitfulness," Bethlehem means "house of bread," Benoni means "son of my sorrow," and lastly, Benjamin means "the son of my right hand." Now, let us put the prophetic storyline together.

The Son left the house of God (heaven), was born in Bethlehem (Luke 2:15) of a Jewish virgin and, thus, became "the bread of life" offered to mankind for eternal life (John 6:35). His earthly ministry transpired after departing His home in heaven but before presenting a fruit harvest of souls to God through the work of His cross (Isa. 53:10-11). He was born to be the man of sorrows (Isa. 53:3), but after Calvary, the Father raised Him up to the seat of honor at His right hand (Heb. 1:3). Therefore, Christ, His work and exaltation are clearly revealed in the various aspects of Benjamin's birth.

Joseph

Perhaps the only other Old Testament characters who would rival Joseph's personal typology of Christ would be Isaac and Joshua. C. H. Mackintosh writes, "There is not in Scripture a more perfect and beautiful type of Christ than Joseph. Whether we view Christ as the object of the Father's love, the object of the envy of 'His own,' – in His humiliation, sufferings, death, exaltation and glory – in all, we have Him strikingly typified by Joseph."[2] A. W. Pink devotes seven chapters of his forty-seven chapter book *Gleanings in Genesis* to this typology – he lists 101 similarities between Joseph and Jesus. Joseph, the morally right and favored son of Jacob, was mocked, mistreated, and stripped by his brethren, then sold for twenty pieces of silver. Joseph accepted his fate in Egypt and remained faithful to God. Joseph was exalted to the second place over the land and through God's wisdom and power preserved the lives of all his brethren through a seven-year famine. Ultimately, all his brethren fell down and reverenced Joseph. This narrative wonderfully depicts the nation of Israel's relationship with Jesus Christ. Though they rejected and crucified Him, He is highly exalted, and in a coming day, they will acknowledge Him as Messiah (Zech. 12:10).

The Rock Moses Struck

From the opening pages of Genesis, the Bible presents a uniform lesson concerning God's rest and work. When God rested from His work of creation, a river that flowed out of Eden provided the whole land with the blessing and refreshment of God's presence. Symbolically speaking, a river is often connected with God's rest and blessing – He being the fountain of both. Years later, Moses smote a rock to provide much needed living water to the children of Israel in the desert – it saved their lives (Ex. 17:6). Shortly after, Moses received the rebuke of God for striking another rock in the same manner – he had been instructed by God to simply speak to the rock in order to receive the needed water (Num. 20:7-13). Israel desperately needed water, so what did it matter if Moses struck the rock or spoke to it? It mattered to God, because it broke the "type" of Christ He wanted to be conveyed to the nation of Israel. Christ was to suffer for sin only once, then the blessing of his work would be received through asking Him personally (Heb. 10:10-18). Both the work and the blessing of Christ are pictured in the rock. In the New Testament, the Lord likened the blessings of the Holy Spirit in a Christian's life to a river of flowing water (John 7:37-39). As a believer yields to God's will for his or her life, the full joy, peace, and blessing of God is experienced.

The Levitical System

Leviticus was Israel's worship manual from God. No Jew could approach God, except in the exact manner God prescribed in Leviticus, which consisted of hundreds of laws. All that related to the place of worship (the tabernacle), including its furniture, coverings, veils, colors, numbers of things, and purification procedures, presents spiritual truths concerning Messiah. The seven feasts of Jehovah relate to the timing of events pertaining to Christ's first and second advents (Lev. 23).

The sacrifices described in Leviticus chapters 1 through 7 present different facets of Christ's future sacrifice at Calvary: the burnt offering – the offering was totally consumed for God, the meal offering – reflected the fine moral character of Christ, the peace offering – the communion of God with man through Christ, the sin offering – God's own payment for the offense of man's sin, and the trespass offering – the demanded payment for the damage that sin causes. In all these, the person and work of Christ are presented in pattern.

The Passover Lamb – The Lamb of God

The Passover was instituted by God as a means of reminding the Israelites that their deliverance from Egypt and bondage and restoration to Him required redemption, the death of an innocent substitute whose blood was then to be personally applied as God described. A male lamb without blemish in the prime of its life was to be tested for four days to prove its healthy condition then killed, roasted, eaten (any remnants were to be burned). The blood of this lamb was applied to the doorway of a household that desired to be spared the judgment of God on Egypt – the death of the firstborn (Ex. 12). The activity marked a clear distinction between the Egyptians and Israelites – applied blood on the door brought life, and no blood brought death.

John the Baptist declared that Christ was *"the Lamb of God which takes away the sin of the world"* (John 1:29). Paul taught that Christ was the literal fulfillment of the Passover Lamb: *"For indeed Christ, our Passover, was sacrificed for us"* (1 Cor. 5:7). Just as the Passover lamb was totally consumed or burnt, Christ was completely judged at Calvary for human sin. The millions of lambs slaughtered up until the time of Christ were a testimony that the blood of animals could never fully atone for man's sin; it was necessary for the perfect, unblemished, fully-tested Man, the Lamb of God, to shed His blood. God sent His beloved Son to bear our sin (2 Cor. 5:21), to taste death for all men (Heb. 2:9), and to redeem anyone trusting in Him alone for salvation once and for all by His blood (1 Pet. 1:18-19).

Leprosy

The deadly disease of sin is pictured by the disease of leprosy in Leviticus 13. Like sin, leprosy existed within an individual long before it worked its way out to be evident to all. There was no cure for leprosy; it brought social isolation and a slow agonizing death. In Leviticus 14, three ceremonial cleansings were to be performed if a Jewish leper was cured of the disease. There is no recorded instance of these ceremonies being performed. Why? Because there were only two lepers healed in the entirety of the Old Testament; Naaman the Syrian was healed of leprosy by Elijah, and God disciplined Miriam with the disease for seven days.

The first cleaning was the miracle itself (which pictures spiritual regeneration through trusting Christ – Titus 3:5). The second cleaning involved two birds. One was killed over running water, and its blood was put upon the second bird, which was then let go. The priest then sprinkled the cleansed leper with the blood-water mixture and declared him "clean." This ceremony pictures God's declaration of a believer's receiving God's righteousness by trusting in Christ as Savior. The birds represent both the death of Christ (the bird that died) and the resurrection of Christ (the released bird that flew up into the heavens). The blood of the first bird links the two aspects together.

The third cleansing detailed in Leviticus 14 required the cleansed leper to repeatedly bathe himself; this pictures the fact the Christians are to keep short accounts with the Lord – that is, confess sin specifically and as quickly as it happens in order to remain in communion with God. (1 Jn. 1:9). During Christ's sojourn on Earth, He healed many lepers so that the priests laboring at the temple would have a testimony of Himself (Luke 5:14). Each time a Jewish leper went to the temple to undergo the Leviticus 14 ritual, the priests understood something which had never happened before was now occurring regularly. Consequently, Luke records the fact that a large number of priests turned from the Law which was to point them to Christ (Rom. 3:20; Gal. 3:24) and trusted Jesus Christ for salvation (Acts 6:7).

In biblical times, leprosy was a deadly disease with no cure. The damage to the nervous system by leprosy often prevented individuals from properly treating bodily injuries, as no pain was felt and they were often unaware of the injury. Likewise if an individual sins enough he or she will become numb to the pangs of the conscience and further injure his or her soul. Pain is generally a good thing because it alerts us to what needs attention. Today there is a cure for leprosy; likewise, there is a cure for sin – Jesus Christ.

The Uniformity of Content

Christianity is quite unique in that its *founder*, Jesus Christ, did not Himself write any of the books of the Bible, whereas each world religion has its own religious book which was developed by a single individual claiming unique revelation. The Bible, however, as previously mentioned, was written by forty writers from different cultural, geographic and social settings over a 1600 year period, yet the agreement of the message is so uniform that it could only be possible if orchestrated by one mind – God's. Here are a few examples.

Principle of First Mention

This facet of hermeneutics implies that the first mention of a particular *key word* or phrase in the Bible usually establishes that word's general application throughout all of Scripture. For example, the words "love," "worship," and "lamb" all first occur in Genesis 22, which records the story of Abraham, at God's command, venturing to the land of Moriah to sacrifice his only beloved son, Isaac. God never intended for Abraham to actually offer Isaac; instead, He tested Abraham's faith and presented a story line that would depict God's own sacrifice of His Son for humanity's sake. The initial meanings of love, worship, and selfless sacrifice are defined in Genesis 22, then developed throughout the remainder of the Bible.

Before the events of Genesis 22, the principle of first mention is witnessed in the life of Abraham in Genesis 15. The word of God came to Abraham, without any associated signs and wonders. God affirmed that, though Abraham didn't have any children, He would make him the father of many nations and, subsequently, bless all the Earth through him. The word of God was good enough for him – he simply trusted what God said and believed. God responded by accrediting a standing of righteousness to Abraham's account.

This accrediting, or accounting, of divine righteousness to a sinner exercising faith is seen throughout the Bible and is thoroughly explained by the Apostle Paul in Romans 4 and 5. Obviously, God wanted no confusion on this matter for the words "believe," "counted," and "righteousness" all occur for the first time in the Bible in one verse (Gen. 15:6) and in one divine declaration just after the first reference to "the word of the Lord" in the Bible (Gen. 15:1). Genesis 15:6 also appears three times in the New Testament: Romans 4:3, Galatians 3:6, and James 2:23. In Abraham's case, what preceded imputed righteousness? His faith. In Noah's case, what preceded imputed righteousness? God's grace (Gen. 6:8). Combining these two important truths, we have *"For by grace you have been saved through faith; and that not of yourselves, it is the gift of God"* (Eph. 2:8). Both God's means of salvation through grace and man's responsibility to lay hold of this gift by personal faith are clearly presented in Genesis, as throughout the Bible.

The Fourfold Gospel Presentation of Christ

The number "four" is the number of *earthly order*, as created by God – four winds, four directions, four phases of the moon, four seasons, and four places creatures dwell (upon, above, and beneath the earth and in the sea). How does *four* then relate to God's presentation of His Son to humanity? When the Son exited the dimensionless and timeless realm of majesty on high and descended to the Earth, He willingly placed Himself under earthly order. As a man, He became subject to the natural laws of creation, even though, as God, He still maintained the order of all things (Col. 1:17).

With Christ's journey to Earth in view, the Old Testament often presents Christ from the earthly number of four, in the same way the four Gospels upholds the brilliancy of the Lord from different perspectives. The following table summarizes the Old Testament fourfold pictures of the coming Savior to earth.

Gospel	Matthew	Mark	Luke	John
Perspective	King	Servant	Human	Deity

Four unique "behold" statements are found within the Old Testament that prepare the way for Christ's first earthly advent; each one emphasizes one of the main Gospel themes. "Behold" means to earnestly look upon with regard; it may convey a connotation of surprise or wonder. These four "Behold" statements are God the Father's invitation to mankind to gaze upon and admire His dear Son.

Behold your King (Zech. 9:9) – Gospel of Matthew
Behold My Servant (Isa. 42:1) – Gospel of Mark
Behold the Man (Zech. 6:12) – Gospel of Luke
Behold your God (Isa. 40:9) – Gospel of John

Occasionally, non-conscious living things are used to symbolize some aspect of the Lord's activities. Examples would include a fruit-bearing vine, an olive tree, and the gopher trees used by Noah and his family to build an ark to escape the imminent flood. In the Old Testament, the Lord speaks prophetically of His Son being a Branch in four ways, which align with the unique vantage points of Christ in the four Gospels. These four divine titles of the Lord align with the four Gospel presentations of Christ.

Unto David a Branch ... a King (Isa. 11:1) – Gospel of Matthew
My Servant, the Branch (Zech. 3:8) – Gospel of Mark
The Man ... the Branch (Zech. 6:12) – Gospel of Luke
The Branch of the Lord (Isa. 4:2) – Gospel of John

The Bible informs us that classes of spiritual beings do indeed exist in heaven for the purpose of declaring God's glory. Furthermore, God describes to us what many of these spiritual beings do and how they appear before God's throne in heaven.

The scriptural accounts of the cherubim in Ezekiel 1 and 10, of the seraphim in Isaiah 6, and of the four living creatures in Revelation 4 all disclose that these beings have the same faces – four kinds of faces to be more exact. Apparently, the cherubim each have all four, that is, the face of a lion, the face of an ox, the face of a man, and the face of an eagle. The faces of these beings reflect the same glories of the Lord Jesus that are presented in the main themes of each Gospel. The *lion* is the king of the beasts, which reflects Matthew's perspective. The *ox*, as a beast of burden, is harnessed for the rigors of serving, and pictures Mark's presentation. The face of the *man* clearly agrees with Luke's prevalent theme of the Lord's humanity. Lastly, the *eagle* flies high above all the other creatures – in view is the divine essence of the Savior.

The four faces of the cherubim, seraphim, and the four living creatures as seen in heaven:

137

Lion – King – Gospel of Matthew
Ox – Servant – Gospel of Mark
Man – Humanity – Gospel of Luke
Eagle – Deity – Gospel of John

The fourfold presentation of Christ witnessed in the four gospel accounts in the New Testament beautifully conforms to the various fourfold prophetic announcements of Christ contained in the Old Testament.

Symbols

Besides the divine message contained in the normal narrative, God also uses numbers, symbols, metals, colors, names, etc. to convey information. These more abstract forms of revelation do not substitute for or supplement the clear teaching of Scripture, but rather reiterate the obvious message of Scripture through metaphor. This general understanding hinders over-zealous theologians from abusing typology, numerology, and general symbolic representations in the Bible. When God initially introduces an object, a number, a color, etc. in a metaphoric presentation, that symbolic meaning is held consistently throughout all sixty-six books of the Bible. For those interested, I have included about three dozen biblical metaphors which are used in a consistent fashion in Appendix III.

A brief example of numerology is provided for the reader's consideration. Though most numbers in Scripture have a literal meaning (Christ arose from the grave on the *third* day.), some numbers also serve a figurative purpose. The Lamb with *seven* horns before the throne of God in Revelation 5:6 symbolically represents the Lord's omnipotence, as *seven* is the number of perfection, and a *horn* represents *power* in Scripture. Sometimes both a figurative and a literal meaning may be understood, especially when the obvious literal sense is within a personal narrative and the figurative sense conveys a future meaning verified elsewhere in Scripture. For example, the seven-year famine in Joseph's day was both an actual event that literally affected the whole land, and a forewarning of a yet future seven-year tribulation period that would devastate the entire planet. *Egypt* figuratively speaks of "the world" in Scripture.

The consistent use of symbols, numbers, analogies, names, first-mention occurrences, fulfilled prophetic types and shadows, plus the plain and consistent teachings of the Bible prove it to be the orchestrated genius of one Mind – the Bible is God's oracle to mankind.

Apparent Contradictions

Skeptics often use the argument that apparent contradictions within Scripture prove that the Bible is fallible and, therefore, not the Word of God. Sometimes this supposition is then used to prove that the God of the Bible Himself is fallible. While a few scribal errors will be found within the Bible as it exists today, no contradictions of context will be found in the Bible. If we think we have found a contradiction, it is because we have not properly discerned God's meaning of Scripture; *"For as the heavens are higher than the earth, so are My ways higher than your ways, and My thoughts than your thoughts"* (Isa. 55:9). Natural man will assume contradictions because he cannot attain to the height of Scripture. The spiritual man will search all of Scripture for an understanding which is upheld by all of Scripture – the truth is in the whole.

Concerning actual scribal errors in the Bible the most noticeable are found in some Old Testament numbers. For example, about one sixth of the numbers in the parallel narratives of the Kings and Chronicles do not agree. C. I. Scofield explains:

> Some discrepant statements concerning numbers are found in the extant Hebrew manuscripts. Error by scribes in transcription of Hebrew numbers was easy, whereas preservation of

numerical accuracy was difficult. Inspiration extends only to the inerrancy of the original autographs.[1]

This type of scribal error is generally easy to identify, and reason should guide the proper interpretation. For example, given Hebrew number construction, it would be logical to conclude that only seventy men from the small village of Bethshemesh died for the offense of peering into the Ark of the Covenant, in lieu of 50,070 (1 Sam. 6:19). Let us not forget that the Bible has been scientifically proven to be 99.5 percent authentic to the autographs and that the autographs were inspired by God – not translations of the autographs. The following examples are just some of which cynics promote to create doubt about the validity of the Bible.

Christ's First and Second Advents

In Bertrand Russell's book *Why I Am Not a Christian*, he surmised that Jesus could not be the Christ predicted by the Bible because He died, and the true Messiah, the heir to the throne of David, would rule forever. Russell wrote:

> For one thing, he [Christ] certainly thought his second coming would occur in clouds of glory before the death of all the people who were living at that time. There are a great many texts that prove that. He says, for instance: "Ye shall not have gone over the cities of Israel till the Son of Man be come." Then He says: "There are some standing here which shall not taste death till the Son of Man comes into His kingdom"; and there are a lot of places where it is quite clear that He believed His second coming would happen during the lifetime of many then living.[2]

Russell's error was that he failed to see the two advents of Christ prophesied in the Old Testament (Isa. 53:10) and clearly taught by Christ Himself. The Lord Jesus said that He would not return to the Earth until all the cities of Israel had been visited with the gospel message (implying that all Jews would have an opportunity to hear the Kingdom message). When would this be accomplished? His teaching, recorded in Matthew 24, states that this would be accomplished during the tribulation period, just prior to the anti-Christ stopping the Jewish sacrifices and proclaiming himself to be God in the temple (Matt. 24:15-16; 2 Thess. 2:3-8). The individual standing with Christ as He was speaking, who would see the Lord Jesus come into His kingdom was John. He saw it in vision form, as an old man banished on the Isle of Patmos, and wrote the entire book of Revelation to document the fact that Christ's words had been fulfilled (those which Russell said were not).

Jesus Christ clearly taught (in Matt. 25:14-19; Luke 20:9-18; 19:11-15) that His kingdom would not be established now, but after an interim period following His death. These teachings by Christ Himself were conveyed to the disciples just a few days before His death. Why? *"Because they [the disciples] thought that the kingdom of God would appear immediately"* (Luke 19:11), and He wanted to correct their wrong assumption. Christ personally told the disciples on a number of occasions that He was going to die: *"From that time Jesus began to show to His disciples that He must go to Jerusalem, and suffer many things from the elders and chief priests and scribes, and be killed, and be raised again the third day"* (Matt. 16:21; also see 17:22; 20:17-19).

Why did the Lord Jesus tell His disciples ahead of time what was going to happen to Him? *"Now I tell you before it comes, that when it does come to pass, you may believe that I am He"* (John 13:19; also see John 14:29). The Lord Jesus wanted His disciples to know that His sufferings and His death were preplanned so that they would not lose faith when they witnessed these things happening – He was in control of every detail.

At His first advent, He came as the sacrificial Lamb of God to offer peace to mankind, but at His second advent, He will execute vengeance and judgment on the Earth, set up His kingdom, and rule over the nations with a rod of iron (Rev. 19-20). Russell's erroneous interpretation resulted for two reasons: (1) He did not "rightly divide" the Word of God (i.e. comparing Scripture with Scripture; see 2 Tim. 2:15), and (2) He did not have the Holy Spirit to guide the process; naturally speaking, man cannot understand Scripture without God's help (1 Cor. 2:14). Consequently, each assertion posed in his book is answerable by good hermeneutical study. Unfortunately, his heresy has led many away from the truth!

Time

Each Gospel presents a unique vantage point of Christ to a particular audience. The Gospel of Matthew presents Christ as the rightful heir to the throne of David and was primarily written to the Jews. Mark was written to the Romans (half of the empire were slaves) and conveys the lowly servant nature of Christ's ministry. Luke upholds Christ's humanity and, therefore, had a Greek identification. John, which presents Christ's deity, is addressed to the entire world. John refers to the world eighty times in his Gospel, compared to eighteen references in Matthew, five in Mark and ten in Luke. John has over twice as many references as the other three Gospels have combined. Unlike the synoptic Gospels, John used the world's reference of time (Roman versus Jewish reckoning). This difference is important to understand, otherwise, there would appear to be serious disagreement between the Gospel writers on major events in the Lord's life. For example, John records that Christ was in the judgment hall before Pilate at the sixth hour, but Matthew states that while Christ was on the cross, darkness covered the land at "the sixth hour." The sixth hour by Roman reckoning would be six o'clock, but the Jews would understand it to be twelve o'clock.

The Temptation (Testing) of Christ

If the accounts of Matthew 4 and Luke 4 are examined closely, one would notice that the order of Satan's specific attacks upon Christ are different. The skeptic deplores such inconsistency: "See, you can't trust the Bible – it does not agree with itself." However, the order maintained by each writer is for the purpose of upholding the prevalent theme of each Gospel. In Matthew, Satan first asks the Lord Jesus to turn the stones into bread, then bids Him to cast Himself down from the pinnacle of the temple, and thirdly offers to Christ all the kingdoms of this world if Christ will only worship him. Luke's order, however, is the request to turn the stones into bread first, then the offer of the kingdoms of the world, and finally Satan adjures Christ to cast Himself down from the pinnacle of the temple to prove that the angels will protect Him. Why the different order? Arthur Pink explains:

> The reason for this variation is not hard to find. In Matthew, the order is arranged climactically, so as to make Rulership over all the kingdoms of the world the final bait which the devil dangled before the Son of David. But in Luke we have, no doubt, the chronological order, the order in which they actually occurred.[3]

Sovereign design accounts for the variation of the temptation accounts, which serves to further declare the wisdom of God and the distinct glories of the Son. Luke's order of temptations is chronological, while Matthew's is climactic unto kingship.

Years Preceding Solomon's Temple

1 Kings 6:1 states that Solomon began construction of the temple in the fourth year of his reign, some 480 years after the children of Israel came out of Egypt, but Acts 13:18-21 denotes many more years between the two events. By plugging other in-

formation from Scripture into some of the missing details of Acts 13:18-21, the actual duration of time is found to be 569 years – which would include 40 years for Israel's wilderness experience, 27 years for the conquest of Canaan and land allotment, 450 years for the era of the Judges, 12 years for Samuel the prophet, 40 years for Saul's reign, 40 years for David's reign. Solomon reigned after David, and the temple was started in the fourth year of his reign; therefore, according to Acts 13:18-21, the total time from Israel's exit from Egypt to the building of the temple was 573 years.

This total seems to be a contradiction with the 480 years recorded in 1 Kings 6:1, but not if you understand the lesson Israel learned during the era of the Judges. The book of Judges records the following repeated cycle: The Jews rebelled against God; they were punished; they cried out to God for deliverance, and God sent a judge to liberate them from their oppressors. How long were the Jews under judgment during this 450 year period? They were ruled by Mesopotamia 8 years, Moab 18 years, Canaan 20 years, Midian 7 years, and the Philistines 40 years – for a total of 93 years. As His people were rebellious and outside of His will for them, God did not count the time He was punishing them – the time they were estranged from Him. The 1 Kings reference records the years from Egypt to the building of the temple in which the Jews were not under God's discipline (573 years – 93 years = 480 years). The purpose of this reckoning served as a warning to the people not to repeat the mistakes of the past! It went unheeded.

Understanding Context

It is usually people who know nothing or very little about the Bible who identify contradictions in the Bible – especially those in our higher institutions of education. Usually, it is because they lack an understanding of proper context or the differing economies of revealed truth that God has placed upon man throughout the Bible. The skeptic complains, "The Bible teaches 'Eye for an eye and tooth for a tooth,' but in another place the Bible says, 'pray for your enemies and do good to them who persecute you.' Therefore, the Bible obviously disagrees with itself." The former truth was expressed to the Jews to teach them that disobedience must be punished if the Law was not kept, whereas the latter statement reflects a deeper truth pertaining to the New Testament, for Christians who had already realized that no one could earn heaven by law keeping and had trusted Christ as Savior. These believers, having received the Holy Spirit, now had the wherewithal to both *keep* the Law (i.e. sin is a conscious choice for a true Christian), and *fulfill* the Law (which would actively demonstrate both God's character and the outworking of His grace).

Throughout the human time line, God has diligently worked to cause man to be more aware of his sin and of the divine solution for it – Christ. It is not that God is changing absolute truth, rather He is methodically unfolding it for man's benefit. The purpose of the Law was to make the Jews conscious of their sin and their personal need for a Savior (Rom. 3:20; Gal. 3:24). However, instead of humility before God for not keeping the Law, they responded by adding a do-it-yourself scheme of self-justifying works. Logically speaking, since they could not keep the Law, they should have looked to God for a solution, rather than create one through religious dead works. The focus of much of the Old Testament was on Law keeping, not Law fulfilling, for this was not even possible in the Old Testament because the faithful were not regenerated and indwelt by the Holy Spirit. Christ's death and resurrection precipitated these realities in the New Testament (John 14:15-20, 16:8). Law keeping demanded that one not steal, but Law fulfilling is not not stealing (double negative intended), but rather to give sacrificially of one's self to others. Paul writes:

> *Owe no one anything except to love one another, for he who loves another has fulfilled the law. For the commandments, "You shall not commit adultery," "You shall not murder," "You shall not steal," "You shall not bear false witness," "You shall not covet," and if there is any other commandment, are all summed up in this saying, namely, "You shall love your neighbor as yourself." Love does no harm to a neighbor; therefore love is the fulfillment of the law* (Rom. 13:8-10).

Many of the "contradictions" in the Bible posed by skeptics are merely the picking and choosing of random statements which have been drawn out of their proper context and meaning, as determined by the whole of Scripture. Many books have been written on this subject, one being *Answers to Tough Questions – What Skeptics Are Asking About the Christian Faith*, by Josh McDowell and Don Stewart. This book address dozens of supposed contradictions by using the whole of Scripture to explain each one. I have been systematically studying the Bible for decades; the supposed contradictions in the Bible are just not there! The truth is in the whole; private interpretations may not reflect the whole truth.

Science in the Bible

Many fascinating scientific details are described in the Bible, some of which date back thousands of years ago – before the various fields of science were developed. Approximately 2700 years ago, Isaiah stated that the Earth was circular, perhaps even spherical (Isa. 40:22); he also described the water cycle that maintains life on Earth (Isa. 55:10; also Job 36:27-28).

Some 3000 years ago, David wrote concerning "the paths in the sea" (Ps. 8:8). This verse prompted 19th century naval officer Matthew Fontaine Maury to explore the oceans for prevailing sea currents. He found them, pioneered the science of oceanography, and revolutionized the trade routes for sailing ships. Within approximately the same time frame, the Bible records that valleys exist on the bottom of the oceans (2 Sam. 22:16) and that the wind blows in circular paths about the Earth (Eccl. 1:6).

The book of Job is perhaps the oldest book in the Bible, dating back some 3500 years. Job records many scientific facts, which we now know to be true. He states clearly that the Earth is suspended in space, hanging in nothing (Job 26:7), and that there are vents in the floor of the ocean (Job 38:16). Job refers to air having weight (Job 28:25) and to light being in motion (Job 38:19-20). One of the most interesting astronomical features in Job is found in a question God poses to Job, *"Can you bind the cluster of the Pleiades, or loose the belt of Orion?"* (Job 38:31). We now understand what God was sharing with Job. Within the Taurus constellation is a tight grouping of stars in gravitation lock; they are called "Pleiades." Although many stars are in this cluster (about 440 light years away), only seven are discernable with the naked eye on a clear night; sometimes these are referred to as the "seven sisters." Just as the Bible states, these stars are bound together; they cannot pull apart from one another. However, the constellation Orion is composed of stars throughout our galaxy, and we know that the Milky Way is expanding. As the years roll by, Orion's belt is literally *letting out a notch*. The answer to God's question to Job was that only God can arrange and control the constellations in such a way that He binds some stars together and loosens others. The Bible is full of such details – it is simply an amazing book!

Summary and Challenge

Over 100 years ago, William Ramsay, a young English scholar, went to Asia Minor with the expressed purpose of proving that the history given by Luke in his gospel and in the Acts was inaccurate. His professors had confidently said that Luke could not be right. He began to dig in the ancient ruins of Greece and Asia Minor, testing for ancient terms, boundaries, and other items which would be a dead giveaway if a writer had been inventing this history at a later date as claimed. To his amazement, he found that the New Testament Scriptures were accurate to the minutest detail. So convincing was the evidence that Ramsay himself became a Christian and a great biblical scholar. We still look upon his books as being a classic as far as the history of the New Testament is concerned.[4]

If you have not explored the Bible, I challenge you to read it and to try to avoid being brought under its influence. The writer of Hebrews states, *"The word of God is living and powerful, and sharper than any two-edged sword, piercing even to the division of soul and spirit, and of joints and marrow, and is a discerner of the thoughts and intents of the heart"* (Heb. 4:12). Many profound atheists have sought to disprove the validity of the Bible and have become absolutely convinced of its message. Some who once rejected the Christian message, such as C. S. Lewis, Josh McDowell, and Lee Strobel, have since written their own defenses of the Christian faith. After experiencing the transforming power of the Bible, C. S. Lewis wrote: "A young man who wishes to remain a sound atheist cannot be too careful of his reading. There are traps everywhere – 'Bibles laid open, millions of surprises,' as Herbert says, 'fine nets and stratagems.' God is, if I may say it, very unscrupulous."[5]

Dear reader, if you want to remain in the darkness of atheism or be blinded by some humanly concocted religion, do not read the Bible, for if you do, you will never be the same – you may even be changed forever. Many have dared, and many are glad.

#5 Prophecy the Proof of Inspiration

We have reviewed the Bible's authenticity and uniformity, now we focus on its third unique quality; its prophetic content. There are many unique qualities of the Bible, but these three (authenticity, uniformity, and prophecy), are the most prominent aspects which demonstrate supernatural origin.

The Bible repeatedly proves its validity by accurately foretelling thousands of future events; many of which are now verifiable history. This same prophetic content is not apparent in the Hindu Vedas, the Quran, the sayings of Buddha or Confucius, the scriptures of Shintoism, the Book of Mormon or any other religious writings. Approximately one fourth of the Bible is prophetic in content; in this distinction, it is in a class by itself as compared to any other "religious book." Through prophetic statements, God puts His name on the line again and again to show the world that He is the one true God and that the Bible is His message to humanity. Ignorance is not bliss; man is without excuse! Irwin H. Linton says it well in his book, *A Lawyer Examines the Bible*: "To doubt is not sin, but to be contented to remain in doubt when God has provided 'many infallible proofs' to cure it, is."[1]

Philosophy and Prophecy

Humanistic philosophy denies the existence of the supernatural. Consequently, all supposed divine revelation via visions, prophecy, miracles, etc. is refuted. How profound is man's wherewithal not to believe in the supernatural? Even when God took on flesh, sojourned among men, and personally explained divine truth, the masses rejected the message and nailed Him to a tree. Humanism would have us conclude that extraordinarily bizarre events are never supernaturally sourced; furthermore, one must accept either an unusual natural cause for such events (no matter how improbable) or a natural explanation that has yet to be determined. But is this logical?

Suppose I stood before you and said, "I have complete control over this silver coin such that it obeys my will instead of known physical laws. I will now demonstrate this fact by randomly flipping the coin in the air and allowing it to fall to the ground where the 'heads' side of the coin will face upwards on 300 consecutive tosses." Immediately, I proceed to do exactly what I just prophesied to do. The statistical probability of this event is one chance in 2^{300} (i.e. the odds of flipping 300 consecutive 'heads' is one in 2.037 x 10^{90}). After about one hundred tosses, I noticed that you no longer appear to be a cynic, but I still complete the 300 tosses anyway, every toss being "heads."

Have I sufficiently proven to you that I have complete control over the coin when it is flipped? Before answering this question, it would be good to verify that the coin does not have two heads or that I am not using some electromagnetic gimmick or learned method of tossing the coin which would cause it to behave according to natural laws and still produce the "heads" reality. Just to ensure the coin is legit, you toss it several times yourself to verify a "tails" flip is possible. After all known natural explanations are evaluated and disproved, you can safely conclude that I control the end result of randomly flipping the coin into the air (though I have not proven to be in control of other facets of the coin, e.g. its molecular composition).

Now suppose that there was such a deplorable situation in which your life depended upon obtaining a "heads" result in tossing the same coin I just tossed 300 times (i.e. "heads" = you live; "tails" = you die). Who would you feel more secure with in the flipping of the coin – yourself, or me? Remember, I have just demonstrated a *naturally unexplainable* ability to flip a "heads" result. Logically, you realize that, if you flip the coin, you have but a mere 50-50 chance of survival, yet you have never witnessed me obtain anything but a "heads" result after tossing the coin into the air. You would rightly determine to allow me to flip the coin, though logically you cannot explain why I always secure a "heads" result. You have exercised a *justified belief* which did not entail trusting in a naturally explainable cause. Some would call this *faith*.

We exercise experientially-based faith in known natural cause everyday. For example, I don't think about whether the chair that I sat in yesterday will still hold me today – I just plop down into it. My nearly unconscious decision was based on historical evidence; thus, no statics calculation or load test was required. In the same way, you will logically favor experience (e.g., my coin flipping track record) over proven natural cause (the even odds of achieving a "heads" result in a coin toss). Consequently, you allow me to perform the 301st flip of the coin. Unless stronger unnatural cause intervenes (someone or something which has greater influence on the coin than I), you should be safe – I will flip a "heads" for you, and you are quite glad!

Applying the same conclusion to biblical prophecy, let us suppose that a particularly extraordinary event was spoken of hundreds of years in advance by a dozen different prophets who had no contact with each other, all of whom were experientially shown to have a 100 percent prophetic track record. Would not experience dictate that I should expect the event to happen even though natural cause provides no reason to believe it will happen? Yes. Furthermore, what if these dozen prophets uttered some two hundred distinct prophecies pertaining to one future event just to ensure that the particular situation would be recognized as a supernatural occurrence? Would not that scenario of past experience and improbable odds demand our belief in a supernatural cause? *Theoretically*, the option of an unknown natural explanation would remain open, but overwhelming practical experience and statistical improbability demands that we avail ourselves of the more reasonable option.

Philosopher David Hume conjectured that the most such experience could establish is that an extraordinary event had happened; therefore, he denied the possibility of supernatural revelation (i.e. prophecies and miracles are naturally explainable or would be at some point in time). Hume's conclusion requires the suppression of good reason and commonsense based on experience. The outcome means that God will never be able to get his attention no matter what medium of communication is used. Those who do not want to see God, never will – and God will honor that decision until judgment day. I will illustrate this point by quoting from *Why I Am Not A Christian* by Bertrand Russell (natural law argument):

> There is, as we all know, a law that if you throw dice you will get double sixes only about once in thirty-six times, and we do not regard that as evidence that the fall of the dice is regulated by design; on the contrary, **if the double sixes came every time we should think that there was design.** The laws of nature are of that sort as regards a great many of them. They are statistical averages such as would emerge from the laws of chance; and that makes this whole business of natural law much less impressive than it formerly was. Quite apart from that, which represents the momentary state of science that may change tomorrow, the whole idea that natural laws imply a lawgiver is due to a confusion between natural and human laws.[2]

According to Russell, someone could repeatedly role two dice and obtain two sixes from now to eternity and believe the sole explanation is unknown natural design, though it clearly violates well understood natural law. Russell saw human law, which is subject to change according to our increased understanding of natural order, and natural law which was absolute, and for the most part unknowable. But if natural law is unknowable, how can one assert that there is no supernatural explanation for the unknowable, when logically speaking known and verified natural law of probability counters that position.

Prior to being engaged in full-time Christian ministry, I worked as an engineer in the aerospace industry. It might be possible to design an airplane that will never experience mechanical failure resulting in a crash, but to do so would result in an airplane so heavy that it may not fly; from an economic standpoint, it certainly would not be practical to build. Much engineering time is spent in failure modes analysis to minimize the threat of catastrophic failures modes (including multiple failure scenarios), but reason dictates that a balanced design must include both the practical aspects of flying the plane and the design reliability of the aircraft. Consequently, in aircraft design, one catastrophic event in every few hundred million flight hours is generally considered an acceptable design. The difference between engineering and philosophy is that engineering functions well in a realm of the probable cause and effect, while humanistic philosophy imposes absolutes (e.g. "There is no God – life came from nature.") where commonsense dictates otherwise.

A Prophetic Portrait of Messiah

Many irrefutable evidences prove that the Bible is God's truth, but none is more convincing than fulfilled prophecy. Much of the Bible's prophecy has to do with the nation of Israel, but the most significant are the hundreds of prophecies pertaining to the coming of the Jewish Messiah. Over two hundred prophecies pertain to Christ's first advent to the Earth and twice that number for His second return to rule and reign. As the second advent of Christ has yet to occur, those related prophecies are unverifiable. First advent prophecies have been fulfilled, however, and may be analyzed.

We all enjoy looking at family pictures and reminiscing of bygone days. Though our outward appearance changes as we age, we are still able to identify certain characteristic features of loved ones in photographs and video clips. Through prophetic Scripture, God has likewise brought various writers together, over a huge span of time, to create a timeless prophetic portrait of the Messiah. They didn't use paint, but each one dabbed a bit of prophetic color in words into the canvas of Holy Scripture to depict Christ. Those willing to gaze upon the prophetic portrait embedded in Scripture would recognize Messiah's features when He arrived. In this way, God removed all doubt as to who the Messiah actually is. The one claiming to be Messiah would indeed be Messiah, proving *every* detail in the prophetic portrait was fulfilled.

For a number of years, I have read or heard several Christian writers and speakers refer to enormous, even astronomical, probability numbers to substantiate the claim that Jesus Christ is the Messiah of whom the Bible foretold. Rarely is their evidence shown, which causes the engineer in me to wonder if such numbers are legitimate or sensationalized. Perhaps you have had the same quandary.

This chapter presents a thorough statistical review of the prophecies concerning Christ's first advent to the Earth some 2000 years ago. Over 200 such prophecies may be found in the Old Testament, which were written by more than a dozen prophets some 1,600 to 400 years prior to Christ's first coming to the Earth. To do a fair evaluation, I have removed redundant prophecies and the more vague ones (which the skeptic might argue against) from consideration. By my reckoning, sixty-nine major unquestionably Messianic prophecies, which are historically quantifiable, remain. Just as a picture confirms that no two people are exactly alike, no one could possibly fulfill all sixty-nine of these prophecies but Messiah Himself.

Each of these sixty-nine Messianic prophecies has been allocated to one of four prophetic categories and then assigned a realistic probability of occurrence by chance. The probability numbers are conservative and represent a "fair" commonsense value. The four prophetic categories are: *Genealogical Prophecies*, *Geographic Prophecies*, *Time Prophecies*, and *Miscellaneous Prophecies*. Another thirty-three prophecies are listed in a fifth prophetic category, *Other Fulfilled Prophecies*, which is a list of significant Messianic prophecies where no probability assessment was attempted as the parametric data is not available to quantify the likelihood of fulfillment by chance. In all, about 150 Old Testament prophecies concerning Messiah's first coming are listed in the five categories (Redundant prophetic Scripture references are supplied, but not counted as part of the sixty-nine major prophecies.).

The actual listing of these biblical prophecies and their statistical evaluation are contained in Appendix IV. The combined probability that the Lord Jesus Christ fulfilled all sixty-nine of the major prophecies listed above, by chance, is estimated to be one chance in 5.32×10^{72} attempts. The actual composite number would be much higher if the fifth table of miscellaneous prophecies were statistically quantifiable and the prophecies which are beyond statistical probability could realistically be assessed (e.g. What probability of chance does one ascribe to a prophecy which predicts that Christ would raise the dead back to life?).

So just how big of a number is 5.32×10^{72} (that is 532 with 70 zeros behind it)? The total mass of all of the Earth's oceans is estimated to be 1.35×10^{21} kg. We obviously need a much bigger number to compare with. The total mass of the Earth is estimated to be 6.0 x 10^{24} kg (or 6,000 billion billion tons).[3] It is evident that 10^{24} is not even in the ball park in comparison to 10^{72}, so we need to look for something a good bit larger. The solar system is dominated by the Sun, which has a mass of about 2×10^{30} kg, which is about 343,000 times the mass of the Earth."[4] Obviously, 10^{30} is still a long ways from 10^{72}; I think we need to start thinking at the atomic level to ever achieve a comparative perspective. Through spectral densities obtained during full solar eclipses, scientists understand the atomic composition of the Sun. If we assume that the atomic weight of the atoms in the Sun is 1.3 (90% hydrogen and 10% helium), factoring in moles per gram and Avogadro's number, it is estimated that the Sun contains approximately 9.032 x 10^{56} atoms, still way short of 10^{72}.

The Milky Way is composed of approximately 200 billion stars; scientists calculate that the total number of atoms in our galaxy is on the order of 10^{68} and, if dark and exotic matter is considered, then the number is closer to 10^{69}. This is relatively close to the Messianic probability number of 10^{72}. By the way, if we assume our galaxy is of average size, the number of atoms in the entire universe would be between 10^{79} and 10^{81} (given the range of galaxies scientist think there are in the universe).[5]

Now that we have some perspective as to how colossal the number 5.320 x 10^{72} is, let us seek a probability illustration we can relate to. What would be the probability of someone randomly choosing a previously marked grain of sand from a child's sandbox? The probability would be extremely unlikely. What would be the chance of randomly choosing one particular grain of sand out of a sandbox the size of a county, or a country, or a continent? The odds would be astronomically impossible. Now let us suppose that we could convert the entire mass of the universe into grains of sand and that one single grain of sand could be marked and hidden anywhere in the universe (which, as stated earlier, some scientists say is nearly 100 billion light years across). What would be the probability of randomly picking out the previously marked grain of sand by chance?

The mass of the universe is estimated to be 1.6×10^{60} kg, while the measured mass of a 2 mm grain of sand is about 9.0×10^{-5} kg.[6] The resulting probability of picking the previously marked grain of sand from somewhere in our galactic sandbox spanning the universe is one chance in 1.78×10^{64} tries. This is beyond astronomically impossible! But as improbable as this seems, the Lord Jesus fulfilling all sixty-nine major Old Testament prophecies is 100 million times *less* likely than randomly choosing that one grain of sand from any location in the universe!

The probability of Christ fulfilling all the Old Testament prophecies by chance is absolutely quantifiably impossible – He fulfilled each one by design. The Lord Jesus was in perfect control of every detail of His life and death. His control during his arrest in the Garden of Gethsemane is a good example. Even though Peter tried to kill the high priest's servant with a sword (managing only to remove an ear), he was not arrested. Why? Because the Lord told those arresting Him, *"If you seek Me, let these go their way"* (John 18:8). Jesus Christ foretold of His death and the details of it several times prior to it occurring – He was in full control of all the events of His death.

The prophetic portrait of the Messiah painted centuries earlier on the Holy Page proves beyond any shadow of doubt that Jesus Christ is who He said He was – He is God's Messiah. Some might say, Jesus knew the Old Testament Scripture, and He was trying to fulfill each one by human effort. Please examine the lists of prophecies in Appendix IV again; the vast majority would not be within the control of human effort. How does one control his or her genealogy, time of birth, birth place, childhood travels, means of personal torture, the method of one's death, and his or her burial place? Only God could control such details!

Some of the scribes and religious leaders of Christ's time memorized large portions of Scripture. Yet, knowing Scripture, they still paid Judas the betrayal money in silver, not gold, and it was the exact amount that Zachariah had prophesied 700 years earlier. Christ was crucified, not stoned, which was the normal means of execution under Jewish law; this fulfilled what David wrote in Psalm 22, a thousand years earlier (Messiah's hands and feet would be pierced). If these religious leaders had been able to void one prophecy, it would have proven that Jesus Christ was not the Messiah; instead, their religious blindness made them available instruments in the hand of a sovereign God. God proved to the world that His Son was the long awaited Messiah.

The Jews of Christ's day refused to compare the prophetic portrait of Messiah to the life of Jesus Christ; thus, they missed Messiah's coming, and stiff-necked men and women have been doing the same ever since. How about you, are you willing to consider that Jesus Christ is God's Messiah, the Savior of your soul? If not, no amount of evidence on Christ's behalf will make any difference. The problem is not evidence, but a willingness to fairly contemplate it.

Summary

Nostradamus published his book of prophecies over four centuries ago, but their vague content has allowed various interpretations to fit a number of historical situations. Accordingly, most of his prophecies are unverifiable. For those prophecies which may have been fulfilled this is really of no concern, for Satan himself (allowed by God) is able to induce great wonders to deceive man, thus providing a test of man's resolve to adhere to God's Word (2 Cor. 11:13-15). The test of divine prophecy is not that many future proclamations of a particular prophet come true, but that one hundred percent of what was prophesied actually happens. Any thing less is not of God (Deut. 13:1-5).

As stated earlier approximately one fourth of the Bible is prophetic in nature. Most world religions, such as Islam, Buddhism, and Hinduism shun specific prophetic utterances. Why? Unfulfilled prophecies and wrongly predicted events provide evidence of deceit and not of divine truth. Consequently, the failed prophecies of Joseph Smith and Brigham Young (founders and so-called prophets of Mormonism) or the numerous false prophecies of Charles Russell (the founder of The Jehovah's Witnesses) serve as examples of what is not of God. The planned sequel to this book, *Hiding God*, will document dozens of failed prophecies by the founders of these two cults.

In contrast, the Bible is full of specific and verifiable prophecies. In this regard the Bible is unique; no other secular or religious prophet can compete with the Bible's prophetic content or clarity. As further examples please consider the following two prophecies: First, the prophet Isaiah named Cyrus, a future Persian king, two centuries prior to his birth. Cyrus was to be, and indeed was, God's instrument to topple the Babylonian empire, release the Jews from captivity, and rebuild the temple in Jerusalem (Isa. 44:28-45:1; Ezra 1:1-2). It is noted that neither the Babylonian, nor the Persian empires existed at the time of this prophecy. Secondly, King Josiah was named by a godly prophet nearly three centuries before he would reign over Judah; God would use him to drive idolatry out of Judah and, as the prophecy states, he would burn dead men's bones on the pagan altar to desecrate it and void its future usability (1 Kgs. 13:2; 2 Kgs. 23:14-20).

If the Bible is God's revelation to mankind would we not expect archeology and scientific discovery to be in agreement with Scripture? Archeological findings continue to validate por-

tions of the Old Testament, such as the recent discovery of a
Babylonian financial account among the British Museum's collection of 130,000 Assyrian cuneiform tablets, which documents
the payment of 0.75 kg of gold to the temple in Babylon by
Nebo-Sarsekim. The tablet is dated to the 10th year of the reign
of Nebuchadnezzar II, 595 B.C., several years before the siege of
Jerusalem. Jeremiah 39:3 identifies Nebo-Sarsekim as one of
Nebuchadnezzar's generals present at the fall of Jerusalem in
587 B.C. Michael Jursa, an Assyriologist professor from Vienna,
called the tablet the most important find in Biblical archaeology
in a 100 years.[7]

Would not what science has learned from the preserved history within the Earth, the mysterious life on the Earth, and the
glory of celestial bodies above the Earth all be consistent with
the revelation found in Scripture, if the Bible were divinely inspired? Bible commentator William MacDonald answers these
questions:

> No true finding of science will ever contradict the Bible, be-
> cause the secrets of science were placed in the universe by the
> same One who wrote the Bible, God Himself. But many so-
> called facts of science are in reality nothing but unproven theo-
> ries. Any such hypothesis which contradicts the Bible should be
> rejected.[8]

As previously noted, the Bible's declarations have prompted
some scientists to look for the unknown reality in nature, thus
leading to significant scientific discovery. The Bible's evident
authenticity, uniformity, and demonstrated prophetic content offer astounding proof of its supernatural origin. Science and history verify the Bible to be true! Many have tried to destroy the
Bible in centuries past, but God has accurately preserved His
Word so that man might know Him and understand what is required of him.

#6 The Human Conscience

We turn our attention from the unique evidence of the Bible for supernatural cause, to evidence of God that is internally within each of us.

Have you heard people say: "That's not fair!" "Hey, don't cut in line!" "I was here first!" "You must do it – you promised." "It's your turn to ...." "How would you like it, if you were treated like that?" "You should share with others." The one speaking is not just inferring inappropriate or appropriate conduct but is appealing to some conventional sense of right behavior. This mysterious standard of moral practice is not written down anywhere per se, yet it is recognized. From where did it come? How is it possible for man to say "You ought to ...." or "Be reasonable." without referring to a previously understood moral protocol? Why does mankind generally affirm this moral protocol as binding? Why does man not perfectly obey it?

Which culture would you say had a higher ethical standard in their day – the 1st century Roman Empire under Nero, or the Christian populace the Romans persecuted and murdered? During World War II, which social standard reflected higher ethics – the Nazi society which slaughtered millions of innocent people or that of the United States? If you made a choice, to what standard are you comparing? How does one rightly scrutinize and pass judgment on the moral behavior of a people?

Many atheists and Christians use the same terminology: "good," "bad," "wicked," "holy," "evil," "right," "wrong," "moral," "immoral." But what is the appropriate meaning of these words? Without an agreement as to moral etiquette, these words have no quantifiable meaning – each is as flexible as rubber hose, bending and stretching as each person constrains it by whim. The idea of a *hero*, someone who willingly risks his own life for the good of others, is not a concept supported by naturalism; self-sacrifice is not honorable; in fact, it is illogical behavior. Yet many naturalists readily apply such terminology in contradiction to their worldview.

If you heard a child screaming for help from a burning building, your first inclination certainly would be to help, for you have been taught not to be selfish since you were a toddler. But a second and more powerful urge grips your feet to the ground – it is the intrinsic constraint of self-preservation. To run into an inferno to assist the distressed child means the possibility of personal harm or even death. So, what is that internal quality that compels a person to overcome the restraint of self-preservation and dash into a burning building to help another? Why is it the morally right thing to do?

The evolutionist has difficulty explaining these natural and unlearned facets of our being, which venture well beyond acquired ethics through parental or civil training. The Bible teaches that all men have a consciousness which monitors moral absolutes located in his spirit (the deepest part of his being). I believe that it is this facet of our existence that properly answers the above questions.

Morality and Anthropology

In her book *Patterns of Culture*, anthropologist Ruth Benedict documents the ethical diversity of some cultures, even on issues such as homicide. While the moral practices of various societies do differ somewhat, the foundational moral principles upholding these practices do not – they are absolute. For example, Benedict found that some societies believed it to be ethically permissible to kill one's parents after they had reached a certain age; the practice stemmed from the belief that people were better off in the afterlife if they entered it while still physically active and vigorous.[1] While this specific practice would be condemned in most societies, we would agree that the underlying moral principle of caring for one's parents is commendable – it is the fifth of the Ten Commandments.

Societies, then, may differ in their *application* of fundamental moral principles while still maintaining a common moral basis of *substance*. For example, in some societies where murder would be prohibited, it might be considered an act of love to euthanize a dying person suffering immense pain. A society in which suicide is unlawful could still be sympathetic towards a man with a terminal illness who commits suicide rather than strap his family with enormous medical bills. It is possible then to demonstrate behavior that nearly all cultures would consider honorable (e.g. unselfish love to others) while at the same time committing acts that most societies would consider immoral (e.g. suicide and euthanasia).

In his book *The Abolition of Man*, C. S. Lewis shows that the moral fabric of past cultures is similar to each other, though the *application* of how the fabric is utilized does differ. A seamstress might produce a skirt or a shirt from the same fabric – the end product is different, but the material, color, print, etc. are the same. The evidence indicates that there is an inherent moral compass within man that is independent of time and experience, and is something that he cannot rid himself of. Societies following the moral standard of their conscience have a better likelihood of thriving and surviving than those who reject it and assume a different ethical standard. Lewis challenges his readers to ponder what a society would be like if it did have a totally different morality:

> Think of a country where people were admired for running away in battle, or where a man felt proud of double-crossing all the people who had been kindest to him. You might as well try to imagine a country where two and two made five. Men have differed as regards what people you ought to be unselfish to – whether it was only your own family, or your fellow countrymen, or everyone. But they have always agreed that you ought not to put yourself first. Selfishness has never been admired. Men have differed as to whether you should have one wife or four. But they have always agreed that you must not simply have any woman you liked.[2]

The fact of the matter is that we *do not* observe radically different ethical systems in earthly societies. Can you imagine a culture in which lying, cheating, hostility, corruption, rape, and murder were acceptable behaviors and where pride, greed, arrogance, selfishness were admired character bents? Such a culture would quickly collapse into ruin, because trust is a fundamental component for cultural survival. While entering an intersection in which I have the *right of way*, I trust that the person approaching from the right will obey the traffic signal – my life depends on it. When I hand over my pay check to the bank teller, I trust him or her to deposit the appropriate sum of money in my checking account. When a contract is signed, I am putting my trust in the other party to complete what has been committed to do. A society cannot effectively operate without a high level of trust in fellow man – this social trust could not develop if stealing, cheating, lying, adultery were mainstream behaviors.

Civil laws establish order in a society to advance prosperity. That order may vary widely in the realm of social convention, especially where a single personal influence controls a society, but not in moral foundation. For example, in England people drive left of the centerline, but in North America people drive right of the centerline. Both conventions are acceptable, yet social order necessitates agreement on the matter – otherwise driving would be very dangerous! But even with the convention understood, an unwritten phenomenon guides its outworking. For example, you should feel differently towards someone who had suffered a heart attack while driving, crossed over the centerline, and wrecked your brand new red pickup truck, versus someone who intentionally crossed the centerline because they dislike red trucks. In the former situation, sympathy soon smothers your momentary anger, while in the latter case hanging might not be too great a punishment for the culprit! So actually, inherent moral reckoning will guide the various permutations of social convention, as well as moral issues beyond civil legislation.

It is also understood that the ethical standards for various societies are derived from specific cultural practices, such as dress, social mannerisms with the opposite gender, punctuality, curfews, and other social customs pertaining to decency. If you were a man visiting Mexico or Italy, it would not be uncommon to be kissed on the cheek while being greeted by a woman; in the US a handshake is acceptable; in China a simple nod of the head is appropriate; in some Arab countries a woman would not be permitted to speak or establish eye contact with you. What constitutes offensive and decent behavior in social greetings may vary, yet each of these cultures would agree that any act conveying a sensual gesture would be wrong. The point is that simply because some social practices are relative does not mean that all ethical practices of a society are relative.

No amount of social legislation can fully regulate the moral inclination of a people any more than volumes of Internal Revenue Service tax laws can tighten all the loopholes against tax evasion. Man naturally spies out the wiggle room between the permitted and forbidden and is inclined to venture there. The wiggle room however, is still governed by a common sense of what is right and wrong behavior, which extends beyond understood social norms. But from where does this curious idea of moral integrity come?

Morality and Philosophy

One of the corollaries of materialism, and naturalism in general, is a flat denial of *absolute morality* (i.e. the view that moral values are inherently and absolutely fixed in human nature). Advocates of evolution claim that the development of innate tendencies of right and wrong would be necessary to assist man to survive, reproduce (promote his genes) and socially thrive (social order is necessary to prosper). The book *Good Natured*, by primatologist Frans de Waal is one of several books propagating this notion that we learn the secrets of human behavior from observing the survival and social tendencies of our reported ancestors (monkeys). If it is important to learn how human ethics developed through naturalism, why not start at the very beginning – How did a conscious *need to survive* develop from random chemical processes over time? It remains an unexplainable mystery. Unconscious plants survive quite well.

Does the need to survive pose a good standard for morality? Ayn Rand writes, "An organism's life is its *standard of value;* that which furthers its life is the *good;* that which threatens it is the *evil.* "[3] In this ethical system, *survival of life* replaces the theistic view of *sanctity of life*. Survival puts the needs of an individual above the needs of others – it precludes personal sacrifice on the behalf of others. Thus animals, living only to survive would become extinct, if it were not for the instinctive programming and inherent biological control within them (e.g. maternal instinct).

The moral outcome of evolution is some form of *moral relativity*, the position that moral standards are flexible and fluid, depending upon the social dynamic from which they are derived. In this system of thinking, man is taught to be in complete moral control of himself, or as Greek philosopher Protagoras put it, "Man is the measure of all things." Freidrich Nietzsche wrote in *Thus Spoke Zarathustra,* "I am a law only for my kind, I am no law for all." Moral relativity allows man to temporarily affix what is acceptable and unacceptable, and then judge himself for possible infractions as he sees fit. Man becomes his own god – answerable to no one but himself! The obvious problem that arises in a society composed of equally relevant self-proclaimed gods is, who wins when there is a conflict? If everyone holds an equally valid moral position, what framework exists to resolve contrasting moral positions?

One method would be that the majority decision of the people determines what is right and wrong (i.e. the moral norm). Although democracy is perhaps man's best chance to rule himself, there are several problems with democratic form when used to determine moral standards. First of all, historically speaking the majority is often wrong. Did U.S. society in pre-Civil War days establish good ethical conduct concerning slavery? No. Did the South African society of the last century establish good ethics in practicing apartheid? No. Therefore, a majority or judicial consensus in a society does not guarantee that a society is behaving ethically.

U.S. History has witnessed a multitude of *flip-flop* judicial decisions on moral issues, such as the *Dred Scott Decision* handed down by the U.S. Supreme Court in 1857. The court ruled that people of African descent (whether free or slave) could never be U.S. citizens. Several years later this ruling was reversed by the addition of the Thirteenth and Fourteenth Amendments to the U.S. Constitution. During those distressing years as Dred Scott fought for his freedom in the Missouri court system, lower and higher courts' rulings were completely opposite after considering the same evidence. So which judicial system at which time represented the moral good of a society?

A second problem with the concept of moral majority is that the majority often changes its mind. Societies have done relatively quick reversals on ethical issues such as polygamy, slavery, cannibalism, women's rights, racism, human experimentation, feminine circumcision, abortion, war, terrorism, capital punishment, the definition of marriage, the relevance of marriage, and homosexuality. The present rate of ethical change in western cultures is so swift that what is recognized and accepted today as ethical behavior is notably different than what our great grandparents acknowledged as being so. This observation begs the questions, "Which generation was more ethically correct?" "Why the radical shift in ethics?"

Thirdly, compelling personalities can easily sway public opinion to affirm a minority view of what is good ethical behavior. For example, it was Thomas Huxley who propagated and popularized Darwin's theory of naturalism. If the rightness or wrongness of an action depends on a society's norms, it follows that an individual of that society must obey all those norms or be guilty of committing an immoral act. But what if I belong to a society in which an influential individual has convinced the general populace that practices such as abortion, euthanasia, and racism are morally permissible? According to moral relativity, even though I disagree with these practices, I must nonetheless conform to the norm or be considered immoral. How is social reform or betterment of the society (a supposed corollary of naturalism) ever to occur when unpredictable relativity governs the robotic ethical wherewithal of a society? History has shown that most social reforms originated with an individual or a few individuals who were willing to stand up against amoral dominance, yet these individuals would be considered outlaws by the moral majority.

Fourthly, if a society's moral protocol (ethics) were truly relative, it would be quite easy for a dictator to brutally control the morality of a culture. Absolute morality would act as a social defense mechanism to resist a tyrant from leading an entire society into immoral behavior. Yet Hitler, Castro, and Lenin are 20th century examples which prove that, despite absolute morality, it is still possible to shape the thinking of whole societies with only a small contingency of highly-motivated followers in an immoral cause. Under their influence, did the majority of the people in their related societies substantiate the social norm of proper ethics?

Does the slaughter of innocent people for their ethnic ties or their lack of perceived profitability to society seem ethical? Is it morally acceptable to experiment on pregnant women and children like laboratory rats, to sterilize men and women because of imperfections or physical features, or to breed women like cattle to obtain selective genetics for super-class society? Did the German majority, therefore, under Hitler's influence, establish a superb ethical society? If you can answer "absolutely not" to these questions, from what ethical compass are you obtaining your *absolute* moral bearing? If indeed the prevailing social mores establish the ethical norms, wouldn't the Nazi majority be as valid as any other social majority in establishing good morality? If you cannot answer "absolutely not" to the questions concerning Nazi relative morality, what sort of holocaust would you condone for your children and grandchildren to suffer? Dietrich Bonhoeffer, who suffered and died under the Nazi brutality wrote, "The test of the morality of a society is what it does for its children."[4] The holocaust happened before, and it can happen again if moral relativity and not absolute morality guides a society.

If moral reckoning is truly derived from developed self-preservation and self-propagating protocol, as evolution postulates, would not the same core of self-focused needs be naturally relied on to resolve moral conflict with others? Would not selfishness, abuse of power, manipulation, and violence characterize conflict resolution? Furthermore, if survival is the chief incentive for morality, why would anyone want to show compassion to a retarded child, the elderly, the sick, the injured, the orphan, the handicapped, the widow, the poor, the defenseless, etc. *Survival of the fittest* is where moral relativity drives a society, the end result of which is either the Third Reich or social anarchy.

From the atheistic point of view, some actions, such as stealing or rape, may be socially unacceptable, but yet be determined necessary to better promote the survival of the species. So is it morally wrong to steal from another or to rape someone? Given the atheistic worldview, there is nothing intrinsically wrong with these behaviors – each act might be deemed necessary; whereas, absolute morality condemns both behaviors. It is morally wrong to steal or to rape.

Consequently, from a theoretical standpoint, a society adhering to absolute moral reckoning rather than moral relativity would be characterized by less violence. If naturalism were true, more aggression would be expected in a society in which each individual pressed for his or her own personal security and survival over the wellbeing of others. If naturalism were not true, this realization may still be observed, for as a people ignore their moral programming (their consciences), that society will primarily be occupied with pursuing personal gain and selfish indulgences, rather than the good of others. In either case, moral inclinations where self is pre-eminent and the welfare of others is ignored will lead to the demise of a society, not to its beneficial development.

Historically speaking, this very situation occurred in the Jewish culture during the era of the Judges (11th to 15th century B.C.). After the conquest of Canaan, we read of a new generation which no longer knew or obeyed God. *"When all that generation had been gathered to their fathers, another generation arose after them who did not know the Lord nor the work which He had done for Israel. Then the children of Israel did evil in the sight of the Lord ... and they forsook the Lord God..."* (Judg. 2:10-12). What was the problem? The Jews rejected the divine moral commands imposed upon them and instead chose moral relativity as a guide, *"everyone did what was right in his own eyes"* (Judg. 17:6). Consequently, for several hundred years, the Jews were a splintered people, immorality was rampant, and they were regularly abused and conquered by other nations. The Bible warns, *"As righteousness leads to life, so he who pursues evil pursues it to his own death"* (Prov. 11:19). *"Righteousness exalts a nation, but sin is a reproach to any people"* (Prov. 14:34). Moral relativity devolves human society into chaos, while pursuing divine righteousness leads to prosperity – God's blessing.

It is interesting that the term "ethics" is used in philosophy to refer to what is good for an individual and a society as a whole (i.e. what are "good" choices that people should make in relationship to each other). The word "ethics" is derived from the Greek *ethos*, meaning "moral character." The word "morality" is derived from *mores*, which originally meant "social rules or etiquette or inhibitions from the society." In modern times, the meanings of these words are often interchanged, with ethics being the external "science" and morals referring to one's inmost character or behavioral choices.[5] The contrasting contemporary and original meanings of these words indicate that there is both an inner-driven and an outer-driven view of what makes moral choices consistent.

Is man able to agree and develop a scheme of ethics which will guide the good of mankind? Hardly. Presently, some fourteen major ethical doctrines, or competing systems of morality have been developed or identified by philosophers.[6] In the realm of philosophy, no one system has gained universal assent, because there is not universal agreement on what is best for an individual or a society. Even if a humanly developed system of ethics were to be agreed upon, it would not be both consistent and complete to address the various permutations of moral propositions facing man on a day-to-day basis. Such a system would ultimately be contradictory, confusing, or nonspecific enough to render right moral decisions in every case. What then would be the determining factor for executing "good" moral choices for the *gray zone* circumstances? Practically speaking, I don't see how man can socially survive, let alone thrive, in a world of moral relativity.

Morality and Psychology

The materialist's version of consciousness equates the mind and the brain as one, thus all choices are conditioned (B. F. Skinner's view). Therefore, at birth one's brain is a blank slate awaiting all the programming necessary for life. It is a wonder an infant doesn't die of starvation before it learns to suckle. The materialist flatly denies a moral conscience or any other instinctive qualities. However, all thought and behavior is clearly not purely derived from learned qualities within a developing brain for a variety of species are observed to be guided by unlearned instinctive knowledge. What brain process, for example, constrains a hunting dog to point, or ants to raid other ants for slaves, or butterflies to annually migrate thousands of miles to a specific location where they have never been before? Instinct! Guided by instinct, animals make better choices in reacting to various situations and circumstances than would be expected through chance probability.

The tsunami that devastated parts of Indonesia, Thailand, and Sri Lanka in December 2004 provided evidence of a survival instinct within many animals, which man apparently does not have. The tsunami destroyed an animal reserve at Yala, Sri Lanka which contained monkeys, leopards, buffalo, elephants, and 130 species of birds. Though many tourists unfortunately were killed by the tidal wave, virtually no animal carcasses were found after the flooding subsided. Why did the animals largely escape death? There were many reports of animals behaving strangely long before the tsunami struck. Some observations were that elephants screamed and ran to higher ground. A dog refused to go for its beachside walk. Flamingos breeding at Point

Calimere wildlife sanctuary in India abandoned their nests for higher ground before the tidal wave struck. And zoo animals remained in their shelters.[7] What caused these unusual behaviors? The National Science Foundation offers this explanation:

> According to sound expert Elizabeth von Muggenthaler, nature often sends warning signals before it goes on a rampage. To an elephant, for example, the magnitude 9.0 Sumatra earthquake probably made a loud noise, even though it was far away and under water. That, Muggenthaler said, is how animals knew to seek higher ground hours before the tsunami struck. Animals apparently often use signals imperceptible to humans to avoid danger.[8]

It seems likely that animals heard or felt something which caused them to perceive danger, but why run to higher ground? Devastating tsunamis are not frequent occurrences and certainly not to any one area to promote a learned behavior among so many species of animals. The answer seems to be an internally programmed safeguard – instinct!

Darwin devoted a whole chapter in *On the Origin of Species* to this subject and even alluded to the fact that instinct was a perplexing obstacle to his theory:

> Many instincts are so wonderful that their development will probably appear to the reader a difficulty sufficient to overthrow my whole theory.... I may here premise that I have nothing to do with the origin of the mental powers, any more than I have with that of life itself. We are concerned only with the diversities of instinct and of other mental faculties in animals of the same class.[9]

Observations of various animal behaviors indicate a reliance on instinct as well as learned information in rendering a decision. Many animals seem to have inherent programming for their protection in the same way that man has a moral conscience to guide his decision making and advance his survival. Consequently, the natural ability to determine moral judgments is a characteristic that is found only in humans. Even the next highest creature below humanity, according to the evolutionary scale, does not execute moral judgments beyond the basic instincts that the Creator placed there (e.g. a mother caring for her young). Dr. Jerome Kagan concludes, "Not even the cleverest ape could be conditioned to be angry upon seeing one animal steal food from another."[10] In the field of psychology, R. A. Shweder states, "There are no non-human animal models for human pride, shame, and guilt."[11]

Morality and the Bible

Over two hundred years ago, German philosopher Immanuel Kant, who attempted to disprove God's existence through philosophical arguments, concluded, "Two things fill the mind with ever new and increasing wonder and awe—the starry heavens above me and the moral law within me."[12] Why do we feel guilt after engaging in certain behaviors which no written law forbids? We have a moral law implanted within us which forces its way into the reasoning mechanics of the brain.

The Bible says, *The fool has said in his heart, 'There is no God.' They are corrupt; they have done abominable works; there is none who does good"* (Ps. 14:1). Though the atheist may be a socially moral person, one significant motivation for atheism is that man is enabled to do as he pleases when he pleases; if he chooses to pursue a life of sin there is no divine consequence, only the *possibility* of a social one. An individual who denies God's existence, regardless of intellectual rationale, ultimately does so to obtain moral liberation from divine authority.

This may seem like a harsh conclusion, but from God's perspective, outside of being a new creature in Christ, there is nothing, naturally speaking, that man can do to please God (Rom.

174

7:18). Why? Because the value of goodness is not only defined by righteous deeds, but in that God initiated and controlled the activity to ensure that only the purest motives and attitudes were present. No activity is considered a *good work* unless God's character is thoroughly manifested in every aspect of the deed; in other words, man doing good things with wrong motives does not reflect the holy nature of God. This is why the Lord Jesus Christ clarified the meaning of "good" for the benefit of a self-justifying young man, *"No one is good but one, that is, God"* (Matt. 19:17). The Bible concludes that man apart from God cannot *perfectly* do good deeds to please God (Rom. 3:10-12). God declares that the *sum total* of man's self-working is putrid in His sight (Isa. 64:6). So, whether atheist, agnostic, unsubmitted theist, etc., the reality of not being good is fostered in rejection of divine truth. From a natural perspective, all mankind, no matter what the religious bias or social backdrop, suffers the same moral ill; we cannot continue doing good even when we try our best, a fact to which our conscience bears witness.

So why do world cultures, even isolated societies, generally agree that it is morally wrong to kill, to steal, to commit adultery, to lie, to be disrespectful to parents, etc. Why is there a uniform code of ethics that spans the globe and is observed to be independent of time and culture? The answer is that the One who designed us has integrated a moral code of ethics within our being to beckon each person to look inward for evidence of a Creator. The Creator is commanding each of us to behave in a certain way, that is, all of us in one perfect way. Unfortunately, none of us behaves perfectly – that is, as God does. *"For all have sinned and fall short of the glory of God"* (Rom. 3:23). The "glory of God" is a direct reference to the moral law of God within God's character. This moral law instinctively resides in each one of us and is monitored by our conscience. When this ethical programming is violated, we feel guilt and impending judgment – we have acted in a way that is contrary to God's nature – we have sinned against God (Rom.

175

2:14-15). These strong feelings are to prompt man to look beyond himself for answers. Soren Kierkegaard wrote:

> A man could not have anything upon his conscience if God did not exist, for the relationship between the individual and God, the God-relationship, is the conscience, and that is why it is so terrible to have even the least thing upon one's conscience, because one is immediately conscious of the infinite weight of God.[13]

Unfortunately, many have learned to ignore their conscience and the feelings of guilt it produces. At this very moment, there is background noise, no matter how faint, that you have become oblivious to in order to concentrate while reading this book. Perhaps it is a ticking clock, the hum of a ventilation blower, the fan in a computer, the compressor in the refrigerator, street noises or just the wind blowing through the trees. Now that I have made you aware of it, you are again conscious of the noise(s). God's Word sharpens the conscience and ensures that man is more aware of His moral standard of right and wrong – it causes us to think and examine ourselves. If the human conscience is ignored, in time it becomes easier to violate it with diminishing guilt. The personal confession of a pirate called Gibbs, as reported by J. H. Bomberger, well illustrates this point:

> The pirate Gibbs, whose name was for many years a terror to commerce with the West Indies and South America, was at last taken captive, condemned and executed in the city of New York. He acknowledged before his death that when he committed the first murder and plundered the first ship, compunctions were severe; conscience was on the rack and made a hell within his bosom. But after he had sailed for years under the black flag, his conscience became so hardened and blunted that he could rob a vessel and murder all its crew, and then lie down

and sleep as sweetly at night as an infant in its cradle. His remorse diminished as his crimes increased.[14]

It is the conscience deep within our essence that produces feelings of guilt when we transgress the moral law God placed within us. *"Therefore, to him who knows to do good and does not do it, to him it is sin"* (Jas. 4:17). Natural man cannot identify the source of these intense feelings of guilt. What can be done to quiet the deafening apprehension of a wounded conscience? Pondering his loathsome situation, man rationalizes, "If doing something I know to be wrong induces mental anguish, then doing what I know to be right should ease my guilty pangs."

As a result, except for Christianity, the religions of the world are founded on the "need of doing" to obtain a supernatural blessing. Works-based religion is a natural product of a depraved human conscience trying to ease its own grieving. The fact that we feel guilt is evidence to us that we did not continue in well doing; we did not obey what we instinctively knew was appropriate behavior (Rom. 2:15). Thus, we prove to ourselves that we are sinners, that we fall below the perfect standard of righteousness needed to enter heaven (Rom. 3:23).

If we are honest about the matter, each of us has a natural propensity to engage in sinful thoughts and deeds – we gravitate to that which we know is wrong. When we see a posted sign that says "Don't touch – wet paint," our flesh naturally wants to touch what is forbidden. "Is it really wet paint? It doesn't look like wet paint." "Yep, it was wet all right." To become a Christian, one must acknowledge that he or she is dead in his or her trespasses and sins, repent from all he or she thought would earn him or her a right standing before God and receive Jesus Christ as his or her Savior.

Christianity declares that you cannot "do" something to earn your way to heaven – you could never do enough, and what is necessary to gain entrance has already been "done" at Calvary.

The world's religion cries "do," while Christianity declares "done." Consequently, we must realize that every aspect of our being has been affected adversely by sin, and only through Jesus Christ and the power of the Holy Spirit can the matter be resolved. My conscience bears witness to me that I need a Savior!

> Religion is humans trying to work their way to God through good works. Christianity is God coming to men and women through Jesus Christ offering them a relationship with Himself.
>
> — Josh McDowell

In his lecture and subsequent book *Why I Am Not A Christian*, Bertrand Russell argues against absolute morality (that man has a God-given conscience) on the basis that God could not be a good God if He created both right and wrong:

> It [the moral argument for God's existence] has all sorts of forms. One form is to say there would be no right or wrong unless God existed. I am not for the moment concerned with whether there is a difference between right and wrong, or whether there is not: that is another question. The point I am concerned with is that, if you are quite sure there is a difference between right and wrong, then you are in this situation: Is that difference due to God's fiat [decree] or is it not? If it is due to God's fiat, then for God himself there is no difference between right and wrong, and it is no longer a significant statement to say that God is good.[15]

Russell did not recognize that God is inherently good and all God's decrees are good; His character and Word define all that is good. Just as darkness is created by the absence of light; evil is that which is not of God (Isa. 45:5-7). God implanted within man the knowledge of right (that which aligns with His character) and wrong (that which does not align with His character) for a reason – to instinctively guide appropriate free-will conduct. If disobeyed, the human conscience causes feelings of guilt; in a personal and tangible way God's holiness has been affirmed and our depravity proven.

The evidence of the human conscience has convinced many of a divine moral law giver. Francis Collins, author of *The Language of God*, concluded that the moral law and moral conscience within him was overwhelming proof of the existence of God and its logical derivatives pointed only to biblical Christianity as reflecting the true revelation of God. C. S. Lewis came to understand that his arguments against the existence of God were really forged in the moral principles of right and wrong which originated within him:

> My argument against God was that the universe seemed so cruel and unjust. But how had I got this idea of just and unjust? A man does not call a line crooked unless he has some idea of a straight line. What was I comparing this universe with when I called it unjust? If the whole show was bad and senseless from A to Z, so to speak, why did I, who was supposed to be part of the show, find myself in such violent reaction against it? A man feels wet when he falls into water, because man is not a water animal: a fish would not feel wet. Of course, I could have given up my idea of justice by saying that it was nothing but a private idea of my own. But if I did that, then my argument against God collapsed too--for the argument depended on saying that the world was really unjust, not simply that it did not happen to please my private fancies. Thus in the very act of trying to prove that God did not exist-- in other words, that the whole of reality was senseless--I found I was forced to assume that one part of reality--namely my idea of justice--was full of sense. Consequently atheism turns out to be too simple. If the whole universe has no meaning, we should never have found out that it has no meaning: just as, if there were no light in the universe and therefore no creatures with eyes, we should never know it was dark. Dark would be without meaning.[16]

Speaking through the prophet Isaiah, God proclaims of Himself, *"That they may know from the rising of the Sun to its setting that there is none besides Me. I am the Lord, and there is no other; I form the light and create darkness ..."* (Isa. 45:6-7). Light and darkness cannot exist together – darkness is defined by the absence of light. Wickedness is defined by what is not declared holy by God's very character. God did not create sin, but He did bestow upon angels and humans the capacity of choice to willingly reflect His righteous glory or to oppose it. In this design – not of sin, but of opportunity – the concept of love is forged.

Love and obedience are intimately tied together throughout Scripture. John explains the importance of this and also from where sin came:

> *Do not love the world or the things in the world. If anyone loves the world, the love of the Father is not in him. For all that is in the world – the lust of the flesh, the lust of the eyes, and the pride of life – is not of the Father but is of the world* (1 Jn. 2:15-16).

What opposes God did not originate from God; it originated from creatures in the world who have free choice to obey God or not. If a person has no choice but to do right, the will is not exercised, and love cannot be demonstrated. It cost God greatly (the life of His own Son) to give us this capacity to choose between right and wrong – to choose to love Him or not. In this, the importance of known moral law is demonstrated: It is not just having the capacity to choose that demonstrates love, but one must also have the wherewithal to understand what is morally right. If God created us as robots with no power of choice, Russell's argument (quoted above) would have some merit.

Without an absolute reference point, man will wander in the realm of insecurity as to who he is, what he is, and why he exists. The human conscience is God's gift to humanity to provide a moral bearing and a reference point to relate to. "Without God," R. C. Sproul acknowledges, "man has no reference point to define himself. [Modern] philosophy manifests the chaos of man seeking to understand himself as a creature with dignity while having no reference point for that dignity."[17] The moral fabric within the human conscience serves as a personalized testimony of God's holy character. No other earthly creature was bestowed with that privileged revelationship. God personally breathed it into Adam, and it has been passed down from generation to generation.

> History is a voice forever sounding across the centuries the laws of right and wrong. Opinions alter, manners change, creeds rise and fall, but the moral law is written on the tablets of eternity.
> — James A. Forude

Naturalism Poses an Inconsistent Worldview

As materialistic naturalism holds the idea that values do not exist in any ontological sense, any reference to right and wrong ultimately promotes an inconsistent worldview. In short, the *ethic* of materialists is an oxymoron; one cannot shift from empirical statements to moral value judgments without inferring an inconsistent ethical system. Whether based on personal preference, survival impulse, or social coherence such a value system will be variable and thus a pitiful guide for personal morality. The term *variable* implies that no atheist or agnostic can consistently live within his or her worldview; eventually divine morality squeezes into his or her "no God" thinking. Consider Bertrand Russell as an example.

Russell was an outspoken pacifist, but yet publicly promoted the idea of a preemptive nuclear strike on Russia that would murder millions of people. What was his justification for this position? He wrote in the *New York Times* magazine (September, 1953): "Terrible as a new world war would be, I still for my part would prefer it to a world communist empire."[18] Personal interests above the lives of millions – what kind of ethic promotes strong pacifism and also mass murder?

In *Marriage and Morals*, Russell expressed his conviction that sex between an unmarried man and woman is not necessarily immoral if they truly love one another. He advocated "trial marriages" or "companionate marriage," formalized relationships whereby young people could legitimately enjoy sex without being expected to remain married or to have children. He advocated easy divorce, but only if the marriage had produced no children (Russell's view was that parents should remain married but be tolerant of each other's sexual infidelity if they had children).[19] This reflected his life at the time, as his second wife Dora was having an open affair, and would give birth to two children by another man. Yet Russell divorced Dora. What was the result of Russell's confusing sexual morality? Four different wives, children from multiple marriages, several mistresses, and other inappropriate relationships.[20]

Russell publicly admitted that his own morality was logically inconsistent and irreconcilable in content. From one vantage point he surmised, "Life is nothing but a competition to be the criminal rather than the victim." But on another occasion he wrote, "One should as a rule respect public opinion in so far as is necessary to avoid starvation and to keep out of prison."[21] How can one be a criminal and respect public opinion at the same time? No matter how staunch an atheist may be, the absolute morality within will eventually confront and contradict a no-God worldview.

Summary

The human conscience is not God's interference with man's ability to enjoy life on Earth, rather it is a provision to secure a peaceful existence on Earth. Hypothetically speaking, if this moral order were obeyed, no social chaos or personal breakdown would exist; peace would characterize man's existence. But unfortunately, man does not always obey his internal ethical protocol and society after society give testimony that man is incapable of ruling himself rightly. No matter what lofty achievements are obtained through human intellect and effort, these eventually collapse into ruin. Why? Because man eventually disobeys his conscience – he does not have the good character required to maintain the good accomplishment. This observation affirms two facts: First, man does not need new moral teaching, but he needs to be constantly reminded of that which he fails to keep and the past consequences for not doing so; secondly, mankind is not morally improving, or else we would have some lingering testimony of a peaceful ordered society somewhere on the planet.

The human conscience provides as much evidence for God as any microscope or telescope – in the deepest part of being, we know right from wrong and that we are accountable to the One from where that knowledge came. If God does exist and He did desire fellowship with man, would it not be necessary for man to have some internal reckoning of God's moral behavior? Otherwise, God would be constantly offended by man, and fellowship could not be established. If God and absolute moral law did not exist, then any and every human behavior would be permissible; the end result of such moral relativity would be rapid social decline into chaos. If God does exist but man chose to ignore his moral programming, the same result would eventually be realized (Rom. 1:20-32). The reader can decide for himself or herself which reality is readily observed in the world.

Man's tendency is to peer outward to gain knowledge, but the conscience beckons him to look inward for moral reckoning then outward for the answer. The only answer is God's solution to man's sin – the Lord Jesus Christ. Only the applied blood of Jesus Christ can cleanse a sinner's conscience (Heb. 9:11-14).

It has been said that a guilty conscience is "as a snake in the heart" and "more powerful than a thousand witnesses" and that "a good conscience is like a soft pillow." The problem is that no child of Adam can naturally continue in well-doing to maintain a good conscience. Consequently, a guilty conscience is a hell on earth and points to the eternal one beyond.

#7 The Human Spirit's Need

German philosopher Karl Marx, the founder of Communism, pompously declared, "The first requisite for the happiness of the people is the abolition of religion. ... Religion is the sigh of the oppressed creature, the heart of a heartless world, and the soul of soulless conditions. It is the opium of the people."[1] It took less than a century to demonstrate his vain philosophies were in error – Communism has failed the people and is collapsing all over the world. Man has a deep need, a void in himself, which Communism, Socialism, Fascism, Capitalism, or any other contrived human philosophy will never satisfy. God is the only solution. Much of what God reveals to us about our origin, purpose, and essence is contained in the book of Genesis.

> *Then God said, "Let Us make man in Our image, according to Our likeness; let them have dominion over the fish of the sea, over the birds of the air, and over the cattle, over all the earth and over every creeping thing that creeps on the earth." So God created man in His own image; in the image of God He created him; male and female He created them* (Gen 1:26-27).

> *And the Lord God formed man of the dust of the ground, and breathed into his nostrils the breath of life; and man became a living being* (Gen. 2:7).

Man was created in both God's image and likeness. Someone may remark to a new mother concerning her baby boy, "He's the spitting *image* of his father." This comment implies that the baby boy is a visible representation of his father. In the New Testament, the Greek word for "image" is *eikon*, which is derived from the word *eiko,* meaning "to be like or to resemble." In a figurative sense, it means "a representation." Our English word "icon" is derived from *eikon*. Icons have become a common part of computer operating systems. The user is able to click on an icon to initiate or to open a desired program or file. The icon is not the program or file, but is an image that represents the program or file. Paul implies by the use of *eikon* in 1 Corinthians 11:7 that man figuratively "represents" God. Adam was not God, but he was an icon representing Him.

In what form does man possess the image of God? First it is noted that *"God is Spirit"* (John 4:24) and *"the Father of spirits"* (Heb. 12:9). Man is also a spiritual being. *"The Lord ... forms the spirit of man within him"* (Zech. 12:1). The human spirit possesses God consciousness (Prov. 20:27; Job. 32:8). It is thus apparent that the spirituality of man's nature is in the image of God. Man's spiritual nature is seen in other ways:

1. Intuitive knowledge and cognitive abilities (Col. 3:10; Isa. 1:18).
2. Moral consciousness (Rom. 2:15).
3. Initially innocent and upright (Eccl. 7:29).
4. Immortality of soul (Rev. 14:10-11; John 5:24).
5. A will – free moral agent (Matt. 16:25; John 19:11; Rev. 22:17).
6. Capacity to labor apart from struggling for existence (Eph. 4:28).
7. Capacity for marriage vs. the mating of beasts (Gen. 2:22-24).
8. Communication and distinct speech (Gen. 2:23).
9. Communion and worship of God (Gen. 4:4, 22:5).
10. Distinct dignity of presence (Gen. 9:5-6; 1 Cor. 11:7).

Referring back to our baby boy illustration, suppose the wee lad has matured to manhood and has become a workaholic like his father. The same individual, who years earlier said, "The boy is the spitting image of his father;" might now say, "He is just like his father." In other words the boy exhibits the character and behavior of his father – he acts like his father. Besides being created in the *image* of God, man was also created in the *likeness* of God; before he sinned Adam exhibited the moral likeness of his Creator. He was created to be a living representative of God and to declare the moral righteousness of God while ruling over the Earth on God's behalf. Jesus Christ taught that a coin displayed the image of someone in authority to which taxes were rightfully due; in the same way, man bears God's image and is to render himself to God (Matt. 22:17-21).

Adam did not become a living "soul" apart from a physical body or the life-giving breath of God (Gen. 2:7; 1 Cor. 15:45). Body, soul, and spirit are not opposing terms, but rather supplementing dimensions that together describe aspects of the inseparable whole person. Originally, Adam had a soul similar to that of an angel in that he was created innocent, possessed personhood (individuality), and could freely exercise moral choice (Eccl. 7:29; Gen. 3:6). Yet, Adam's outward man more resembled earthly creatures than spiritual heavenly beings. But what differentiated him from all other created things? He alone was created in God's image and, thus, represented God in this New World. His created position was higher than all creatures who call Earth, home, yet lower than those spiritual beings of God's habitation (Heb. 2:7-8). As God's representative, he was to rule over the Earth (Gen. 1:28; 2:19).

Before the Fall

Before the fall of mankind, Adam and Eve enjoyed a life of felicity and harmony with their Creator. Feelings of significance and security permeated every fiber of their being. They felt significant because they were fulfilling God's intended purpose for them: to keep His garden (Gen. 2:15), to exercise authority over the creatures of the Earth, and in God's timing, to procreate. As all their physical, emotional, and spiritual needs were amply provided for, a deep sense of security characterized their existence. Man and his Creator walked hand in hand. Man's spirit completely ruled his mind. The human "will" knew only to do what God had decreed, and his emotions were a replica of his Creator's. His flesh had no control over his mind, other than what was normal in creation order. All was at peace.

After the Fall

God had informed Adam shortly after his creation, *"Of every tree of the garden you may freely eat, but of the tree of the knowledge of good and evil you shall not eat, for in the day that you eat of it you shall surely die"* (Gen. 2:16-17). Life was wonderful until that horrible day that changed the course of humanity forever. Satan externally solicited Adam and Eve to do evil, and they chose to believe the "father of lies" instead of the Father of all. The same satanic deception and desire for knowledge presently blinds many from heeding the truth that would liberate their souls from the bondage of sin.

Our first parents listened to seducing words instead of the quiet voice of their spirits. Paul informs us that Eve was deceived and that Adam knowingly followed the lead of his wife and sinned (1 Tim. 2:13-14). Adam sinned with his "eyes open." God held his representative, Adam, directly accountable for the error (Rom. 5:12). Just as God said, mankind died that day and would continually die. Adam and his wife experienced spiritual death the moment the sin was committed, but they would gradually die physically, their bodies eventually returning to the ground from which man came.

Because of disobedience, Adam and Eve's fellowship with God was severed. They now felt uneasy with God and even tried to hide from His presence. Billows of guilt and waves of shame relentlessly pounded their awakened conscience. The anguish of impending judgment swept over them like a flood. God would judge them and thrust them out of the garden to struggle for survival on what would now be a cursed planet. Instead of significance, they felt rejection. Gone, too, was their security; they were now on their own, having to rely on their own strength and self-control to live. In a brief moment, their secure and significant communion with God was forfeited. Now feelings of rejection, shame, and helplessness overwhelmed them. Suddenly, many new choices became available. The human spirit no longer ruled the mind, which had successfully maintained the emotions and the will of man in check; therefore, the flesh soon bombarded the mind with base lusts and wanton desires. The immensity of that moment for our first parents was staggering. The spirit of man would continue to speak within, but the competition to be heard suddenly became fierce.

Even now, it is our spirit that confesses to our soul that there is a God and life after death. During a nighttime stroll, man will invariably gaze heavenward, and while beholding the starry host upon a canopy of blackness, a voice deep within him whispers, "There is Someone out there – there is a God." The Psalmist writes, *"You will light my lamp; the Lord my God will enlighten my darkness"* (Ps. 18:28). God is seeking the rebel and calling him back to Himself. God's Spirit pleads through our own human spirit to draw near and be restored to our Creator. The Lord Jesus said that it is impossible for man to worship God except through his spirit and in divine truth; this necessitates trusting the truth of Christ's message in order to be spiritually restored to God (John 4:24).

The human spirit's longing for God is so compelling, that at times self-proclaimed atheists and agnostics cannot constrain these innermost feelings from outward expression. Some have personalized the universe, or ascribed feelings to nature, or even deified the cosmos. Carl Sagan always spelled cosmos with a capital "C." The late astronomer wrote of profound loyalty and reverence for the Universe: "The Cosmos is all that is or ever was or ever will be."[2] "Our obligation to survive is owed, not just to ourselves but also to the Cosmos, ancient and vast, from which we spring."[3] Material matter somehow evolved into deity, travailed, and gave birth to humanity? That is how far man's spiritual need for God will push him; if unsatisfied by God's fellowship, man will become an idolater in one form or another.

Our human spirit desperately needs God and communion with Him to be satisfied. Being impoverished of two senses, a blind and deaf Helen Keller acknowledged eloquently what her spirit cried out from within, "I believe in the immortality of the soul because I have within me immortal longings."

It is only through man's spirit that worship can be rendered to God (Phil. 3:3). Consequently, at the spirit level of man resides his most intense need – to be one with his Creator. Many will try to fill this void with religiosity, others with momentary thrills that satisfy base lusts – drugs, amusements, unlawful sex – others with more sophisticated fascinations of the soul – fame, power, intellect, and wealth. What temporal stimulus could ever satisfy man's deepest spiritual need to be one with his Creator? None. My spirit has a deep longing that only God can satisfy.

> So it is that men sigh on, not knowing what the soul wants, but only that it needs something. Our yearnings are homesickness for heaven. Our sighings are sighings for God just as children that cry themselves to sleep away from home and sob in their slumber, not knowing that they sob for their parents. The soul's inarticulate moanings are the affections, yearning for the Infinite, and having no one to tell them what it is that ails them.

> — Henry Ward Beecher

#8 The Inflammatory Name of Jesus

Let us ponder together several social observations. Generally speaking, why are the various biblical names of God often vainly used in public and in private speech to convey disgust and contempt, but not the names of religious founders and their associated god(s)? There are three reasons. First, these expressions only communicate disdain if there is perceived value in the associated name. Man does not blaspheme or become enraged with that which is imaginary or fictitious, but rather with what he knows to exist. It would be ludicrous to bellow out curses in the name of Mickey Mouse, Big Bird or Barney the purple dinosaur. In general, to swear effectively, men make reference to God or the Lord Jesus. Imagine an atheistic evolutionist swearing in the name of a prehistoric amoeba or slimy amino acid – it just doesn't happen.

Secondly, only those who are insecure in what they believe become angry when their "belief system" is attacked. What would you think if, while enjoying a meal together in my home, I volunteered the following to you, "I have a giant pet marshmallow in my basement which I converse with every day"? You would either laugh at my preposterous proclamation or be genuinely concerned about my mental faculties, but you would not be angry with me. I have not challenged your belief system or personally insulted you, yet every conscious fiber of your being believes me to be in error. Someone secure in their faith (belief system) need not be angry with those with differing opinions. So why do many atheists become angry while discussing evidences for God's existence, if there is no God?

The religious leaders, namely the Pharisees, often became enraged at Jesus' teachings and resorted to slander to demonstrate their contempt for His message. They called Him "the son of a fornicator," a "Samaritan," and told Him that He was possessed by a demon. Anger of this type is a practical demonstration of fear and insecurity. The fact that people become infuriated at the name of Jesus Christ proves their own insecurity and that there is some validity to the name which they intrinsically understand, but outwardly reject.

Thirdly, government controlled schools in the United States celebrate Halloween (a pagan holiday), but not so-called Christian holidays. Many of these institutions of learning apply New Age teaching techniques used in Buddhism and Hinduism, but the God of the Jew and the Christian has been willfully shoved out of the classroom. God's Word, the Bible, is shunned in school, but witchcraft practices that exalt Satan are permitted. Conservation is promoted in reverence to *Mother-Earth* and to save the planet, but man's stewardship to a Creator is denied. Cultural and religious diversity are endorsed, but don't dare speak the name of Jesus Christ. If you want to get a rise out of people, just start preaching the gospel message of Jesus Christ on a street corner. Something about *Jesus* and His message invokes strong emotions – "Jesus" is a powerful name.

Franklin Graham tells the story of praying at a memorial service connected with the April 20, 1999 Columbine High School massacre. After the service, he was publicly criticized by print and the broadcast media for praying in Jesus' name.[1] The shunning of the name of Jesus Christ, while other religious figures are freely and favorably batted about, should provide some indication as to what is real. Satan does not care what man believes as long is it is not the truth. Speaking to Jewish religious leaders, the Lord Jesus said *"You are of your father the devil, and the desires of your father you want to do. He was a murderer from the beginning, and does not stand in the truth, because there is no truth in him. When he speaks a lie, he speaks from his own resources, for he is a liar and the father of it"* (John 8:44). If this statement is true, we must expect that Satan will try to deceive mankind into believing anything but the truth, for Satan's grip on a person is loosened when he or she embraces the truth. The Lord Jesus said, *"I am the way, the truth, and the life. No one comes to the Father except through Me"* (John 14:6). The Christian message has no religious diversity, but it has full cultural diversity, *"For God so loved **the world** that He gave His only begotten Son, that **whoever** believes in Him should not perish but have everlasting life"* (John 3:16).

An Historical Figure

It is a common ploy of some atheists not only to deny the central message of the Bible (i.e. Jesus Christ, the Son of God, came to Earth to seek and save the lost), but to further assert that Jesus Christ of Nazareth likely never even existed. Although a slight digression, it is important for the reader to consider the external biblical evidence for the historical figure Jesus Christ, otherwise this chapter will offer no real evidence for supernatural cause within human history (i.e. if Jesus Christ actually never existed).

Writing shortly after the time of Christ's death, Jewish historian Flavius Josephus wrote: "Now, there was about this time Jesus, a wise man, if it be lawful to call him a man, for he was a doer of wonderful works – a teacher of such men as received the truth with pleasure."[2] Conveying the story of the stoning of James the half brother of Christ, Josephus wrote: "So he [Ananus the High Priest] assembled the Sanhedrin of judges, and brought before them the brother of Jesus, who was called Christ, whose name was James...."[3] The reference to James, a leader in the early Church and the half brother of Christ, agrees with

Scriptures' reckoning (Matt. 13:55; Mark 6:3; Acts 15:13; Gal. 1:19). Josephus was referring to a genuine historical Jesus.

Some have asserted that Josephus' statements were "refined" by a Christian editor centuries later. While this is possible, it doesn't undermine that Josephus refers to a historical Jesus. Furthermore, in 1972, a Jewish scholar found a copy of the above passage in an Arabic translation of Josephus's Greek writings. The original translator must have been a Moslem. Since neither medieval Jews nor medieval Moslems would have had any reason to authenticate the historic life of Jesus, the mention of Jesus in Josephus's writings appears authentic.[4]

Reporting on Emperor Nero's decision to blame the Christians for the fire destroying much of Rome in A.D. 64, the Roman historian Tacitus wrote:

> Nero fastened the guilt ... on a class hated for their abominations, called Christians by the populace. Christus, from whom the name had its origin, suffered the extreme penalty during the reign of Tiberius at the hands of ... Pontius Pilatus, and a most mischievous superstition, thus checked for the moment, again broke out not only in Judaea, the first source of the evil, but even in Rome ....[5]

A third important historical source of evidence concerning Jesus Christ and those who believed on Him is found in the letters of Pliny, a Roman governor of Bithynia (then a province of Asia Minor) to Emperor Trajan asking for advice on how to legally prosecute those accused of being Christians. In one letter (about 112 A.D.), Pliny relates to Trajan what he has learned about these Christians (who were quite numerous in Bithynia):

> They were in the habit of meeting on a certain fixed day before it was light, when they sang in alternate verses a hymn to Christ, as to a god, and bound themselves by a solemn oath, not to any wicked deeds, but never to commit any fraud, theft or

adultery, never to falsify their word, nor deny a trust when they should be called upon to deliver it up; after which it was their custom to separate, and then reassemble to partake of food – but food of an ordinary and innocent kind.[6]

Lucian of Samosata was a second century Greek satirist. While his flippant remarks in one of his works were meant to ridicule early Christians, he does supply significant comments about their founder Jesus Christ. He wrote:

The Christians ... worship a man to this day – the distinguished personage who introduced their novel rites, and was crucified on that account. ... [It] was impressed on them by their original lawgiver that they are all brothers, from the moment that they are converted, and deny the gods of Greece, and worship the crucified sage, and live after his laws.[7]

Suetonius mentions Christ in his biography of the Roman Emperor Claudius and repeatedly observes, in his biographies of Caligula and Vespasian, that the Romans knew about Christ's prophecy of a King rising in the East who would rule the entire world. The Lord Jesus is even mentioned, albeit obliquely, in the Jewish Talmud.[8]

Besides Josephus, Tacitus, Pliny, Lucian, Suetonius, and the Talmud, other non-biblical first century writers have documented the unique life of the Lord Jesus Christ. Men such as Clement of Rome (a leader in the Church at Rome and likely a companion of Paul), Hermas (likely referred to by Paul in Romans 16:14), Ignatius (a personal disciple of one or more of the original apostles), Papias (a disciple of John the apostle), and Polycarp (a disciple of John the apostle). All these men had access to information pertaining to Jesus Christ from direct eye-witness accounts.

Besides these, there are ample second century writings still in existence which collaborate the biblical accounts of the life of

Christ. These accounts are from writers such as: Apollonarius, Aristides, Athenagoras, Celsus, Clement of Alexandria, Dionysius of Corinth, Hegesippus, Hippolytus, Irenaeus, Julius Africanus, Justin Martyr, Marcion, Melito, Montanus, Polycrates, Tatian, Tertulian, and Theophilus. Both the historical and the biblical evidence is overwhelming to substantiate the unique teachings, miracles, and character of Jesus Christ. He really died after being nailed to a Roman cross and arose from the grave three days later just as He said He would. Clement of Rome wrote just a few years after Christ's resurrection, "God has made the Lord Jesus Christ the first-fruits by raising Him from the dead."[9] His contemporary Ignatius recorded this statement: "For I know that after His resurrection also, He was still possessed of flesh. And I believe that He is so now."[10]

The World's View of Jesus Christ

With both the biblical and non-biblical historical evidence for the existence of Jesus Christ before us we now return to the discussion of the world's natural disdain for Him. What is meant when someone refers to the "world?" The world has different forms: political, artistic, musical, religious, entertainment, business, etc. Biblically speaking the "world" may speak of the world we live in (the physical planet), the world of things, the world of people, or the world system controlled by Satan. In the latter instance, the world represents a human society built up apart from God; it is human civilization with base motives and desires, the outworking of mankind's depraved state. For this reason, you may hear Christians say, "We are in the world, but not of the world." A true Christian's allegiance is to the Lord Jesus, and his or her citizenship is in heaven (Phil. 3:20).

Worldliness, then, is any sphere in which the Lord Jesus is excluded. The Lord Jesus told His disciples the night before He was crucified, *"If the world hates you, you know that it hated Me before it hated you. If you were of the world, the world would love its own. Yet because you are not of the world, but I chose you out of the world, therefore the world hates you"* (John 15:18-19). James likens worldliness to the sin of spiritual adultery. *"Adulterers and adulteresses! Do you not know that friendship with the world is enmity with God? Whoever therefore wants to be a friend of the world makes himself an enemy of God"* (Jas. 4:4). Worldliness is the love of passing things – things have no eternal value, except in how they are used to please God. Worldliness opposes God, and God hates it.

Ponder for a moment how the world's standard of success is in direct opposition to what the Lord Jesus taught:

The world wants service, but Christ says humble yourselves and serve others.

The world says save your life, but the Lord says lose your life to gain one worth living.

The world exclaims "live for the moment," but Christians are to live for eternity.

The world says live for self, but the Lord says die to self.

The world is into power, but the Lord uses weak things to confound the mighty.

The world permits greed to rule distribution, but Christians are to give according to need.

The world says acquire wealth, but God says don't seek to be rich.

The world uses money and power to rule, but Christians are to pray and use Scripture in love.

The world says retaliate and get even, but the Lord says repay evil with good and be forgiving.

The world uses violence, but Christians are to turn the other cheek.

So why is it that the world generally ignores religion, but stands in opposition to Jesus Christ and His message? Why is it that He is excluded from conversations, education, professional realms, etc., while it is permissible to speak about any of the world's religions? Because Satan is behind the scene controlling the various systems of the world, and he despises Christ and those who take His name. Paul properly identifies Satan as *"the god of this age"* (2 Cor. 4:4) and *"the prince of the power of the air"* (Eph. 2:2). The Lord Jesus says on three different occasions that Satan is *"the prince of this world."* The world is Satan's delegated domain, but he must function within the boundaries which God allows. God is holy, and He cannot tempt anyone to sin (Jas. 1:13), but Satan is allowed to test man's resolve to faithfully trust God.

Satan has been effective in deceiving humans into self-elevating religions and self-seeking practices. Through spiritual blindness (2 Cor. 4:3-4), Satan is able to convince man that his deep spiritual void can be satisfied with religious facades. These serve to effectively lock the participant into a fear-based, work-based belief system, which can only serve to stimulate man's flesh to further sin against God, be high on self, and vent rage towards God. Without Christ, man has absolutely no hope of salvation and no hope of pleasing God.

Speaking of Christ, Peter proclaimed to the Sanhedrin (the Jewish judicial body): *"Nor is there salvation in any other, for there is no other name under heaven given among men by which we must be saved"* (Acts 4:12). They didn't like the Christian message and prohibited the apostles from speaking or teaching in the name of Jesus Christ (Acts. 4:18). Because the message of Christ confronts the sinner to look honestly at his or her condition and to take sides with God against himself or herself, the name of Jesus Christ will always be inflammatory for those rejecting His message. The power of Jesus' name to invoke both radical hatred within the rejecter (Luke 10:22) and immense love in the heart of a believer (1 Jn. 4:15-21) is suggestive of an influence beyond the natural realm.

#9 Miracles

When someone blurts out, "That's a miracle!" what do they really mean? In the casual sense, such an announcement might refer to an event which excites wonder, such as the birth of a baby, or to some unexpected outcome such as cashing in on a long-shot stock investment or surviving a natural disaster. A storyteller might apply the term to better exaggerate the abilities of a fictional hero in his tale. In the formal sense, a miracle refers to supernatural intervention that defies natural law to accomplish divine purpose in time.

Unusual incidents are witnessed regularly in the world, much of which is not supernaturally caused, otherwise natural law would be difficult for man to determine and depend on. Without a thorough understanding of natural law, a miracle could not be identified; therefore it stands to reason that miracles are not commonplace. Uncommon phenomenon might then be caused by supernatural influence, unknown natural law at work, or just improbable situations adhering to natural order.

If naturalism were true, then certainly all miracles must be denied; how can something intrude upon natural law when there is nothing which exists outside of nature? If supernaturalism were true, then we may expect there to be irregularities within natural order which express both blessing and revelation to man from beyond his physical realm. If miracles can be shown to have occurred, then such events must be considered as direct supernatural influences within natural order.

Biblical Terminology

In reference to supernatural cause within man's realm of existence, the Bible applies three main terms which are intricately related: signs, wonders, and miracles. W. E. Vine suggests the following meanings for each of these terms:

> A Sign: "Signs" confirmatory of what God had accomplished in the atoning sacrifice of Christ, His resurrection and ascension, and of the sending of the Holy Spirit, were given to the Jews for their recognition, as at Pentecost, and supernatural acts by apostolic ministry....

> A Wonder: "something strange," causing the beholder to marvel, is always used in the plural .... A sign is intended to appeal to the understanding, a "wonder" appeals to the imagination, a power (*dunamis*) indicates its source as supernatural. "Wonders" are manifested as divine operations in thirteen occurrences (9 times in Acts); three times they are ascribed to the work of Satan through human agents, Matt. 24:24; Mark 13:22; and 2 Thess. 2:9.

> A Miracle: "power, inherent ability," is used of works of a supernatural origin and character, such as could not be produced by natural agents and means.[1]

A *wonder* is an event which simply confounds the imagination, but a *sign* has the purpose of causing man to deeply ponder the message being validated by the extraordinary event. Miracles generally speak of God's supernatural operations within nature and may be classified in two categories, *providential* and *super-providential* events. God's sovereign plan for man will be accomplished either *through* natural law or supernaturally working *within* or *above* natural law. *Providential* events are often unnoticed by man, but at other times are more evident because of the improbable likelihood of certain situations

200

occurring naturally. For these events a feasible explanation is possible, though unlikely.

God's sovereign purposes and providential care ensure His intimate and intricate involvement in the daily affairs of humanity (Ps. 113:5-9); He maintains all the various aspects of our lives accordingly. We read in Matthew 18:10 that children have guardian angels; Peter instructs Christians to cast all their cares upon God because He cares for them (1 Pet. 5:7); James confirms, *"The effective, fervent prayer of a righteous man avails much"* (Jas. 5:16). Unfortunately much of God's supervision goes undetected or is labeled as "coincidence." For example, was it a providential miracle for George Washington's army to cross the Delaware River at night in a snowstorm to surprise the British? What of the incredible escape of trapped British soldiers at Dunkirk during unusual weather conditions? Some think these were providential miracles, but there is no way to prove this assertion, because bad weather often hampers war.

The second group of miracles, *super-providential*, would consist of irregularities so extraordinary that there is no possible natural explanation. All *true* miracles, *providential* and *super-providential* are supernatural in origin, but the latter are spectacular events which obviously do not adhere to known natural order. Numerous *super-providential* miracles are recorded in the Bible: the Lord Jesus feeding thousands of people by multiplying a boy's sack-lunch, calming the wind and the sea during a raging storm, and raising the dead back to life, etc. Science would readily explain *providential*-type miracles as either a hoax, a situation which validates newly exposed or yet-to-be-discovered natural order, or a series of understandable circumstances which are unusual and perhaps even improbable.

For the *super-providential* category, science would not offer a conclusive explanation because the event completely baffles science. As science focuses on empirical evidence to derive natural order, technically speaking, a *super-providential* miracle could never be validated as supernatural in origin. Why? Because it is impossible for man to acquire complete knowledge of all natural order, even over the vast expanse of time. Accordingly, science may **identify** *super-providential* miracles, but not **validate** them. Reasons for scientific rejection of such events would then include: fictitious hearsay, sensationalized folk tales, hallucinations, misunderstood natural order or an instance of a yet-to-be-discovered natural law. It seems almost humorous that we have science to thank for identifying miracles, yet it requires some measure of faith to actually validate that a miracle occurred. Perhaps that is the very test God intended!

Philosophy and Miracles

Thomas Aquinas (*Summa Contra Gentiles*, III) states that, "those things are properly called miracles which are done by divine agency beyond the order commonly observed in nature."[2] Dr. Eric Mascall declares that the word miracle "signifies in Christian theology a striking interposition of divine power by which the operations of the ordinary course of nature are overruled, suspended, or modified."[3]

Aristotle rejected the idea that God would or could personally intervene in the natural order of the world. But, as mentioned earlier, philosopher and theologian Thomas Aquinas used Aristotelian logic to write *Summa Theologica*, a work which reconciles faith with reason, proving the existence of God as the logical "uncaused cause."[4]

Some have argued that, if God intruded into the natural order He established, He would not be a perfect God: "What kind of a righteous god violates his own laws?" Let us remember that God is immutable and eternal; He existed prior to creation, and He is not bound by the natural order He created, including time. He is independent of natural order – natural order depends on Him (Col. 1:16). Therefore, any divine acts within natural order are immediately absorbed into nature's framework by adapting all interrelated events and mechanisms to the caused irregularity in the same way that random and extremely rare events are compensated for.

Man was created in God's image – and, therefore, possesses moral agency and freewill bestowed by God. Man was not created to robotically articulate superficial gestures of praise to God; on the contrary, God bestowed on man a genuine opportunity to express love back to Him, after first receiving it from Him (1 Jn. 4:19). So, if the universe is God's cosmic stage to affect His merciful plan of reconciliation, would not God have the right to effect sovereign acts to accomplish that predetermined reality? Furthermore, would we think any less of God if He extended greater blessing to man and revelation of Himself in the process of executing such acts?

Could not the director of a play change the script during a final rehearsal to ensure the end result was an unsurpassed theatrical production? Some would argue, however, that a sovereign God would get it right from the start. This point of view is time-limited and self-focused. We would expect a truly sovereign and gracious God to control the numerous permutations of the events of our lives in accordance with His foreknowledge, in such a way as to accomplish the greatest good for humanity (Rom. 8:28). In our play example, might the director have purposed the alteration in the script from the beginning but, in order to draw out a frustrated disposition in the actors' final performance, wait to the last-minute to announce the change? Yes. Might he invoke the predetermined change to provide a wider field of training for developing actors? Certainly. Perhaps the preplanned change by the director was to convey a "wing it" opportunity to a particular actor or to reveal more about his style of directing to the cast. Therefore, to state that God cannot intrude within or contradict natural order is to say, "I don't want an omnipotent and omniscient God using His full capabilities to interfere in my life and I don't need His blessings either." This type of attitude conveys rank humanism.

The *locus classicus* for the modern philosophical discussion of miracles is Chapter X (entitled "Of Miracles") of David Hume's *Enquiries Concerning Human Understanding*, first published in 1748. Hume argued that it is *always* more likely that a particular claim of a miracle is false than it is that the miracle actually occurred. He believed that it was more warranted given "firm and unalterable" laws of nature to believe that those who had witnessed a miracle were in error (lying or in ignorance) rather than telling the truth. This is close-minded methodological naturalism at its worst. Since generally natural laws are mysterious before they are characterized as such, does it mean that the scientist is not telling the truth when describing an irregularity to others he or she has observed? Because it is unusual does not make it untrue!

Hume was a chief proponent of the "regularity theory of causation."[5] He proclaims, "A miracle may accurately be defined, *a transgression of a law of nature* by a particular volition of the deity, or by the interposition of some invisible agent."[6] His premise that a miracle is "a violation of the laws of nature" seems to be his central argument against defensible belief in miracles. "A miracle is a violation of the laws of nature; and as a firm and unalterable experience has established these laws, the proof against a miracle, from the very nature of the fact, is as entire as any argument from experience can possibly be imagined."[7] Michael Levine (contributor to the *Stanford Encyclopedia of Philosophy*) explains Hume's philosophical view and also the flaws in his logic:

> A law of nature cannot be violated by natural forces. It can only be undermined as a genuine law. This happens if something natural occurs that the law was supposed to account for but in fact could not. But neither can a law of nature be violated by a

nonnatural force. Nor can it be undermined, assuming we can distinguish natural from nonnatural occurrences. A law of nature is, whatever else it may be, a true description of both the physically and logically possible occurrences within its scope, in the actual world *only* if it is assumed that no nonnatural forces could exist or interfere. Otherwise, a law describes only what can happen as a matter of physical possibility. Its presupposed scope is limited to what can happen given only natural forces. It allows for the possibility that the physically impossible remains logically possible, assuming the possibility of nonnatural forces capable of interaction in the actual world. Thus, nonnatural interventions are not, strictly speaking, violations of laws of nature....

A statement that a miracle occurred, usually – as in the case of many of the biblical miracles – refers to God as causing something that is not the sort of occurrence that one would expect to be explainable in terms of laws of nature, if it could be explained at all. I am here supposing supernatural explanation to be a viable alternative and the one that might plausibly be chosen in a case like the Red Sea parting.... Miracles are contrary to laws of nature, *not* "violations" of them and *not* instances of them. Note that it is not simply a miracle's *uniqueness* that rules out such reference to laws of nature. It cannot be uniqueness since even miracles that are supposed to be repeatable, such as raising one from the dead, cannot in principle refer to laws of nature for a complete explanation of their occurrence. Presumably they must also refer to divine intervention.[8]

Bible commentator A. R. Fausett also takes issue with Hume's definition of a miracle being a violation of natural law, then acknowledges that God's sovereign purpose for man necessitates direct intervention in human affairs:

A miracle is not a "violation of the laws of nature" (Hume), but the introduction of a new agent. Such introduction accords with human experience, for we see an intelligent agent often modifying the otherwise uniform laws of nature. "Experience" informs us of human free will counteracting the lower law of gravitation. Infinitely more can the divine will introduce a new element, counteracting, without destroying, lower physical law; the higher law for a time controls and suspends the action of the lower. Or, "law" being simply the expression of God's will, in miracles God's will intervenes, for certain moral ends, to suspend His ordinary mode of working.[9]

What is the value of God's handiwork accomplished through miracles? Besides counteracting the free agent of sin that is opposing God's activities in the world (1 Jn. 2:16), miracles are an issuance of providential care and supernatural blessing to man. In this sense, God is providing a unique testimony of Himself to mankind through the miracles He invokes. By countering natural laws, He is providing revelation of Himself. A. R. Fausett further explains this truth:

Hume alleged against miracles their contrariety to "experience," and that experience shows testimony to be often false. But "experience" is not to be limited to our time and knowledge. The "experience" of the witnesses for Christianity attests the truth of miracles. However improbable miracles are under ordinary circumstances, they are probable, nay necessary, to attest a religious revelation and a divine commission. "In whatever degree it is probable that a revelation should be communicated to mankind at all, in the same degree is it probable that miracles should be wrought" (Paley, *Evidences of Christianity*). That they are out of the ordinary course of nature, so far from being an objection, is just what they need to be in order to be fit signs to attest a revelation. It is as easy to God to continue the ordinary course of the rest of nature, with the change of one part, as of all the phenomena without any change. It is objected, miracles "interrupt the course of nature." But as that course really comprises the whole series of God's government of the

206

universe, moral as well as physical, miracles are doubtless included in it. The testimony to Christian miracles is that of concurrent and contemporaneous witnesses.[10]

It is inconceivable that we would experience the inconceivable and not ever venture an assumption as to why it happened. Naturally speaking, there is no way that science can prove that miracles do not occur, nor that nature, as Hume suggests, *always* behaves uniformly. Certainly, nature must normally behave uniformly or man would find it difficult to anticipate anything as based on experience or reason. But on such rare occurrences where an observed anomaly simply baffles natural law and all human reason, would it not be permissible to ponder the possibility that God is personally demonstrating His presence and accomplishing sovereign purpose? Miracles demonstrate God's personal attention to the particulars of our lives – He desires us to be aware of His interest and concern for us.

> A thing is not necessarily against reason because it happens to be above it.
>
> — Charles Caleb Colton

Religion and Miracles

If legitimate miracles do occur can Christianity claim a monopolizing ownership of their use? In response to this subject matter C. S. Lewis writes:

> I do not think that it is the duty of the Christian apologist (as skeptics suppose) to disprove all stories of the miraculous which fall outside the Christian records.... I am in no way committed to the assertion that God has never worked miracles through and for pagans or never permitted created supernatural beings to do so....[11]

In other words, God is God; He may, to demonstrate His compassion and mercy, work a miracle to heal an individual or deliver someone from a tragic circumstance. The focus of the miracle may be to provide a singular blessing to an individual and/or to accomplish a wider development in His overall plan for mankind. For God to show kindness to an individual in a pagan religion does not mean God is endorsing that religion. In the case of John Newton, a vile slave trader, God preserved his life during an extended raging storm at sea. Newton's experience as a sea captain confirmed in his mind that everyone on board should have perished. Based on previous experience, Newton concluded supernatural intervention had saved his life, and the lives of nearly all his crew. Consequently, Newton turned from his wicked ways to embrace Christ as Savior and became a notable preacher, abolitionist, and hymn writer.

Lewis went on to explain, "But I claim that Christian miracles have a much greater intrinsic probability in virtue of their organic connection with one another and with the whole structure of religion they exhibit."[12] Dr. Art Lindsley of the C. S. Lewis Institute summarizes Lewis' statement:

For instance, in Hinduism, the principle of non-distinction (All is One) rules out any validity to the distinction between natural and supernatural. Since all is "maya" or illusion, how can it be important to demonstrate power over the illusion? Granted, there have been claims of gurus levitating or healings in New Age circles, but within the system of thought how important are these "illusory" acts?

There are stories in late Buddhism about the Buddha doing miracles. But since he held that nature is illusory, why would he be concerned with miraculous demonstrations on the level of nature? ...

In the Koran, Mohammed does not do any miracles … whereas, Jesus is reported there to have done 16 miracles. Only in later Islamic tradition are there reports of miracles done by Mohammed.

As Lewis says, miracles in the New Testament are greater in their "intrinsic probability" because of the credibility of the historic claims and their "organic connection" – they fit together and converge on Christ. Jesus' miracles are not just powerful acts but also demonstrate who He is. So the healing of the man who was born blind (John 10) leads to the revelation that He is the light of the world. The resurrection of Lazarus from the dead (John 11) leads to the proclamation that He is the resurrection and the life, and so on. Miracles are often not only indicative of God's power but have symbolic significance as well.[13]

So, instances of actual divine intervention will undoubtedly occur in a variety of ways and within any religious framework that man might devise for the purposed of awakening individuals to some spiritual understanding, or simply to further accomplish God's sovereign plan for humanity. While miracles recorded in the Old Testament often are associated with validating God's prophets or affirming His glory to the nation of Israel, in the New Testament most miracles have a specific purpose – the validation of Jesus Christ as Messiah. In comparison to world religious systems, Christianity is quite unique both in the number of recorded miracles in Scripture and in their intended purpose of certifying the credentials of God's divine messenger, in this case Jesus Christ. Peter's very first sermon to the Jews focuses on this point:

Men of Israel, hear these words: Jesus of Nazareth, **a Man attested by God to you by miracles, wonders, and signs which God did through Him in your midst,** *as you yourselves also know – Him, being delivered by the determined purpose and foreknowledge of God, you have taken by lawless hands, have* *crucified, and put to death; whom God raised up, having loosed the pains of death, because it was not possible that He should be held by it* (Acts 2:22-24).

Christ's Miracles in Review

Nearly all the miracles that the Lord Jesus performed while on Earth were of the super-providential variety, preventing the skeptic from asserting a natural cause for the miracle. The Jewish religious leaders understood this fact, and elected rather to attribute the miracle to Satan than natural cause; thus, they affirmed that the miracle was supernatural in origin. A detailed biblical overview of all Christ's miracles is contained in Appendix V.

Providential miracles performed by Christ would include His instructions to Peter concerning casting a fishing line into the sea to catch a single fish (the first fish caught). The Lord told Peter that the fish would have a piece of money in its mouth and that he was to use that money to pay their taxes (Matt. 17:27). Another such situational miracle would be the bizarre way that the Lord directed His disciples to the unknown location He had chosen to keep the Passover (Luke 22:8-13). The Lord Jesus knows the future better than we understand the events reported in yesterday's newspaper. Foretelling a series of statistically improbable events is miraculous, but not beyond the realm of natural explanation. It is extremely unlikely that such events could happen by chance, but it is plausible.

To prove His credentials as Messiah and Savior, the incarnate Son of God worked many super-providential miracles – each one a sign to the Jews and a warning if rejected. Jesus Christ changed, controlled and multiplied the elements, healed the sick, rebuked evil spirits, raised the dead, and affected His own death and resurrection. The Jews were never satisfied with Christ's miracles; they continued to request Him to provide more signs. The Lord told them that it was a wicked and adulterous generation who wanted to base their faith on signs alone. The ultimate sign, which would really determine if they would believe on Christ as Messiah, would be acknowledging the Lord's resurrection from the dead, which He refers to as the sign of Jonah (Matt. 12:38-40). No resurrection – no Messiah.

Jesus Christ truly was who He proclaimed to be and His miracles provided evidence to this truth. To say that miracles are not supernatural evidence of God's handiwork beyond the normal of nature is to call Jesus Christ a liar! There is no logical middle ground on this matter; as Thomas Aquinas surmised centuries ago, "Christ was either liar, lunatic, or Lord!"[14] So which is it? Remember you have to live with your conscience. If He is not Lord of all, He is not Lord at all.

Christianity and Miracles

As previously stated, the primary purpose of the recorded miracles in the New Testament was to prove to the Jews that Jesus Christ was their Messiah. The fact that Christ's disciples continued to work similar miracles in His name proved that Jesus Christ had risen from the dead and that the disciples were operating under His authority and power. A secondary emphasis of miracles is for the building up of a believer's faith, after he or she has trusted Christ by personally witnessing God's intervention in difficult circumstances in which nature offers no hope. Prayer aligns the mind of believers with the mind of Christ (1 Jn. 5:14; John 14:13-15) in such a way that God is honored by co-laboring with Christians and working the impossible for His glory. It is not that God is forced to do something by prayer, but rather that believers are forcing themselves to yield to His will. A Christian's prayers and God's foreknowledge cooperate to accomplish what had previously been determined before anything was created. God's foreknowledge is ultimately reality in time; the Christian's prayers in time had eternal consequence prior to time.

Seven times in the Gospel of John, the Lord Jesus instructs His disciples to ask of the Father in His name and it will be done. The disciples were instructed to pray and that God would do something in response to those prayers. It is not that God is doing something that He did not already plan to do, but rather that He desires to be asked and He desires that intercession be made on behalf of others; it is profitable for us to engage in these activities. Abraham pleaded that God would spare wicked Sodom (Gen. 18:23-33), Moses made intercession to preserve Israel from God's wrath (Ex. 32:11-14), and Christ asked His Father to forgive those (i.e. not to judge their offense then) who had nailed Him to the cross (Luke 23:34). It softens the believer's heart to pray for those who have done him or her wrong or for those who desperately need divine intervention in their lives. God longs to hear intercessory prayer – it is like sweet incense ascending up to the throne of God (Rev. 5:8, 8:3).

After Peter was arrested again and sentenced to death, the Christians gathered to pray about the situation and God sent an angel to rescue Peter from prison (Acts 12). Did God hear their prayers? Certainly. Was God done with Peter? No. The result was God's will was done that day and man's prayers were answered. If you are a Christian, keep on praying (Jas. 4:3).

The Rebirth of Israel

The preservation of the Jewish people and the rebirth of the state of Israel is one of the greatest foretold miracles of the Bible. Normally, when a particular people are held captive in a foreign land the social mingling causes them to blend into the new culture. In time, the original identity of the estranged people is usually lost. Not so with the Jews. They were a scattered people without a homeland for 2600 years; but incredibly they maintained their distinction among the nations. God promised that He

212

would gather the Jews back to their own land, and that they would be one nation called "Israel," not two separated kingdoms, Judah and Israel, as previously arranged (Ezek. 37:15-22).

Isaiah states that the rebirth of Israel would come unexpectedly and be fulfilled suddenly – *"Shall a nation be born at once?"* (Isa. 66:8). This prophecy was fulfilled in May 1948. Greatly out-numbered and out-gunned, these outcast people became a self-governing nation again, in the very land God gave them thousands of years ago (Gen. 15:18, 26:3), and under the prophesied name of "Israel." It is noted, that by the end of the Tribulation Period all Jews will be regathered back to Israel (Ezek. 39:28-29).

The Reality of Miracles

It is emphasized that many, if not most of the circumstances posed today as miracles are not really miracles at all. If an unusual event occurs without supernatural cause it is not a miracle. Consequently, those thrilling fancies of our imagination, synthesized events for personal gain, or just misunderstood natural order in bizarre action are not miracles.

In the centuries after Christ's sojourn on Earth, a vast number of His followers were tortured and martyred for their faith; this reality continues to this day. The centuries of brutal inquisitions alone resulted in the deaths of millions of innocent people;[15] most were Christians who determined it better to honor Christ in death than to be a part of religious apostasy. A repeatedly witnessed miracle was that some of those who were burned at the stake were given martyr's grace to endure the judgment without the agony of pain. Martyrdom itself is not the miracle (people down through the centuries have died for what they believed in, whether the matter was valid or not), but to die in such a way that natural laws are suspended is a miracle. I have chosen three such stories to document this point. Each is recorded in

213

Foxe's Book of Martyrs. The first account takes place in the Roman Empire early in second century A.D.:

> Polycarp, the venerable bishop of Smyrna, hearing that persons were seeking for him, escaped, but was discovered by a child. … He was, however, carried before the proconsul, condemned, and burnt in the market place. The proconsul then urged him, saying, "Swear, and I will release thee; – reproach Christ." Polycarp answered, "Eighty and six years have I served him, and he never once wronged me; how then shall I blaspheme my King, Who hath saved me?" At the stake to which he was only tied, but not nailed as usual, as he assured them he should stand immovable, the flames, on their kindling the fagots, encircled his body, like an arch, without touching him; and the executioner, on seeing this, was ordered to pierce him with a sword, when so great a quantity of blood flowed out as extinguished the fire. But his body, at the instigation of the enemies of the Gospel, especially Jews, was ordered to be consumed in the pile, and the request of his friends, who wished to give it Christian burial, rejected. They nevertheless collected his bones and as much of his remains as possible, and caused them to be decently interred.[16]

The second account occurred in December of 1560 when the inquisition found an innocent English merchant man named Nicholas Burton guilty and sentenced him to death for adhering to biblical truth concerning salvation, thus, sequestering his wealth for the Roman Catholic Church.

> Afterward, the twentieth of December, they brought the said Nicholas Burton, with a great number of other prisoners, for professing the true Christian religion, into the city of Seville, to a place where the said inquisitors sat in judgment…. His [Burton's] tongue was forced out of his mouth with a cloven stick fastened upon it, that he should not utter his conscience and faith to the people, and so he was set with another Englishman of Southampton, and divers other condemned men for religion,

as well Frenchmen as Spaniards, upon a scaffold over against the said Inquisition, where their sentences and judgments were read and pronounced against them.

And immediately after the said sentences given, they were carried from there to the place of execution without the city, where they most cruelly burned them, for whose constant faith, God is praised. This Nicholas Burton by the way, and in the flames of fire, had so cheerful a countenance, embracing death with all patience and gladness, that the tormentors and enemies which stood by, said, that the devil had his soul before he came to the fire; and therefore they said his senses of feeling were past him. [17]

The third account took place in England during the early 16th century (just prior to the reign of Queen Mary I). James Baynhan was put to death for trusting Jesus Christ alone for salvation.

The next person that suffered in this reign was James Baynham, a reputable citizen in London, who had married the widow of a gentleman in the Temple. When chained to the stake he embraced the fagots, and said, "Oh, ye papists, behold! ye look for miracles; here now may you see a miracle; for in this fire I feel no more pain than if I were in bed; for it is as sweet to me as a bed of roses." Thus he resigned his soul into the hands of his Redeemer. [18]

There have been a good number of books written to compile instances of God's faithful care of His people. These provide thousands of testimonials of God's miraculous interventions in human affairs. If you have an interest, may I suggest reading *The Wonders of God* or *Our God is Wonderful* by William Mac-Donald, or *Our God is Faithful* by J. B. Nicholson, or a biography of men and women of faith, such as George Mueller, Hudson Taylor, David Livingstone, Fanny Crosby, Corrie ten Boom, William Carey, Anthony Norris Groves, Adoniram Judson,

Gladys Aylward, etc. Such biographies are real stories of real people in connection with a real God. It is an arduous task to narrow the field of these miraculous accounts of God's grace, but perhaps the reader will appreciate the following three missionary testimonies.

George Mueller of Bristol (1805-1898) was widely known as a "man of faith." In the course of his life, he received more than 1,000,000 pounds in gifts for the care of over 100,000 orphans without ever advertising his needs, soliciting donations, or going into debt. Mueller prayed over specific needs and trusted God to supply every penny. By 1870, he had in his daily charge over 2,000 children housed in five orphanages.[19] His detailed diary records the exact needs for the day, his specific prayer for those needs to be supplied and the resultant answers to those prayers. In his latter years, Mueller engaged in an extensive preaching ministry which required him to travel over 200,000 miles, an incredible achievement for pre-aviation times. The following story occurred on such a trip. It is not told by Mueller himself, but by an unbelieving sea captain whose ship had been fogged in for days while crossing the North Atlantic.

"We had George Mueller of Bristol on board," said the captain. "I had been on the bridge for twenty-four hours and never left it and George Mueller came to me and said, "Captain, I have come to tell you I must be in Quebec on Saturday afternoon." "It is impossible," I said. "Then very well, if your ship cannot take me, God will find some other way. I have never broken an engagement in fifty-seven years; let us go down into the chart room and pray."

"I looked at that man of God and thought to myself, "What lunatic asylum can that man have come from, for I never heard of such a thing as this?" "Mr. Mueller," I said, "do you know how dense this fog is?" "No," he replied, "my eye is not on the density of the fog, but on the living God who controls every circumstance of my life." He knelt down and he prayed one of the most simple prayers. When he had finished I was going to pray, but he put his hand on my shoulder and told me not to pray. "As you do not believe He will answer, and as I believe He has, there is no need whatever for you to pray about it."

"I looked at him and George Mueller said, "Captain, I have known my Lord for fifty-seven years and there has never been a single day when I have failed to get an audience with the King. Get up, Captain, and open the door and you will find the fog has gone." "I got up and the fog indeed was gone, and on that Saturday afternoon George Mueller kept his promised engagement."[20]

Hudson Taylor (1832-1905), the famous missionary to China, was also know for his faith and for receiving specific answers to prayer. He began the China Inland Mission, which under Taylor's leadership supervised a thousand missionaries in China. This story, also told by a sea captain, occurred on Hudson's first trip to China when his sailing vessel stalled in great calm very near the shore of cannibal islands:

The ship was slowly drifting shoreward unable to go about and the savages were eagerly anticipating a feast. The captain came to Mr. Taylor and besought him to pray for the help of God. "I will," said Taylor, "provided you set your sails to catch the breeze." The captain declined to make himself a laughing stock by unfurling in a dead calm. Taylor said, "I will not undertake to pray for the vessel unless you will prepare the sails." And it was done. While engaged in prayer, there was a knock at the door of his stateroom. "Who is there?" The captain's voice responded, "Are you still praying for wind?" "Yes." "Well," said the captain, "you'd better stop praying, for we have more wind than we can manage."[21]

Dr. David Livingstone (1813-1873), a Scottish doctor and missionary, is considered one of the most important European explorers of Africa and pioneers in the abolition of the slave trade. Mrs. J. H. Worchester writes in her book, *David Livingstone: First To Cross Africa With The Gospel*, that "as a missionary explorer, [Livingstone] stood alone, traveling 29,000 miles in Africa, adding to the known portion of the globe about a million square miles, discovering lakes N'gami, Shirwa, Nyassa, Morero and Bangweolo, the upper Zambesi and many other rivers, and the wonderful Victoria Falls." By the grace of God, Livingston ventured where no white man had previously dared to and God preserved Him despite the cannibals, deadly snakes, diseases, and wild beasts (though, he was once severely injured in a lion attack). He suffered acute malaria for some twenty years, often bedridden with fever and unconsciousness for days at a time (the fever usually rendered him temporarily deaf). He was a man of faith and witnessed a life-long display of God's grace in answered prayers and miracles.

In 1872, Henry Morton Stanley (1841–1904), the English correspondent for the *New York Herald,* found David Livingstone at Ujiji on Lake Tanganyika in the heart of Africa. He greeted him with the now-classic salutation, "Dr. Livingstone, I presume?" Henry M. Stanley described the famous old missionary:

> Here is a man who is manifestly sustained as well as guided by influences from Heaven. The Holy Spirit dwells in him. God speaks through him. The heroism, the nobility, the pure and stainless enthusiasm as the root of his life come, beyond question, from Christ. There must, therefore, be a Christ;—and it is worth while to have such a Helper and Redeemer as this Christ undoubtedly is, and as He here reveals Himself to this wonderful disciple. [22]

Yes, miracles are evidence of God's presence in the world. Unbelievers may deny that there is a God who intrudes upon natural order by the working of miracles, but they cannot deny the effect that these repeated highly improbable experiences have upon men and women who have been previously beseeching their God to act in their behalf. In this, the sum total of improbable experience overshadows theoretically derived absolutes.

Personal Testimony

A number of years ago, I began a journal to record on an ongoing basis all the wonderful ways my wife and I have providentially seen the Lord's handiwork. In times of distress or difficulty, I reread the accounts to remind myself of God's gracious dealing with His servants. At first, I had narrowed the field to ten personal stories for inclusion in this book, but I realized that it might be viewed by some as out of character with the nature of this work; so please permit me to share with you the following three personal stories of God's providential care; all three pertain to bizarre traveling situations. The reader will find two additional personal accounts of divine providence in Appendix VI.

A Hong Kong Meeting

Mike Attwood is both a trusted friend and a co-laborer in Christian ministry. When divine providence intertwines our courses, the fellowship is sweet and the accountability to continue on high moral ground and the path of faith is invaluable. It had been a couple of months since Mike and I had communicated. In his last correspondence, he indicated that he would be doing some ministry in Africa for a few weeks in January 2004. During that same time, I planned to minister in Mainland China and then go on to Hong Kong for some continuing work among God's people there.

I flew into Hong Kong on a Thursday and a Christian brother

picked me up and took me to my hotel. Though my accommodations were in the downtown area, all the towering buildings made it difficult to see more than a portion of the city from any vantage point. Hong Kong has approximately seven million inhabitants compressed together in a relatively small area, thus much of its metropolitan structure is vertical.

Later that evening, I phoned a local missionary named Sheldon to determine if we could enjoy a meal together while I was in Hong Kong. We were able to find some time to meet during my stay. Before ending the conversation he volunteered, "Guess who I literally bumped into in the Chinese market this evening?" My reply was, "I don't know, as this is only my second trip to Hong Kong and I know but a handful of people here." The missionary continued, "I ran into Mike Attwood." I inquired, "Mike Attwood from Washington, Georgia?" Sheldon said, "Yes, he is here to speak at a Bible Conference this weekend." I replied, "I didn't know that Mike was going to be in Hong Kong; when did he arrive? The missionary responded, "This afternoon." I exclaimed, "I arrived this very afternoon also."

"Do you know where Mike is staying?" I inquired. "No," was the reply. As the conversation drew to a close I was just dazed by the possibility that the Lord could have drawn his two servants halfway around the world to the same city on the same day without either of them being aware of the other's schedule. After pondering the matter for a moment, I decided to call the hotel front desk and inquire if Mike and I were lodging in the same hotel. I was awestruck to hear that he was only three floors below me.

Early the next morning, I knocked on the door to Mike's room. The door opened to reveal an equally stunned occupant. After gawking at one another for a moment or two in speechless wonder, Mike invited me into his room where we enjoyed recounting this providential miracle. After recovering from our surprise, we enjoyed a time of fellowship and prayer with one another. Neither of us knew at that time that there would be some difficulties during the next few days, and that the Lord had already provided his servants to mutually encourage one another.

What is the probability of such events occurring by chance? It is noted that this was Mike's first trip to Hong Kong and that Sheldon resides in the Western Territories, some 45 minutes west of the downtown area, and he doesn't visit the area often. When you consider how I learned of Mike's arrival through Sheldon, where he was staying, and then the mutual encouragement through a difficult situation, I dare say the probability of such events unfolding by random chance is astronomically impossible!

Encouragement for a New Christian

By God's grace, my wife and I were able to see a number of people trust Christ as Savior and start a new Church work in Rockford, Illinois. One of the new Christians, Craig, was also an engineer and had to travel occasionally on business. His countenance was just beaming after returning from such a trip to Hartford, Connecticut. "You will never guess who I met on my trip," Craig said. "Who?" I replied. "A friend of yours, Jack Spender." A bit astounded I said, "Unbelievable! How did you meet Jack?" Craig then relayed the story.

Jack and his wife Ruth are likewise involved in a church planting ministry in Connecticut, but Jack also does some itinerant speaking. He had finished speaking at a Bible Conference in Tennessee and went to the airport to fly home when he found out his flight had been cancelled. He was then booked with a different airline company (to obtain an early morning flight the next day) and put up in a hotel for the night. His new flight plan routed him through Chicago, where as the Lord would have it, he was seated next to Craig on the flight to Hartford. The two men, both being evangelistic, soon started to talk about spiritual matters. When Jack learned that Craig was from Rockford, Jack inquired, "I only know one person from northern Illinois, that is Warren Henderson, do you know him?" Craig said later that for a moment he was speechless. "Yes, he is the man God used to bring me to Christ." What is so ironic about the situation is that at that time in my life, Jack and Ruth were the only people I personally knew in Connecticut. Craig had been going through a difficult time in his life, but that day the Lord greatly encouraged him, he has never forgotten God's specially arranged meeting with Jack.

Anger at 35,000 Feet

In order to participate in a Bible conference in October of 2005, I used air miles from my United Airlines frequent-flyer program to purchase a roundtrip ticket from Minneapolis to Ft. Lauderdale. United originally routed me through Chicago, but about three weeks from the travel date, they notified me that I was to fly through Denver. This change made no sense to me, as I had to get up very early in the morning, and endure four hours of extra flying time. Arriving at the airport on the day of departure, I noticed the flight to Denver was delayed two hours, meaning I would miss my connecting flight from Denver to Ft. Lauderdale. After waiting in line at the United Airlines ticketing counter, I learned that there were no other options that would allow me to arrive when I desired to, so the attendant at the counter instructed me to check with their affiliate, US Air. I waited in line again and learned that they could book me on a flight to Charlotte then on to Ft. Lauderdale, but United had not released my ticket. Hence, I went back and stood in line at the United Airlines counter again. After getting a released ticket, I went back to the US Air counter, waited in line a fourth time, and finally received my boarding pass for a flight to Charlotte – which departed in 30 minutes.

The departure gate was in one of the furthest concourses. Because I had changed carriers, I received extra special treatment through security which already had a long waiting line. After making it through security, I wheeled my luggage as quickly as possible to my departing gate – I had only 5 minutes to make the flight. Arriving at the departure gate, I noticed that the door to the jet-way had already closed and that the plane was already pushed back. After catching my breath and wiping my perspiration off the countertop, I explained my situation to the US Air attendant, who started searching for another flight for me.

A few moments later, she said, "Actually, there is only one option. There was a flight which was to leave for Philadelphia from this very gate 30 minutes ago; it is projected to arrive shortly and depart in one hour. There are just a couple seats left, but I can put you on this flight and get you to Ft. Lauderdale only one hour later than your initial itinerary." I said "It doesn't really matter to me if I go through Chicago, Denver, Charlotte, or Philadelphia as long as I get to Ft. Lauderdale." I received a new boarding pass. Having seen the Lord work through similar bizarre circumstances before, I was confident that He was orchestrating something unusual. I recall being excited about the possibility and prayed expectantly about the forthcoming events while waiting to board the flight to Philadelphia.

The flight was packed, yet I had obtained a window seat. This is unusual, as the middle seats are usually the last to be filled on a full flight. It likely meant that I had received someone else's seat due to a last minute change of plans. After reaching cruising attitude, I noticed that the man sitting next to me was reading a book on anger. In fact, I recognized the book, one written by a Christian author, Dr. Richard Walters, and published some twenty-five years earlier. The reason I recognized it was that particular book was one I reviewed in publishing my own book on the subject *just four months* earlier.

After introducing myself, I asked the man, "How are you enjoying your book?" He replied, "OK so far, I am just getting into it." I continued, "I am familiar with this book; it is excellent, and I see you are at the part about God's anger." For the next several minutes, I shared with the man why God was angry over man's sin, but that He had devised a way to satisfy His righteous anger over man's sin by judging His own Son in humanity's place. The man listened intently, and when I asked if he had any questions, he said, "My wife and I are in the process of getting a divorce; my family life is in shambles." After a lingering gulp to fight back the tears, he continued, "I think God is trying to tell me something. I just flew from Fargo to Minneapolis to catch this flight to Philadelphia, and a man named Bob sat in the same seat you are in and told me how I could receive forgiveness of my sins in the same way you just explained." The man showed me the gospel literature he had received from Bob. While looking at him straight in the eye I replied, "Actually, you have no idea the trouble God has gone to this morning to put two Christians beside you to share the gospel message with you." After explaining to him my chaotic morning, the man started to shake slightly, and for the next hour, I shared with him several passages on salvation from the Bible.

I had one copy of the book I had written on anger (*Be Angry and Sin Not*) with me, so I wrote my personal information on the inside cover and handed it to him. What is the probability, by chance, that my flight schedule would be changed three times, that the man's flight would be delayed to allow me to get on it, that he would sit next to two gospel preachers on two consecutive flights (with the preachers in the window seat and the man in the middle seat), that the man would be reading the same book on anger I had reviewed earlier in preparation to publish my own book on the subject (keep in mind, the book he was reading was published twenty-five years earlier and was out of print), that the man was seeking answers to his problems and would intently listen to the gospel message. And some say there is no God! Might the Lord arrange a "chance" meeting with one of His workers for you someday? Perhaps it will be me.

It would require a book longer than this one to record all the statistically improbable situations I have witnessed of the providence of God at work. These three incidents were taken from just one category of personal stories. Perhaps a person might randomly see one or two of these unique events during his entire lifetime, but what if an individual witnessed these normally? Would not he or she live to expect them? Now you know why Mueller, Taylor, Livingstone, and many more would not trade a single day with the Lord Jesus Christ for an entire lifetime without Him. The abiding presence of Christ and His providential care confirm that life has eternal purpose – though many never know this to be true.

> Miracles are a retelling in small letters of the very same story which is written across the whole world in letters too large for some of us to see.
>
> — C. S. Lewis

Summary

Miracles demonstrate God's existence and presence in different situations, but miracles, themselves, will never *produce* believing faith; miracles can only build up the faith of someone who already believes the truth. The Lord Jesus stated that the unrighteous were the ones who wanted to see a "sign or a wonder" in order to believe in Him. He called these *sign seekers* an evil generation and spiritually adulterous (Matt. 12:38-39). Even those people that witnessed the miracle of the feeding of the 5000 men (plus women and children) were pestering the Lord the very next day: *"What sign will You perform then, that we **may see it and believe** You? What work will You do?"*(John 6:30). Had they not recalled the miracle the day before? Did they not fill their bellies with a boy's multiplied sack-lunch? The Israelites saw miracles every day in the wilderness for forty years, yet it did not increase their spirituality for they constantly murmured against God and His leadership (Ex. 15:24, 16:2).

The Bible's accounts show that miracles – dramatic, show-stopping miracles like many of us still long for – simply do not foster deep faith.

— Philip Yancey

Peter shows us that true faith in God opens our eyes to understand the things of God. When the Lord asked His twelve disciples if they, too, would turn away from Him, as many had done, Peter responded, *"Lord, to whom shall we go? You have the words of eternal life. Also we have come **to believe and know** that You are the Christ, the Son of the living God"* (John 6:68-69). The unrighteous want a sign to believe, but the righteous believe, then understand. Thus, until we exercise faith, we will not understand from where we came. *"By faith we understand that the worlds were framed by the word of God, so that the things which are seen were not made of things which are visible"* (Heb. 11:3).

Life is wonderful when you see the Lord's hand bestowing miraculous provisions along its course. The atheist says, "There is no God." Because I believe and know that there is a God, I am able to witness His repeated personal intervention in the affairs of my life – I *absolutely* know this to be true by continuing experience. These events are beyond natural explanation – God is the only answer. Have you witnessed the unexplainable in your life? If so, don't just dismiss the matter as a coincidence because you don't understand it, look heavenward and ponder the why. Perhaps, God will work the greatest miracle He can on your behalf – to cause you to realize that you are totally spiritually destitute without Him.

#10 Changed Lives

The final evidence of supernatural influence within natural order to be discussed is the personal testimony of changed lives. The personal impact of the gospel of Jesus Christ is perhaps the strongest visible evidence of supernatural power among humanity today.

Lee Strobel, mentioned in a previous chapter, was once a scoffer of the Christian message until one day in the autumn of 1979 his wife Leslie announced that she had become a Christian. He feared the worst for his marriage, but as he recalls:

Instead I was pleasantly surprised – even fascinated – by the fundamental changes in her character, her integrity, and her personal confidence. Eventually I wanted to get to the bottom of what was prompting these subtle but significant shifts in my wife's attitudes, so I launched an all-out investigation into the facts surrounding the case for Christianity.

Setting aside my self-interest and prejudices as best I could, I read books, interviewed experts, asked questions, analyzed history, explored archaeology, studied ancient literature, and for the first time in my life picked apart the Bible verse by verse.

I plunged into the case with more vigor than with any story I had pursued [as a journalist]. I applied the training I had received at Yale Law School as well as my experience as legal affairs editor of the Chicago Tribune. And over time the evidence of the world, of history, of science, of philosophy, of psychology – began to point toward the unthinkable.[1]

What was the result of Strobel's twenty-one months of research? On November 8, 1981, he received Jesus Christ as his Lord and Savior. The research he gathered was subsequently compiled into the book "The Case for Christ." He knew that Christ had changed his wife's life and that the evidence he had accumulated verified the truthfulness of the message she had trusted, so he made a rational choice to do likewise.

Sometime shortly after the turn of the 19th century, Christian author and Bible commentator Harry Ironside was preaching on a street corner in San Francisco when he received a written challenge to a debate. The subject was to be "Agnosticism vs. Christianity," the place was to be The Academy of Science Hall, and the debate was to be at 4:00 pm on the next Sunday. After pausing to read the challenge, Harry, addressing the man in front of a sizable crowed, said he would accept the challenge on the following two conditions.

First, he must promise to bring with him one man who was for years what we commonly call a 'down-and-outer.' … a man who for years was under the power of some evil habits from which he could not deliver himself, but who, on some occasion, attended this gentlemen's meetings and heard him speak, glorifying agnosticism and denouncing the Bible and Christianity, and whose heart and mind as he listened to such an address were so deeply stirred that he went away from the meeting saying, 'Henceforth I, too, am an agnostic!' or words to that effect, and as a result of embracing that particular philosophy he found that a new power had come into his life. The sins that he once loved, now he hates, and righteousness and goodness are henceforth the ideals of his life [Ironside's second request was that the challenger present a morally depraved woman who likewise] won her way back to an honored position in society and is living a clean, virtuous, happy life – all because she is an agnostic.

"Now, sir," Harry continued, "if you will promise to bring with you two such people as examples of what agnosticism will do, I will promise to meet you at the Academy of Science Hall at the hour appointed next Sunday, and I'll bring with me at the very least one hundred men and women who for years lived in just such sinful degradation as I have tried to depict but who have been gloriously saved through believing the message of the gospel which you ridicule. I'll have these men and women with me on the platform as witnesses to the miraculous saving power of Jesus Christ, and as present-day proof of the truth of the Bible.

[After this a Salvation Army captain, who was present during this oration, volunteered to bring forty such saved souls and Harry reiterated he would have no problem finding at least sixty more to come to the Hall at the appointed time.]

His opponent, who had at least some sense of humor, smiled rather sardonically and, with a wave of the hand as if to say, "Nothing doing!" He walked away from the scene of the meeting – while the crowd applauded and cheered the street preacher [Ironside] who had met the challenge of the agnostic and put him to flight. **They recognized immediately that no philosophy of negation, such as agnosticism, could ever make bad men and women good, and yet they knew from observation and experience that this is exactly what Christ has done for centuries and is doing every day.**[2]

I find it amusing to explore the internet and find websites publicizing the stories of Christians converting to Islam, to Catholicism, to Mormonism or to some other cult. But, in general, when you search for Christian conversion stories, you will read of men and women turning from sin, from self-invoked misery to find salvation, hope, and fulfillment in Jesus Christ. The flavor of these websites should indicate what is real and what is not. It is easy for one to change a religious label; it is an entirely different matter for one to be liberated from a life of sin, alcoholism, drug addiction, mental disorders, etc. and willingly live a life pleasing to Christ.

> Atheism never composed a symphony. Never painted a masterpiece. Never dispelled a fear. Never healed a disease. Never gave peace of mind. Never dried a tear. Never established a philanthropy. Never gave an intelligent answer to the vast mystery of the universe. Never gave meaning to man's life on earth. Never built a just and peaceful world. Never built a great and enduring civilization.
>
> —Charles M. Houser

The Testimony of Church History

One of the pleasing distinctions of true Christianity over the major monotheistic religions (excluding Judaism) is that the Founder and His followers did not beset a path of violence in the conversion of others to Christianity. On the contrary, over the centuries a faithful remnant of true Christians have held to the teachings of Christ and were led like sheep to the slaughter for their faith. *Foxe's Book of Martyrs* and *The Pilgrim Church* by E. H. Broadbent are excellent historical resources to document this fact.

A religion based on hate will be sustained by fear and self-preservation, but that which is forged in love will be propagated by sacrificial service. This is the testimony of true Christians for the last two thousand years beginning with the original followers of Christ. What they believed was lived out in selfless sacrifice even unto their death. Being assured of the truth, they did not defend themselves from tyranny, mockery, and martyrdom. The assurance of God's Word resulted in hope for the future and joy while bearing tremendous pain and suffering.

How did those early disciples of Jesus Christ emphatically demonstrate that they had witnessed the resurrection of their Lord? They willingly laid down their lives to show love and obedience to their Savior – men do not peacefully die for a lie – fully convinced of what they knew to be true. Peter, Andrew, James (son of Alphaeus), Philip, Simon and Bartholomew were crucified in various ways. Matthew and James (the son of Zebedee) were slain by the sword; Thaddaeus was struck by several arrows; Thomas was thrust through with a spear, and James (the half-brother of Jesus) was cast over the temple wall and, after plummeting to the ground, was finished off by stoning. John Mark bled to death after being tied to a chariot and dragged through the streets of Alexandria. It is true that some people are conned into dying for religious causes, but the disciples died for what they knew to be true. Sane men don't willing die for what they know is a lie.

History records that Aegeas crucified Andrew, Peter's brother, for his faith in Christ. Seeing his cross before him, Andrew bravely spoke, "O cross, most welcome and longed for! With a willing mind, joyfully and desirously, I come to thee, being the scholar of Him which did hang on thee: because I have always been thy lover, and have coveted to embrace thee."[3] Why could Andrew approach his cross with joy? He had watched the Lord approach His cross in the same manner. During the deepest trials of life, it is possible to have present joy in God's future promises. Each of the Lord's disciples faced death with the same hope and endured tremendous suffering for the joy set before them. John was the only disciple not to experience martyrdom; his latter years were spent in exile on the Isle of Patmos.

> The peace and joy that belong to deepest suffering are the miracles of faith.
>
> — Ralph W. Emerson

Perishing to Become Preachers

Since the early days of Christianity, men and women have surrendered their lives to Christ in all sorts of circumstances and places. God worked specifically and individually to bring about conversion and radical change. In some cases, those coming to Christ for salvation became tremendous preachers of righteousness.

John Newton was a vile God-mocking man employed in the slave trade during the mid 18th century. Early in life, Newton had been exposed to the Christian message through his mother, but had rejected it. While at sea, however, a raging storm beset his sailing vessel for days. The timbers of the ship were shattered; the rigging was in shambles, and the sails tattered. In attempt to keep the ship from sinking, bedding and clothes were used to plug up holes in its battered hull. The sailors pumped tirelessly; one man died of exhaustion. When Newton was too exhausted to pump any longer, he strapped himself to the wheel of the ship. He prayed and read the Bible during free moments, and he sought God for the forgiveness of his sins (which he had earlier concluded were "too great to be forgiven"). John Newton trusted Jesus Christ as His Savior on March 21, 1747. He was transformed into a kind captain and led Christian meetings on his ship. Later (after realizing the slave trade was wrong), he became an abolitionist and a minister of the Gospel. Reflecting back on his violent and brutal life, he wrote one of Christianity's greatest hymns: "Amazing grace, how sweet the sound that saved a wretch like me."

Dwight L. Moody had a fifth grade education; his spelling and grammar were awful, and his manners were often brash and rough. He was raised in a home embracing Unitarianism (which denies the deity of Christ and de-emphasizes man's need for salvation from sin). As a teenager living in Northfield, Massachusetts, Moody was desperate for work. His uncle graciously offered him a job selling shoes, if he promised to attend the Mt.

232

Vernon Congregational Church; Moody agreed. He had been living in spiritual darkness, but that all changed on April 21, 1855, when Moody's Sunday School teacher Edward Kimball came to the shoe store and asked Dwight to repent and commit his life to Christ. Moody listened intently to the gospel message, trusted Christ as his Savior and immediately began sharing his faith with others. Moody later moved to Chicago, where he wandered the streets to find children to bring to his Sunday School class. He had a passion for saving souls and determined never to let a day pass without telling someone the gospel of Jesus Christ. He later founded Moody Bible Institute to properly equip those desiring to serve Christ. By some estimates, D. L. Moody is thought to have led as many as a million people to confess faith in Christ.

Charles Haddon Spurgeon is referred to as the "prince of preachers." Warren Wiersbe relates the following story of Spurgeon's conversion:

On January 6, 1850, a snowstorm almost crippled the city of Colchester, England; and a teenage boy was unable to get to the church he usually attended. So he made his way to a nearby Primitive Methodist chapel, where an ill-prepared speaker was substituting for the absent preacher. His text was Isaiah 45:22 – *"Look unto Me, and be ye saved, all the ends of the Earth."* For many months this young teenager had been miserable and under deep conviction; but though he had been reared in church (both his father and grandfather were preachers), he did not have the assurance of salvation. The unprepared substitute minister did not have much to say, so he kept repeating the text. "A man need not go to college to learn to look," he shouted. "Anyone can look—a child can look!" About that time, he saw the visitor sitting to one side, and he pointed at him and said, "Young man, you look very miserable. Young man, look to Jesus Christ!" The young man did look by faith, and that was how the great preacher Charles Haddon Spurgeon was converted.[4]

Unshackled

The Pacific Garden Mission in Chicago has a radio ministry called "Unshackled." In 1950, *Unshackled* began airing the testimonies of changed lives using the popular radio drama format of the day. The first program was about Billy Sunday, the famous Chicago baseball player turned evangelist (Sunday saw tens of thousands of souls won for Christ).

At the time of this writing, "Unshackled" is heard on over 1,550 radio outlets in 147 countries, on six continents, in eight languages (more than 6,500 times a week worldwide). The ministry is nearing its 3000th program; each program has provided vivid presentations of a changed life through the gospel of Jesus Christ.

Darwin Witnesses the Power of the Gospel

In 1833, Charles Darwin went to the South Sea Islands looking for the so-called "missing link." As he studied what he thought to be cannibals who resided there, he concluded that no creatures anywhere were more primitive, and he was convinced that nothing on earth could possibly lift them to a higher level. He thought he had indeed found a lower stratum of humanity that would fit his theory of evolution. Darwin wrote:

> I could not have believed how wide was the difference between savage and civilized man; it is greater than between a wild and domesticated animal.... Viewing such man, one can hardly make oneself believe that they are fellow creatures and inhabitants of the same world.[5]

Thirty-four years later, he returned to the same islands. To his amazement, he discovered church buildings, schools, and homes occupied by some of those former so-called cannibals. In fact, many of them wore clothes and frequently gathered to sing hymns. The reason was soon learned: Missionary John G. Paton had been there proclaiming the truths of salvation! Darwin was so moved by their transformation that he made a generous contribution to the London Missionary Society. [6]

Darwin had wrongly surmised that the Fuegans were cannibals, as an extensive study by those living with the Fuegans failed to disclose a single case of cannibalism. Darwin also wrongly concluded that the Fuegan grunt language, Jahgan, had a tiny vocabulary. Through the missionary work accomplished among the Fuegans more than 32,000 words were learned, including more than 50 names that described family relationships alone. The conclusion: Darwin's "missing link" remained missing and the gospel of Jesus Christ had miraculously changed the Fuegans. [7]

Tribal Salvation

Besides the Fuegans, many other primitive and often brutal tribes have been completely transformed by trusting the gospel message of Jesus Christ. The Hmar in India and the Auca in Ecuador serve as good examples.

Hmar Tribe of Northeast India

Bibles for the World ministry provides this report concerning the people of the Hmar tribe of Northeast India who were once fierce headhunters:

In 1910, a missionary named Watkin Roberts sent a copy of the Gospel of John to a Hmar chief. The chief invited Roberts to come and explain the Scriptures. He went despite a ban by the British Colonial government to keep him out of the area, and five young tribesmen chose to follow the Lord Jesus. These converts grew in faith and became leaders of a new and growing church. Within two generations, the entire tribe was evangelized. Headhunting stopped and *heart*hunting became the fervent pursuit of the people.[8]

Auca (Huaorani) Tribe in the Ecuador Rainforest

In 1956, tribesmen from the Auca (a Quechua word for "savage") tribe in Ecuador speared five American missionaries: Peter Fleming, 27; Jim Elliot, 28; Ed McCully, 28; Roger Youderian, 31, and Nate Saint, 32. The headlines of their martyrdom circulated worldwide. In 1959, Nate Saint's sister, Rachel and Jim Elliot's widow, Elisabeth, made contact with this fierce tribe. Rachel Saint remained with them for 30 years. The movie *Beyond the Gates of Splendor* (2002) and the writings by Elisabeth Elliot highlight the historic details of the martyrdom, but few people know that these women were instrumental in leading the actual killers of their loved ones to Christ, effectively ending generations of tribal revenge killings, which in recent years had wiped out 60 percent of the tribe.[9]

James Boster, an anthropologist from the University of Connecticut, studied the history of Auca revenge murders, and concluded that Christian conversion prevented self-extinction (The tribe had dwindled down to 600 members in 1958, but at present numbers about 2,000.). He notes:

> Deadly cycles of revenge had scattered them into small, paranoid factions. Attempted truces failed because their language had no words for abstractions such as "peace." Because Christianity was brought by kin of men they had killed, but who befriended them in return, it became a powerful way to signal commitment to nonviolence.[10]

Summary

"Do you really believe the miracles in the Bible?" a skeptic asked a new Christian who had been a terrible drinker. "Of course I do!" the believer replied. The skeptic laughed. "Do you mean that you really believe that Jesus could turn water into wine?" he asked. "I sure do! In my home He turned wine into food and clothing and furniture!"[11]

It has been the awesome experience of my wife and myself to witness the transforming power of the gospel message in saving men and women from their sins and from the most corrupt and perverse situations. Some have been delivered from alcoholism, drug addiction, immoral lifestyles, emotional disorders, suicidal tendencies, the blindness of humanism, and the darkness of religiosity. These lost souls were reached for Christ in the work place, in the home, in the streets, and in jail cells. After salvation was received, we have seen marriages on the brink of divorce be rescued and shattered lives be restored, all in joyful submission to and dependence upon Christ.

Five years ago, we witnessed a man and woman (who were living in fornication) profess Christ as Savior in our home. She was enslaved to alcohol, and he to drugs; both were immediately freed – the debilitating desire was gone. They continue to this day to live for the Lord. These are supernatural events; no man-made religion nor human effort can manufacture such miraculous transformations. Changed lives are a sacred testimony of God's handiwork in human affairs!

We are not talking about people who have changed from one religion to another; we are speaking of men and women who were dead in trespasses and sins and now experience the abundant life in the Lord Jesus Christ. The Lord Jesus said, *"I have come that they may have life, and that they may have it more abundantly"* (John 10:10). This abundant life reality cannot be explained by logic; it is supernatural. It cannot be rationalized by the human intellect; it is understood only by faith. Those experiencing spiritual life in Christ know and understand what the truth actually is by first exercising faith in God's word – faith bridges the gap between the unexplainable influences in our lives and the invisible God who creates each one. *"By faith we understand that the worlds were framed by the word of God, so that the things which are seen were not made of things which are visible"* (Heb. 11:3).

Is God Reason-able?

Is God *reason-able*? God certainly reasons with men, but man cannot fully reason with God apart from faith. This is not to say that God has not provided infallible evidence of Himself for man to contemplate; He has, as previous chapters gave testimony. There is ample evidence to know of God's existence for all of nature demands a Creator. *"For since the creation of the world His [God's] invisible attributes are clearly seen, being understood by the things that are made, even His eternal power and Godhead, so that they are without excuse* (Rom. 1:20).

But believing in the one true God alone does not merit salvation. James, an apostle of Christ, used a bit of sarcasm to punctuate this warning: *"You believe that there is one God. You do well. Even the demons believe – and tremble!"* (Jas. 2:19). Believing in something and trusting in something are two different somethings. I may believe that the ice is thick enough to keep me from falling into the frigid lake below, but if I am terrified to step out upon the ice, do I really believe the ice will support me? True faith is evidenced by action – it is lived out (Jas. 2:17, 20). The temporal excites the flesh; intellectualism stimulates the soul, but faith in divine truth allows man's spirit to commune with God.

Our intellect is involved in rendering a decision to trust in God, but intellectualism alone will never cause man to render a decision in which God states faith must be a part. Certainly, some have closed their minds to the prompting of God through their own spirit, but I believe many more are still wrestling with divine persuasion. This book has identified ten evidences of God's influence within natural order. Each of these represents *open door* opportunities to peer into the supernatural realm – each beckons the human mind to consider something beyond nature, to consider that which is superior to nature.

By way of a summary, the previous investigated evidences which I believe identify God's influence within nature are:

- The Uniqueness of the Earth

- The Testimony of Nature

- The Authenticity of the Bible

- The Uniformity of the Bible

- The Prophecy of the Bible

- The Human Conscience

- The Human Spirit's Need

- The Inflammatory Name of Jesus

- Miracles

- Changed Lives

These evidences for the supernatural realm do not compose an exhaustive list; there are indications of supernatural influence in the natural realm such as ministering angels, and demonic opposition (my book entitled *Mind Frames* addresses this subject).

The Cost of Doubt

Rejection of the evidence God has provided of Himself has a serious spiritual consequence (discussed in the next chapter) and strongly degrades one's worldview of life. Disbelief in the true

God ensures the absolute belief in nothing resulting in the quasi-belief of anything. This allows the human mind to both fabricate and operate within a relative world of make-believe, an adequate description of the post-modern culture of our day. Unfortunately Bertrand Russell realized the truth too late; just before he died, he glumly proclaimed, "Philosophy has proven a washout for me."[1]

Voltaire said that it took centuries to build up Christianity, but "I'll show how just one Frenchman can destroy it within 50 years." Taking his pen, he dipped it into the ink of unbelief and wrote against God. Twenty years after his death, the Geneva Bible Society purchased his house as a site for the printing of Bibles. It later became the Paris headquarters for the British and Foreign Bible Society. The Bible is still a best-seller; an entire 6-volume set of Voltaire's works was once sold for just 90¢. Just before his death, the noted atheist swore: "I wish I had never been born!"[2] Atheists die hard.

Thomas Paine, an immigrant to America in 1787, leaped from obscurity to fame after writing some brilliant pamphlets on freedom. Later, this founding father in US history unfortunately changed his focus from fighting for freedom to pungent declarations of atheism. Paine wrote his "masterpiece" called *The Age of Reason* which scoffed at Christianity. "This will destroy the Bible," he predicted. "Within 100 years, Bibles will be found only in museums or in musty corners of second-hand bookstores." His book was published in London in 1794, but it brought him so much misery and loneliness that he once said: "I would give worlds, if I had them, had *The Age of Reason* never been written." Paine became a bedridden invalid, friendless and alone, until his death in 1809. The Bible still remains a best-seller year after year.[3]

Russell, Voltaire, Paine, and others have concocted a self-imposed reality through human philosophy which somehow was to eliminate God from human awareness. Humanism cajoles man into a blasé awareness of reality, a sort of pacified existence that lacks both moral fortitude and inspirational hope. This is why humanistic propaganda, such as Richard Dawkin's recent book *The God Delusion*, will always fail to assure man of a purposeful and meaningful existence.

What hope is there for pain and suffering, if there is no God working all things out for a greater good (Rom. 8:28)? What hope is there for an afterlife if there is no eternal God? What hope is there for a joyful life upon the Earth without personally knowing the sweetness of the blessed Savior – the Lord Jesus Christ? What did the theories and the philosophies of the four revered heroes of atheism – Darwin, Huxley, Nietzsche, Freud – accomplish for them? A life of dread, mental illness, physical suffering and an obsessive fear of death. But unfortunately, the despair of a hopeless life will never adequately prepare man for the horror of a hopeless eternity without Christ. *"It is appointed for men to die once, but after this the judgment"* (Heb. 9:27). Why do atheists die hard? The Bible states, *"'There is no peace' says the Lord, 'for the wicked'"* (Isa. 48:22) and that those without Christ will naturally fear death (Heb. 2:15).

Finding God and Being Found

Naturally speaking, if we were left to ourselves, we would never know God personally because we would never know how to seek after Him. After our first parents sinned, spiritual death (separation from God) passed down to all their descendants (Rom. 5:12). That is why Scripture states that an individual is already condemned even before he or she might reject the gospel message of Jesus Christ (John 3:18). Paul summarizes our natural spiritual condition, *"There is none righteous, no, not one; There is none who understands; There is none who seeks after God. They have all turned aside; They have together become unprofitable; There is none who does good, no, not one"* (Rom. 3:10-12). Man is hopelessly lost and separated from God as a result of human sin.

The Matter of Sin

Sin is not a popular word. It describes "lawlessness, rebellion, not doing what we know is right, falling short of God's standard of righteousness" (Rom. 3:23; James 4:17). Though God never placed the Gentile under the law (nor is the believing Jew still under the law; Rom. 7:4-6), the law still declares His moral standard for right and wrong – the Ten Commandments show us our sin (Rom. 3:20) and affirm that we need a Savior.

> *Therefore the law was our tutor to bring us to Christ, that we might be justified by faith. But after faith has come, we are no longer under a tutor* (Gal. 3:24-25).

The first two of the Ten Commandments relate to the subject of recognizing God as Creator and not worshipping creation – a major theme of this book.

The First Commandment: *You shall have no other gods before Me* (Ex. 20:3)

Moses explained how one obeys this commandment – by believing in the one true God and giving Him first place in your life: *"The Lord our God, the Lord is one! You shall love the Lord your God with all your heart, with all your soul, and with all your strength"* (Deut. 6:4-5). The Lord Jesus reiterated this teaching, *"'You shall love the Lord your God with all your heart, with all your soul, and with all your mind.' This is the first and great commandment"* (Matt. 22:37-38).

On another occasion, the Lord explained the commandment's meaning, *"He who loves father or mother more than Me is not worthy of Me. And he who loves son or daughter more than Me is not worthy of Me. And he who does not take his cross and follow after Me is not worthy of Me"* (Matt. 10:37-38). When it comes to having no other god before the Creator, it means that He has first place in your life, your thinking, your allegiance and your affection. There are to be no close seconds concerning our love for God. Do you love the Lord God above all else – including yourself?

The Second Commandment: You shall not make for yourself any carved image ... (Ex. 20:4)

The entire commandment reads:

You shall not make for yourself a carved image – any likeness of anything that is in heaven above, or that is in the Earth beneath, or that is in the water under the Earth; you shall not bow down to them nor serve them. For I, the Lord your God, am a jealous God, visiting the iniquity of the fathers upon the children to the third and fourth generations of those who hate Me (Ex. 20:4-5).

Have you ever heard someone say, "God to me is ...?" The individual is revealing to you his or her self-concocted god, an imaginary god which fits his or her liking and, therefore, will readily condone that person's moral standard for life. In this way, holiness becomes relative; there is no judgment of sin with a self-manufactured God. It may not be a golden calf, but neither is it the Lord revealed in the Bible. God has no varying degrees of holiness and righteousness; His very character defines moral integrity, and all that does not measure up to it will be judged. When an individual replaces the true God, as revealed by Scripture, with a created image (whether visible or imaginary), he or she has violated the second of the Ten Commandments. To reject God as Creator is to violate the first two of the Ten Commandments. Evolutionary teaching exalts man and demotes or denies God – it is an intellectual religion which is high on self and applauds creation's ability to do what only God can do – create life!

The first two commandments alone should be sufficient to prove that each and every one of us has offended God, but just in case you are still not convinced that you have offended God (sinned against Him), here is a paraphrased summary of the remaining commandments (Ex. 20:7-17):

- Do not blaspheme God or use His name disrespectfully;
- Put aside one day in seven to honor the Lord;
- Honor your parents;
- Do not murder;

- Do not commit adultery;
- Do not steal;
- Do not lie;
- Do not covet (lust after what is not yours).

Ask people on the street if they are a good person, and most will say "yes, I am a pretty good person." Their moral standard of reckoning, however, is all wrong and they don't even know it. They have fabricated a self-righteous system of weighing their good deeds against their bad (sin), thinking that their good deeds will somehow offset their sins. God's standard of judgment is quite different – absolute perfection! By His standard one sin will keep anyone out of heaven (Gal. 3:10-12). Someday each of us will be judged by God's standard of perfection (Eccl. 12:14; Rom. 14:10-12; Rev. 20:11-15). How do you measure up against His standard of perfection?

The Bible answers that question for us on two counts. First, as to the matter of sin: *"All have sinned and fall short of the glory of God"* (Rom. 3:23), and secondly as to good works: *"All our righteousnesses are like filthy rags"* (Isa 64:6). So, one sin will tip God's moral scales against us because good works cannot satisfy God's anger for our sin. Imagine for a moment that you are driving a car faster than the posted speed limit and, appropriately, are pulled over by a highway patrolman. While he is writing you a citation for speeding, you boast to the patrolman that you are a good parent and a good spouse, that you do community service work, that you give generously to charities, etc. To your frustration, the patrolman continues writing and hands you the citation – you are fined $250. What is the moral of the story? No amount of good works undoes the fact that we all have violated God's moral law. Now ponder all the self-righteous and religious fabrications that men have concocted to convince God that they do not deserve judgment: water baptism, good works, religious parents, church attendance, repetitious prayers, rubbing beads, reciting vain religious chants, etc.

Imagine for a moment that your son and my son are enjoying an afternoon together, and in the course of play, they decide to go swimming. My son doesn't swim very well though, and, venturing out beyond his ability, he begins to drown. Noticing the dire situation, your son, a good swimmer, risks his own life to save my son. After much effort, your son is able to pull my son to shore and save his life. Unfortunately, however, your son inhaled a lot of water; complications ensued, and a few days later he died. Your son saved my son, but it cost him his life. Now one evening, being very much moved over this sincere sacrifice, I visit your home to personally thank you for your son's sacrifice, "If there is anything I can ever do for you in light of what your son did for our family, please let me know." Then, after pausing for a moment, I pull out my wallet and say to you, "In fact, I would like to show my gratitude now. Do you have change for a twenty dollar bill?" How would you feel in response to my comment? You should be enraged at my insulting gesture, and rightly so – I have ascribed a minimal value to something that cost you greatly. So, how much more must it anger God when humans snub their noses at the sacrifice of His own dear Son and offer feeble gestures of self-works to honor Him? Salvation is by grace alone. Grace is God's unmerited favor, and grace plus a nickel is not grace!

In our natural state apart from God, our good works do absolutely nothing to earn God's favor. The flesh nature opposes God in deed and motive; therefore, there is nothing inherent within the flesh that can please God. Jeremiah states: *"The heart [seat of emotion] is deceitful above all things, and desperately wicked"* (Jer. 17:9). The Apostle Paul speaks about the rankness of his own flesh: *"For I know that in me (that is, in my flesh) nothing good dwells; for to will is present with me, but how to perform what is good I do not find"* (Rom. 7:18). The grand conclusion is that we all are sinners and that we can do nothing to persuade God to love us more than He already does. Our good works are evidence of our true salvation in Christ, not the basis for it (Jas. 2:17, 20).

The Consequence of Sin

How then can man obtain a pure standing with God? The answer is that each individual must be justified (declared right). This is how Abraham received salvation: *"For if Abraham was justified by works, he has something to boast about, but not before God. For what does the Scripture say? 'Abraham believed God, and it was accounted to him for righteousness'"* (Rom. 4:3). If any individuals ever lived who could have merited salvation through personal effort, it would be Paul and Abraham, but Scripture condemns them both apart from receiving the righteousness of God through Christ.

Justification is an accounting term which means "to impute or accredit to another's account." When an individual trusts Christ, God imputes a righteous standing to that individual's account (he or she is declared righteous before God, though in practice he or she will still sin). This reality is a positional truth which the Christian is exhorted to live out practically each day (Rom. 6:11-12, 13:14).

If you die without being justified (i.e. receiving forgiveness of your sins and a righteous standing in Christ), there is no hope for you (Heb. 9:27). Contrary to what some teach, there is no purgatory – you will spend eternity in Hell. God has done everything He can to save you from eternal judgment, but He will not force you to go to heaven – it is your choice (2 Pet. 3:9). The Bible vividly describes hell, the ultimate fate of the lost (rejecters of God's truth):

- *"Shame and everlasting contempt"* (Dan. 12:2)

- *"Everlasting punishment"* (Matt. 25:46)
- *"Weeping and gnashing of teeth"* (Matt. 24:51)
- *"Unquenchable fire"* (Luke 3:17)
- *"Indignation and wrath, tribulation and anguish"* (Rom. 2:8-9)
- *"Their worm [soul] does not die"* (Mark 9:44)
- *"Everlasting destruction"* (2 Thess. 1:9)
- *"Eternal fire ... the blackness of darkness for ever"* (Jude 7, 13)
- *"Fire is not quenched"* (Mark 9:46)

Revelation 14:10-11 tells us the final, eternal destiny of the sinner: *"He shall be tormented with fire and brimstone ... the smoke of their torment ascended up for ever and ever: and they have no rest day or night."* The Bible's teaching of an eternal place of punishment for unforgiven sinners offends people; consequently, many are watering down the truth – teaching that hell is a state of non-existence or quick annihilation. To the philosopher, like Bertrand Russell, hell is repulsive teaching. He condemned the moral character of Jesus Christ because He spoke of hell: "There is one very serious defect to my mind in Christ's moral character, and that is that He believed in hell. I do not myself feel that any person who is really profoundly humane can believe in everlasting punishment."[1]

Have you ever heard the expression "The truth hurts"? Let's say you are dying of some rare deadly disease and are not even aware of the matter. One day you bump into your physician unexpectedly while shopping. His keen eye and skilled training cause him to identify the disease instantly. He knows that the disease is fatal and that there is only one possible cure, which must be administered immediately to be effective. Would you expect your doctor to tell you that you have a fatal disease and to prescribe the medicine that will save your life, or would you rather that he not disturb you with such tragic news? Obviously, to escape the consequences of reality, you must know the truth, no matter how distressing it is.

The Lord Jesus spoke more about hell than He did heaven, addressing the subject over seventy times. He bore our hell at Calvary and appeased God's anger for our sin so that we would not have to spend eternity there. He did not frighten people for kicks. He lovingly warned them about their deadly disease (sin) and the fatal consequence of the disease (hell), and pleaded with them to internalize the cure (exercise faith in Him for salvation). God will not force anyone against his or her will to receive Christ so that they might live with Him in heaven. Heaven would be hell if you didn't want to be there, but hell will not be heaven for those rejecting Christ. Salvation is like a personal check that has been written out for the full value of our offenses against God which God extends to us in the person of Christ. As an individual believes on Christ, he or she is by faith, endorsing the check and the value of it is imputed to their personal account. The check has value whether we cash it or not, but it only has value in our account if by faith we take action to cash it.

Russell concluded that "Religion is based, I think, primarily and mainly upon fear."[2] I agree with this statement, but only with a clarification – world generated religion is motivated by fear. As stated earlier, biblical Christianity is not about religion it is about a relationship with God through the Lord Jesus Christ. Biblical Christianity is motivated by love – love for the Lord, love for fellow man, and love for enemies. Do not look at the professing church as an example of biblical love; religiosity is a spiritual facade and mockery of the truth! Look to Christ and His Word alone for answers. In so doing you will be able to properly identify true followers of Christ, for their character will remind you of Him (2 Cor. 2:14-16). What world religion on the planet is love-motivated? Most religions of the world historically and/or presently convert by the sword or manipulation; Russell is correct on this point. Biblical Christianity speaks the truth in love and allows God to work on the hearer – end of story.

Since Christ, in Russell's mind, was obviously not the answer to the world's problems, what did he believe was? Science and the Intellect! He wrote:

> Science can help us to get over this craven fear in which mankind has lived for so many generations. Science can teach us, and I think our own hearts can teach us, no longer to look around for imaginary supports, no longer to invent allies in the sky, but rather to look to our own efforts here below to make this world a better place to live in …[3]

So it seems that man's choices for a better existence are but three: to have an intellectual relationship with science; to have a "make me feel good" rapport with religion; or to have an intimate relationship with God through the Lord Jesus Christ. The reader must decide which is more pertinent, reliable, personal, and genuine. If you decide that God is more important than science or religion, you must approach God through Christ alone; there is no other way to be saved. Speaking of Jesus Christ, Peter said: *"Nor is there salvation in any other, for there is no other name under heaven given among men by which we must be saved"* (Acts 4:12). But how does one approach God through Christ?

How to Personally Know God

The Lord Jesus said, *"Unless you repent you will all likewise perish"* (Luke 13:3). Repentance means that you agree with God that you are a sinner deserving His judgment, and that you first turn away from all you thought would earn you heaven; such repentance indicates a deep grief over personal sin and a desire to turn from wickedness (Jer. 8:6). Secondly, you must turn to something – that is you must believe the gospel message of Jesus Christ. To alleviate any confusion about what the gospel message actually is, the Lord Jesus Christ personally conveyed it to Paul: *"I delivered to you first of all that which I also received:*

251

that Christ died for our sins according to the Scriptures, and that He was buried, and that He rose again the third day according to the Scriptures" (1 Cor. 15:3-4). Believing any other gospel than this brings eternal damnation (Gal. 1:6-9).

So if by faith one believes and receives Christ for the forgiveness of his or her sins, he or she is then born again (spiritually; John 3:3; 1 Pet. 1:23) and becomes an adopted child of God (Rom. 8:15-16). Birth and adoption are acts which establish relationship; man's fellowship with God depends upon righteous behavior (1 Jn. 1:5-10). A continuation of godly behavior is now possible through the abiding presence and power of the Holy Spirit; if the believer chooses to walk according to revealed truth, his or her fellowship with God is unbroken. If one sins, fellowship is broken, but relationship is secured in Christ. As Christians confess their sins they are restored to full communion with God (1 Jn. 1:9).

The prophet Isaiah describes humanity as sheep which go their own way and get lost *"We like sheep have gone astray; We have turned, every one, to his own way"* (Isa. 53:6). Praise be to God that he comes seeking and calling to bring us back to Himself. What should be our response? Isaiah says *"Seek the Lord while He may be found, call upon Him while He is near* (Isa. 55:6). But, to seek the Lord one must repent (turn back from going his or her own way). Then, a seeking Savior and a seeking sinner will find each other – we find God when He finds us. Fortunately for us, God is seeking us out through the finished work of Christ and by the wooing ministry of the Holy Spirit to believe on Christ. God's offer for salvation is to whomsoever will respond (Matt. 11:28-30; Rev. 22:17). Why? Because He is *"not willing that any should perish but that all should come to repentance"* (2 Pet. 3:9).

Pascal's Wager

If at this point you're still a skeptic, I would ask you to consider the logic of Pascal's wager. Blaise Pascal (1623–1662) was a French physicist, mathematician and philosopher. He helped develop the barometer and pioneered hydrodynamics and fluid mechanics, which led to his discovery of "Pascal's Principle," the basis of hydraulics. He made invaluable contributions in the areas of probability and differential calculus, with the invention of Pascal's triangle for calculating the coefficients of a binomial expansion. If you are still not convinced that the message of Lord Jesus Christ is true, please consider the logic of one of the most brilliant men in the history of science – take "Pascal's Wager":

> How can anyone lose who chooses to become a Christian? If, when he dies, there turns out to be no God and his faith was in vain, he has lost nothing—in fact, he has been happier in life than his nonbelieving friends. If, however, there is a God and a heaven and hell, then he has gained heaven and his skeptical friends will have lost everything in hell![4]

Although it is impossible for someone to try on Christ to see if He fits into his or her lifestyle, or to embrace Him as some good-luck charm that will mystically bestow tranquility and affluence, I am convinced that, if you will open your mind to listen to God's calling and study the Bible, you will find Christ the most wonderful answer to all your problems, the chief of which is sin. By this I do not mean that your life will be filled with wealth, prosperity and lack of trial and difficulties, but rather you will know a joy and peace beyond these things. Solomon concisely summed up man's purpose on the Earth: *"Fear God and keep His commandments, for this is the whole duty of man"* (Eccl. 12:13).

When we obey the gospel message of Jesus Christ, God rewards us with Christ and all the riches that are in Him (Eph. 1:3). By God's mercy, the believer escapes hell, and by His grace, he or she inherits heaven and all that Christ has (Rev. 21:7). Will you not trust Christ for salvation and know the wonder of God? In this our search to find God ends, and our search to know God begins. The Lord Jesus Christ is both the beginning and the end of man's quest to uncover and believe the Truth! If you hear His pleading voice now, please don't harden your heart; trust the Lord Jesus Christ for the salvation of your soul. You will never regret it!

For God so loved the world that He gave His only begotten Son, that whoever believes in Him should not perish but have everlasting life. For God did not send His Son into the world to condemn the world, but that the world through Him might be saved. He who believes in Him is not condemned; but he who does not believe is condemned already, because he has not believed in the name of the only begotten Son of God (John 3:16-18).

Jesus said ..."I am the way, the truth, and the life. No one comes to the Father except through Me." (John 14:6).

Appendix I – Imperfect Logic

Deduction is the process of deriving the consequences of what is assumed, while *induction* is the process of inferring likely antecedents as a result of observed multiple consequences. Through deductive reasoning, the conclusion is necessitated by, or derived from, a stated premise. If the premise is accurate, the conclusion will be also. If the premise is false, deductive reasoning *may* lead to a false result, and an inconclusive premise will yield an inconclusive conclusion. As far as verifying God's existence, one cannot assume what one is trying to prove. How could derived deductive conclusions be shown to prove that the premise was in conflict with perceived natural law?

This form of reasoning, in relating to the supernatural, will become highly subjective as those who already *believe* in the supernatural will draw conclusions that comply with observed natural order, but supposed supernatural cause. On the contrary, those who do not believe in, or do not need to believe in, the supernatural will formulate conclusions which uphold observed natural law without supernatural cause. The former position results in a poor ontological argument (i.e., because I can conceptualize God, God must exist); this position doesn't prove anything. For example, if the premise was "God creates rain to sustain life on the Earth," those who assume that the premise is true will conclude "It is raining; therefore, God is sustaining life on the Earth." The naturalists, however, will conclude "It is raining; therefore, the hydrological cycle is still functional on the

Earth." Scientific knowledge offers a complete and satisfactory explanation for the observed rain; therefore, the premise of God's existence is not proven to be true, or false for that matter.

Consequently, creationists as well as the naturalist impose into the deductive process their personal belief systems when evaluating particular evidence – pure objectivity in science is unattainable. Sir Arthur Eddington recognized this tendency in scientists: "In science we sometimes have convictions which we cherish but cannot justify; we are influenced by some innate sense of the fitness of things."[1] Deductive reasoning cannot be used to prove or disprove God's existence.

In *abductive* and *inductive reasoning*, the premises may predict with a high probability a particular conclusion, but cannot absolutely ensure it to be true. *Abductive* reasoning is often used by those in the medical profession to diagnose potential ailments given a set of observed symptoms. It is the type of reasoning that infers causes from effects, or explanations from observations in order to determine the best explanations for a set of observations. As there may be a number of possible illnesses from any set of observed symptoms, a physician's task would be to narrow the field of possibilities to the most likely illness that the patient has. For example, a particular patient exhibits symptoms Y, and anybody with disease X shows symptoms Y; therefore, the patient has disease X. Abduction is the process of seeking the best explanations for a set of observations.

Abductive reasoning yields a good degree of accuracy but is problematic in that a conclusion may have been unduly forced from a premise, the observations may have been in error, the link between explanations and observations may have been incorrect, and information discovered in the future will show other and likely better explanations for the initial observations.

Likewise, in inductive reasoning, the premise may predict a conclusion with a high degree of probability, but cannot ensure it. Referring again to our medical illustration, a particular patient has disease X and exhibits symptoms Y; therefore, anyone with disease X will show symptoms Y. Obviously, this may not be true, but the more patients who have disease X and show symptoms Y, the more confidence in the conclusion is increased. It is inductive reasoning, especially in past centuries, that has been widely used by science to identify natural laws; unfortunately, these inductively derived conclusions can never be completely validated. The same reasons of error noted for abductive logic also hold true for inductive reasoning as well. At best, induction provides a refining process in which previous imperfect determinations are made more accurate over time, but never perfect. Here are three examples to stress this point.

Suppose the initial premises were "All boiling water will scald you," and, "This is boiling water." One may conclude by induction, and with a high degree of reliability based on past experience, the following: "This boiling water will scald my finger if I touch it." Although for millennia this conclusion seemed absolute, we now know that at lower pressure (say 0.1 atmospheres) water boils at a much lower temperature; it would feel like bath water to your touch – though you might need the assistance of an oxygen mask or a pressure suit to keep from passing out.

Another famous example of this point occurred in the 20th century. From analytical analysis, Einstein hypothesized that light rays passing through a strong gravitational field would be noticeably deflected from their normal path. Newtonian physics predicted no such effect, and the phenomena had never been observed. Later, advancements in technology allowed Eddington to confirm Einstein's theory of relativity in 1919, which consequently invalidated a portion of Newton's derived laws, though centuries of verification validated these to be accurate. Einstein's theory explained the behavior that Newton's theory explained, and in addition it explained some behavior that Newton's didn't. Einstein's work is a closer approximation of true reality than

Newton's understanding; no doubt Einstein's theories will undergo future refinements as well.

Charles Darwin's naturalistic theories rested heavily upon limited empirical results and inductive reasoning, but time has shown many of his conclusions to be in error. Why? Because he was missing critical information or chose to ignore available information in the fossil record. It would seem that no humanly derived logic system is without its flaws; each is either tainted with human supposition or famished by insufficient information. Consequently, to survive, man has had to devise innovative schemes of reasoning with imperfect logic.

From a humanistic standpoint, man exists upon the Earth because he contemplates available information, draws from past personal experience, assesses a reasonable probability of outcome, and by inductive reasoning renders a decision, which unfortunately, has a certain probability of being a wrong choice – humans make mistakes. Scottish philosopher David Hume was critical of induction as a justifiable scientific method of establishing natural law. However, he did concede that man was justified in reasoning inductively from instances of which he had experience to instances of which he had no experience, but asserted that there was no logical necessity that the future would resemble the past. For example, if man observed the sun rising every 24 hours for thousands of years, he is warranted in assuming that it will do so tomorrow even though a catastrophic event or a solar eclipse may void the predictability of the nature law. Hume concluded that daily induction was absolutely basic to our ideas of rational belief and rational action, but that there was no absolute certainty to any induction.

Hume postulated that man could know nothing about nature prior to experiencing it; hence, all that we say, think, or predict about nature must come from prior experience – this conclusion ensures the necessity of induction. Rather than pursuing unproductive *radical skepticism* about everything, Hume advocated a *practical skepticism* based on common sense, where the inevitability of induction is accepted (but not explained). In other words, life requires practical skepticism based on common sense, where the inevitability of induction is accepted.[2]

Karl Popper, a 20th century Austrian philosopher, accepted Hume's critique of induction (i.e. induction was not a pure scientific method of establishing natural law), but went even further to argue that induction is never actually used in science. What was Popper's point? Science has a long standing tradition of induction development going back to the days of Francis Bacon and Isaac Newton. In a nutshell, the process consisted of the unbiased accumulation of data which may lead to noticeable patterns, the scientist hypothesizes a new natural law, or perhaps a refinement to one previously determined, then sought to prove and refine the hypothesis by conducting further tests and the gathering of more evidence. If *all* the available evidence is conclusive, a new law of nature has been discovered in its infancy; if not, no law has been validated. Popper's objection to this method is that laws of nature cannot be fully validated without access to all knowledge.

Popper's challenge is illustrated with the statement, "All swans are white." He rightly claimed that no amount of observations affirming white swans could ensure that a black one would not be spotted in the future. In other words, the empirically developed theory that "all swans are white" could be shown to be flawed by a single authentic sighting of a black swan in the future. Popper concluded that scientific theories of universal form can never be conclusively verified; they can only be falsified. In other words, science can never fully discover truth; although there is such a thing as truth, it is a regulative notion which man strives to approach but can never reach.

Popper, therefore, promoted the idea that scientists should, when evaluating a theory, give greater credence to data which is in disagreement with the proposed theory than to data which supports it. Though advocating *falsifiability* as the criterion to properly delineate what science should be, Popper allows for the fact that, in practice, a single conflicting instance does not provide sufficient cause to falsify a theory and that scientific theories are often retained even though evidence is found which is in conflict with or inconsistent with them. Maintaining imperfect theories for further development is an acceptable and needful course of science. The *Stanford Encyclopedia of Philosophy* summarizes Karl Popper's position on the variability of scientific methodology:

> Scientific theories may, and do, arise genetically in many different ways, and the manner in which a particular scientist comes to formulate a particular theory may be of biographical interest, but it is of no consequence as far as the philosophy of science is concerned. Popper stresses in particular that there is no unique way, no single method such as induction, which functions as the route to scientific theory, a view which Einstein personally endorsed with his affirmation that "There is no logical path leading to [the highly universal laws of science]."[3]

Popper went one step further to state that a hypothesis which does not allow for experimental tests of falsity is outside the bounds of science; consequently, he viewed naturalism and the inductive theory of science as one and the same.

> A naturalistic methodology (sometimes called an "inductive theory of science") has its value, no doubt. ... I reject the naturalistic view: It is uncritical. Its upholders fail to notice that whenever they believe to have discovered a fact, they have only proposed a convention. Hence the convention is liable to turn into a dogma. This criticism of the naturalistic view applies not only to its criterion of meaning, but also to its idea of science, and consequently to its idea of scientific method.[4]

Though affirming many of Popper's ideas, utilitarian philosopher Peter Singer criticizes Popper's position of falsification as obscuring the role that induction has in scientific development by disguising it in steps of falsification.[5] His meaning is that the very method used to falsify a proposed theory is a form of induction itself. Even if a proposed theory was validated countless times, logically speaking it is unsafe to assume that the proposition would always yield a uniform result for all possible permutations of conditions and circumstances.

Because falsification itself is a form of induction and man does not know all things, it would be theoretically impossible to prove any scientific theory absolutely true or for that matter absolutely false. For this reason, contemporary science tends to regard hypotheses and theories as tentative, then *validation is done in continuing degrees of confidence* rather than absolutely true or false propositions. Consequently, inductive reasoning is very much used today in scientific research though it seems to be better balanced with deductive and abductive logic than in past centuries.

Appendix II – The Fossil Record

The following quotations by scientists (nearly all of which are naturalists) provide an overview of what is seen and not seen within the fossil record. The references are organized by various biological classifications and draw from a wide range of 20th century study. The overwhelming evidence in the fossil record does not support Darwin's naturalistic ideas – a fact that has not changed much in the last 150 years.

Plants

It has long been hoped that extinct plants will ultimately reveal some of the stages through which existing groups have passed during the course of their development, but it must be freely admitted that this aspiration has been fulfilled to a very slight extent, even though paleobotanical research has been in progress for more than one hundred years. As yet we have not been able to trace the phylogenetic history of a single group of modern plants from its beginning to the present.

> — Chester A. Arnold, *An Introduction to Paleobotany* (1947), p. 7.

Most botanists look to the fossil record as the source of enlightenment. But ... no such help has been discovered. There is no evidence of the ancestry [of plants].

> — E. J. H. Comer, *The Natural History of Palms* (1966), p. 254.

Nothing is more extraordinary in the history of the Vegetable Kingdom, as it seems to me, than the apparently very sudden or abrupt development of the higher plants.

> — Charles Darwin, in Francis Darwin (ed.), *The Life and Letters of Charles Darwin, Vol. 3.,* (1887) p. 248.

Again, just as in the case of the absence of pre-Cambrian fossils, no forms have ever been found in pre-Cretaceous rocks linking the angiosperms with any other group of plants. ... The ancestral group that gave rise to angiosperms has not yet been identified in the fossil record, and no living angiosperm points to such an ancestral alliance. In addition, the record has shed almost no light on relations between taxa at ordinal and family level.

> — M. Denton, *Evolution: A Theory in Crisis* (1985) pp. 163, 227, 230.

Invertebrates

[Anthozoa:] Any suggestion is welcome in the attempt to find some evolutionary scheme into which the corals may be fitted. [Echinoidea:] Their number [the unanswered questions] is a measure of our ignorance. [Brachiopods:] Such is the imperfection of the geological record of evolution. [Trilobite:] The Cambrian record ... reveals very little of the evolutionary paths they [the trilobites] followed. [Graptolithina:] The links in the supposed evolutionary chains are not so secure as was thought.

> — John Challinor, "Palaeontology and Evolution," *Darwin's Biological Work* (1959), pp. 80, 81, 82, 88, 87.

Yet the transition from spineless invertebrates to the first back-boned fishes is still shrouded in mystery, and many theories abound.

> — J. O. Long, *The Rise of Fishes* (Johns Hopkins University Press, Baltimore; 1995), p. 30.

Arthropods

"The origin of Arthropods is quite unknown."

> — V. B. Wigglesworth, *The Life of the Insect* (1984), p. 4.

One weakness in the traditional view [of common ancestry for all arthropods] is the lack of evidence for intermediate ancestral types, either as fossils or living forms. By no conceivable route could any one of the types of mandibles (jaws) found in crabs, insects, or king-crabs have 'evolved' from either of the other two.

> — Walter E. Lammerts, "Insect Family May Become a Forest," *Creation Research Society Quarterly* (September 1974), pp. 124-125.

Insects

The fossil record does not give any information on the origin of insects.

> — *Encyclopedia Britannica,* Vol. 7, p. 585 (Macropaedia; 1978 ed.).

Insect wings appear in the fossil record, from the first, fully formed. No evolution, no intermediate forms are found, any more than transitional forms between orders of insects, such as grasshoppers, bees, or damsel flies, are found. Insects have always been numerous and varied; they retain as many types in the present. They do not demonstrate plasticity .... There is no clue from the fossil record as to the origin of the iridescent wings of a dragonfly or the flight of the bee. A leap of faith is needed to believe in the evolution of an eye, a feather, an insect wing or any other special organ.

> — Michael Pitman, *Adam and Evolution* (1984), p. 227.

By and large, the insect population of today remains remarkably similar to that of the earlier age. All the major orders of insects now living were represented in the ancient Oligocene forest. Some of the specific types have persisted throughout the 70 million years since then with little or no change.

> — C. T. Brues, "Insects in Amber," *Scientific American,* Vol. 185, (November 1951), p. 80.

The Trilobites, Paleozoic Arthropods known only from fossils, could have been ancestors [of insects], a belief based on their combination of general structure; but there is no actual proof or even good evidence that they were.

> — A.B. and E.B. Mots, *1001 Questions Answered about Insects* (1961), p. 7.

There are vast gaps in the fossil record covering millions of years, and when we go beyond the Carboniferous period which began about 300 million years ago, the trail [of insect origins] fades completely.... Insect origins beyond that point [the Carboniferous] are shrouded in mystery. It might almost seem that the insects had suddenly appeared on the scene, but this is not in agreement with accepted [evolutionary] ideas of animal origins.

> — A.E. Hutchins, *Insects* (1988), pp. 3, 4.

Over ten thousand fossil species of insect have been identified, over thirty thousand species of spiders, and similar numbers for many sea-living creatures. Yet so far the evidence for step-by-step changes leading to major evolutionary transitions looks extremely thin. The supposed transition from wingless to winged insects still has to be found, as has the transition between the two main types of winged insects, the paleoptera (mayflies, dragonflies) and the neoptera (ordinary flies, beetles, ants, bees).

> — Fred Hoyle, *The Intelligent Universe* (1983), p. 43.

We are in the dark concerning the origin of insects.

> — Pierre-P. Grasse, *Evolution of Living Organisms* (1977), p. 30.

There is, however, no fossil evidence bearing on the question of insect origin; the eldest insects known show no transition to other arthropods.

> — Frank M. Carpenter, "Fossil Insects," *Yearbook of Agriculture: Insects* (1952), p. 18.

Mollusks

Strange as it may seem ... mollusks were mollusks just as unmistakably as they are now.

> — *Austin H. Clark, The New Evolution, Zoogenesis* (1930), p. 101.

The horseshoe crab ... has existed on earth virtually unchanged for 200 million years.

> — James Gorman, "The Tortoise or the Ham?" *Discover*, (Oct. 1980), p. 89.

Brachiopods

It must be significant that nearly all the evolutionary stories I learned as a student ... have now been 'debunked'. Similarly, my own experience of more than twenty years looking for evolutionary lineages among the Mesozoic Brachiopoda has proved them equally elusive.

> — Fred Hoyle, *The Intelligent Universe: A New View of Creation and Evolution* (1978), pp. 131, 132.

Vertebrates

Fossil remains, however, give no information on the origin of the vertebrates.

> — *Encyclopedia Britannica, Vol. 7, p. 587* (Macropaedia; 1976 ed.).

On the other hand, they [vertebrates] are pretty well diversified on this first appearance.

> — James R. Beerbower, *Search for the Past* (1968), *p. 487.*

The gap remains unbridged and the best place to start the evolution of the vertebrates is in the imagination.

> — H. Smith, *From Fish to Philosopher* (1953), p. 28.

Fish

Fish jump into the fossil record seemingly from nowhere: mysteriously, suddenly, fully formed.

> — Francis Hitching, *The Neck of the Giraffe* (1982), p. 20.

To our knowledge, no 'link' connected this new beast to any previous form of life. Fish just appeared.

> — *Marvels and Mysteries of Our Animal World* (1984), p. 25.

[The 100 million year gap between fish and the ancestors they are supposed to be descended from] will probably never be filled.

> — F.D. Ommanney, *The Fishes* (1984), p. 80.

The geological record has provided no evidence as to the origin of fishes.

> — J. Norman, *A History of Fishes* (1963), p. 298.

Tetrapods

To me one of the most astonishing consequences of the furor over statistics is the realization that the current account of tetrapod evolution, shown in a thousand diagrams and every-where acknowledged as the centerpiece of historical biology, is a will-o'-the-wisp. For nowhere can one find a clear statement of how and why the recent groups are interrelated, and the text-book stories are replete with phantoms extinct, uncharacteriz-able groups giving rise one to another.

> — W. Patterson, *Book Review, in Systematic Zoology* (1980), Vol. 29, p. 26.

There are no intermediate forms between finned and limbed creatures in the fossil collections of the world.

> — G.T. Taylor, *Great Evolution Mystery* (1983), p. 80.

Reptiles

One of the frustrating features of the fossil record of vertebrate history is that it shows so little about the evolution of reptiles during their earliest days, when the shelled egg was developing.

> — Archie Cart, *The Reptiles* (1983), p. 37.

[Regarding snakes:] Their family tree is still adorned with question marks rather than branches.

> — C. Pope, *The Great Snakes* (1981), p. 184.

There is no direct proof from the fossil record [regarding the reptile], but we can readily hypothesize the conditions under which it came about.

> — R. Stirton, *Time, Lice and Man* (1957), p. 416.

Amphibians

About 350 million years ago, a number of archaic and now extinct groups of amphibia make their appearance as fossils. However, each group is distinct and isolated at its first appearance, and no group can be construed as being the ancestor of any other amphibian group.

> — Michael Denton, *Evolution: A Theory in Crisis* (1985), p. 184.

The lack of fossil specimens intermediate between anurans or unodeles and the older amphibians has forced paleontologists and students of the living animals to base their speculations about the evolution of the group upon evidence from the anatomy and embryology of modern species. This approach so far proved insurmountable. The structure of the existing amphibians is so specialized that the more generalized condition from which it derived is almost completely obscured.

— B. Stahl, *Vertebrate History: Problems in Evolution* (1973), pp. 240-241.

It is generally presumed that amphibia evolved from fish and even the order of fish, the *Rhipidistia,* has been specified. However, transitional forms are lacking. The first amphibian had well developed fore- and hindlimbs of normal tetrapod type which were fully capable of supporting terrestrial motion.

— Michael Denton, *Evolution: A Theory in Crisis* (1985), p. 168.

Birds

[Concerning the theory that warm-blooded birds came from cold-blooded reptiles:] This stands out today as one of the greatest puzzles of evolution ... [birds have] all the unsatisfactory characteristics of absolute creation.

— Lecomte du Nouy, *Human Destiny* (1947), p. 72.

The transition from reptiles to birds is more poorly documented.

— G. Ledyard Stebbins, *Processes of Organic Evolution* (1971), p. 146.

No fossil of any such birdlike reptile has yet been found.

— *World Book Encyclopedia, Vol. 2,* (1982 ed.), p. 291.

The origin of birds is largely a matter of deduction. There is no fossil evidence of the stages through which the remarkable change from reptile to bird was achieved.

> — W.E. Swinton, in A.J. Marshall (ed.), *Biology and Comparative Physiology of Birds* (1960), Vol. I, p. 1.

Mammals

Fossils, unfortunately, reveal very little about the creatures which we consider the first true mammals.

> — Richard Carrington, *The Mammals* (1963), p. 37.

This is true of all the thirty-two orders of mammals .... The earliest and most primitive known members of every order already have the basic ordinal characters, and in no case is an approximately continuous sequence from one order to another known. In most cases the break is so sharp and the gap so large that the origin of the order is speculative and much disputed.

> — George Gaylord Simpson, *Tempo and Mode in Evolution* (1944), p. 105.

These mammals must have had an ancient origin, for no intermediate forms are apparent in the fossil record between the whales and the ancestral Cretaceous placentals. Like the bats, the whales (using the term in a general and inclusive sense) appear suddenly in early Tertiary times, fully adapted by profound modifications of the basic mammalian structure to a highly specialized mode of life. Indeed, the whales are even more isolated with relation to other mammals than the bats; they stand quite alone.

> — E. H. Calbert, *Evolution of the Vertebrates* (1955), p. 303.

Man

No fossil or other physical evidence directly connects man to ape.

> — John Gliedman, "Miracle Mutations,"
> *Science Digest* (February 1982), p. 90.

Even this relatively recent history [of evolution from apes to man] is shot through with uncertainties; authorities are often at odds, both about fundamentals and about details.

> — Theodosius Dobzhansky, *Mankind Evolving* (1965), p. 168.

[Summarizing the genetic data from humans] Even with DNA sequence data, we have no direct access to the processes of evolution, so objective reconstruction of the vanished past can be achieved only by creative imagination.

> — N. A. Takahata, "Genetic Perspective on the Origin and History of Humans," *Annual Review of Ecology and Systematics* (Vol. 26, 1995), p. 343.

A number of naturalists representing a variety of scientific disciplines have concluded that the fossil record generally does not support the theory of evolution. This admission was published in the March 29, 1982 edition of *Newsweek*; the cover story was entitled "Mysteries of Evolution":

> ... a professional embarrassment for the paleontologists: their ability to find the fossils of transitional forms between species, the so-called "missing link." Darwin, and most of those who followed him, believed that the work of evolution was slow, gradual and continuous and that a complete lineage of ancestors, shading imperceptibly one into the next, could in theory be reconstructed for all living animals. In practice, Darwin conceded, the fossil re-

cord was much too spotty to demonstrate those gradual changes, though he was confident that they would eventually turn up. But a century of digging since then has only made their absence more glaring. Paleontologists have devoted whole careers to looking for examples of gradual transitions over time, and with a few exceptions they have failed.

— Mysteries of Evolution, *Newsweek* (March 29, 1982)

Appendix III – Biblical Metaphors

In concert with the narrative in Scripture, God applies a variety of symbols to convey a consistent meaning to man. The following list provides a few examples of numbers, colors, materials, animals, etc., which are commonly employed throughout the Bible. The consistent use of so many metaphors in a text penned by dozens of men over a 1600 year period is evidence that the Bible was God-breathed – it came from one divine source.

Metals/Materials

Gold – Purity, Holiness, Righteousness: e.g., tabernacle and temple furniture in Holy Places (Rev. 3:18).

Silver – Redemption: e.g., Jesus betrayed for 30 pieces of silver – *"the price of blood"* (Matt. 27:6), and Gomer was redeemed with 15 pieces of silver + 1.5 homers of barley (Hos. 3:2).

Bronze – Judgment: e.g., tabernacle and temple furniture in courtyard (Ex. 27:2), and feet of the Lord Jesus at His second advent (Rev. 1:15).

Wood – Humanity: e.g., Noah's ark, the golden altar of incense, and the Ark of Covenant had gold over wood (Ex. 25:10).

Numbers

Each number, from one through forty, is used symbolically in the Bible; here are just a few examples.

One – Unity (Eph. 4:4-6; 1 Cor. 10:16-17).

Four – Earthly order: God's created order – four winds, four directions, four corners, four phases of the moon, four seasons, and four places creatures dwell (upon, above, and beneath the earth and in the sea).

Six – Man's number: Man was created on the sixth day of creation (Gen. 1:24-31), was to labor on six days of the week (Ex. 9:10), and the mark of the beast is 666 (Rev. 13:18).

Seven – God's number: In the creation story (Gen. 1 - 2), we read seven times *"And God said,"* and *"it was good."* Enoch, a man who walked with God, was the 7th in Adam's line through Seth (Gen. 5). God sanctified the 7th day, 7th year and the year following the 7×7th year (Lev. 25:8-12).

Twelve – Governmental perfection: The number twelve indicates completeness of a government or administration, usually divinely appointed. In the Old Testament the number twelve is often used as the signature of the nation of Israel (12 tribes). In the New Testament twelve is used to show the complete administration of the Church (12 apostles).

Thirteen – Rebellion: First mentioned when five kings rebelled (Gen. 14:4); 13 years of silence after Abraham doubted God's promise and fathered Ishmael – God then reminded Abraham of his covenant 13 times (Gen. 17). Satan/Dragon is spoken of 13 times in Revelation. 13 judges during the time when *"every man did what was right in their own eyes"* (Judg. 17:6). Haman's plot to destroy the Jews on the 13th day of the month (Est. 3:13).

Twenty-four – The Priesthood: David distributed the various roles of the priesthood among the twenty-four descendants of Aaron, the first Levitical High Priest (through Aaron's sons Eleazar and Ithamar, see 1 Chronicles 24:1-8). In John's vision of heaven, twenty-four elders are sitting on thrones in heaven about God's throne; these represent redeemed souls which God has made to be kings and priests in His presence (Rev. 4:4, 5:9-10).

Animals/Man
Lion – King: Gospel of Matthew
Ox – Servant: Gospel of Mark
Man – Humanity: Gospel of Luke
Eagle – Deity: Gospel of John
  Note: Throughout the entire Bible the faces of the cherubim (each cherub has four faces), the seraphim, and the four living creatures are described having these four faces, thus reflecting the before mentioned four glories of Christ.

Colors
White – Purity, Righteousness (Rev. 1:14, 6:11, 19:8)
Red – War, Bloodshed (Rev. 6:3-4)
Scarlet – Humility/service (Ps. 22:6 – the *tola* worm was smashed to yield a scarlet, *tolaath*, colored dye).
Black – Death, Sin (Rev. 6:5-6; Job 3:5; Isa. 45:7)
Blue – Heaven (Num. 40)
Purple – Royalty (Mark 15:17)

Miscellaneous
Fire – Judgment (Gen. 19:24, 22:6; Lev. 10:2; Num. 16:35; Matt. 3:11, 13:39-40, 25:41)
Sword/Knife – Judgment (Gen. 22:6; Rev. 1:16, 19:15)
Stars – Angels or Messengers (Rev. 1:20, 9:1, 12:4)
Lampstand – A Testimony (Rev. 1:20, 2:5; Matt. 5:13-16)
Rainbow – God's Promises (Gen. 9:13; Rev. 4:3)
Eyes – Seeing (Ezek. 1:18; Rev. 5:6; 1 Pet. 3:12; Ps. 33:18)
Circle/Ring – Eternity or Security (Ezek. 1:16-18; Rev. 4:3; Gen. 41:42; Est. 8:2, 8)
Mountain – Kingdom (Dan. 2:44-45; Zech. 6:1; Rev. 17:9)
Horn – Power (Gen. 22:12; Dan. 7:8, 24; Rev. 17:12)
Head – Authority (Dan. 7:6, 17; Rev. 13:1-5, 17:9-10)
Dragon – Satan (Rev. 12:9)
Earth – Israel (Matt. 13:44; Rev. 13:11, 14:3-4)

Sea – The Nations (Matt. 13:47; Rev. 13:1, 17:1, 15)

Barley – Redemption (Ruth 1:22, 2:8-10; Lev. 23:9-14; Hos. 3:2)

Wheat – Blessings of Resurrection Life (Ruth 2:23; Lev. 23:15-22; Matt. 13:24-25, 38; John 12:24)

Appendix IV – Prophecies of Christ's First Advent

The following five tables are organized by subject matter and contain first advent prophecies of Christ as referenced in the Old Testament (first column) and their New Testament fulfillment (a "/" separates O.T. and N.T. references in the second column of each table). The third column provides a brief explanation of the fulfilled prophecy and assesses a statistical probability of fulfillment by chance where possible (e.g. 1:x chances).

Genealogical Prophecies	Reference	Probability of Fulfillment by Chance
Messiah to come through Noah. Noah was a just man who walked with God; he found grace in the sight of God and God established His covenant with Noah prior to the flood.	Gen. 5:8,18/ Luke 3:36	Nine generations from Adam to Noah (over one thousand years). Average number of sons per generation at this time = 4.4 (Adam had at least 3 sons – one died {Abel} apparently without having children, while the early descendants of Adam had a number of children, no specifics are given. Noah had 3 sons; Shem had 5 sons; Ham had 4 sons; and Japheth had 7 sons). The estimated number of male descendents of Adam after ten generations = 2(Adam) x 3 (Noah) x 4.4^8 (unknown, average is assumed) = 280,964; these are potential male descendants of Adam when God confirmed Noah in the messianic line.

Through Noah's son Shem	Gen. 9:25-27/ Luke 3:36	Noah had 3 sons (Shem, Japheth, Ham). 1:3
Seed of Abraham	Gen. 10:21-31; 11:11-26; 12:3/ Matt. 1:1; Gal. 3:8, 16; Heb. 6:14	Ten generations (four and a half centuries) from Shem to Abraham. Average number of sons per generation during this time period = 4.8 (Noah had 3 sons; Shem had 5 sons; Ham had 4 sons; Japheth had 7 sons; Gomer had 3 sons; Javan had 4 sons; Cush had 5 sons; Raamah had 2 sons; Aram had 4 sons; Joktan had 13 sons; and Terah had 3 sons). The estimated number of male descendents of Shem after ten generations = 3 (Noah) x 5 (Shem) x 3 (Terah) x 4.8 [7] (unknown, average is assumed) = 281,793; these are potential male descendants of Shem when God chose Abram (Abraham).
Seed of Isaac	Gen. 17:19; 21:12/ Rom. 9:7; Heb. 11:18	Isaac (named prior to birth) was the second of eight sons of Abraham. 1:8
A star out of Jacob	Num. 24:17-19/ Matt. 2:2; Luke 1:33, 78; Rev. 22:16	Isaac had two sons (Esau & Jacob). Jacob confirmed before birth (Gen. 25:23). 1:2
Of the tribe of Judah	Gen. 49:10/ Rev. 5:5	Judah one of 12 tribes. 1:12
Firstborn set apart for God	Ex. 13:2/ Luke 2:23	Firstborn or 2nd, 3rd, 4th, or 5th born. 1:5
Out of Jesse	Isa. 11:1; Gen. 38:24-30, 46; 1 Chron. 2:9-24/ Matt. 1:6	Ten generations (nearly 6 centuries) from Judah to Jesse. Average number of sons per generation at this time = 5.2 (Judah had 5 sons – two died without children; Perez had 2 sons; Zerah had 5 sons; Hezron had 6 sons; and Jesse had 8 sons). The estimated number of male descendents of Judah after ten generations = 3 (Judah) x 2

Out of Jesse (cont.)		(Perez) x 6 (Hezron) x 5.2[7] (unknown, average applied) = 3,701,058 potential male descendants of Judah when God chose Jesse.
Seed of David	Ps. 89:3-4, 19, 27-29, 35-37, 132:11; 2 Sam. 7:12-16, 25-29/ Matt. 1:1; Luke 1:32; Acts 2:30, 13:23; Rom. 1:3; 2 Tim. 2:8	Jesse had eight sons – David was chosen. 1:8
Descendant of Zerubbabel	Hag. 2:23/ Luke 3:27-31	Luke lists 22 generations from David to Zerubbabel. Six sons were born to David in Hebron (2 Sam. 3:2-5) and eleven more in Jerusalem (2 Sam. 5:14-16). From Nathan to Zerubbabel, it is assumed that there was an average of four sons per generation. 1:7.48 x 10^{13}
Messiah would not be a descendant of Jeconiah (Messiah would not come through royal line of Solomon).	Jer. 22:20-30/ Matt. 1:11; Luke 3:31	Jechoniah was cursed for wickedness – the curse passed down to his generations. Consequently Jesus Christ was a descendant of David through Nathan and not of the royal line through Solomon to avoid the curse. Descendant of Solomon or not. 1:2

Probability of chance fulfillment of genealogical prophecies from Adam to Zerubbabel. It is noted that nearly all Jewish genealogies were lost after 70 AD, meaning that **the Messiah that the Jews are waiting for cannot be validated**.

Total probability of fulfillment is one in 1.100 x 10^{36} chances.

Geographic Prophecy	OT/ NT Reference	Probability of Fulfillment by Chance
Would live in Galilee	Isa. 9:1/ Matt. 2:22	Reside in one of three regions of Israel: Galilee, Samaria, or Judea. 1:3
Would be called a "Branch" (Hebrew = Netzer, Greek = Nazareth)	Isa. 11:1/ Matt. 2:23; Luke 4:16	Live in Nazareth, or in one of some one hundred other towns in Galilee.[1] 1:100
Journey into Egypt	Hos. 11:1/ Matt. 2:15	To escape Herod's wrath – escape to Egypt or to other foreign regions/ countries nearby. 1:12
Born in Bethlehem of Ephratah	Micah 5:1-5/ Matt. 2:1; Luke 2:4, 10-11	Jews had settled throughout the Roman Empire (e.g. One million Jews were living in Alexandria, Egypt.). There were approximately 12,000 town/cities in Roman Empire at the time Christ was born. Scripture names the exact county and city to eliminate confusion of Messiah's birth place (The population of Bethlehem at Christ's birth was less than a thousand – Micah said it would be a "little" town, as compared to Jerusalem which had a population of approximately 250,000).[2] 1:12,000
Triumphal entry into Jerusalem	Zech. 9:9-10/ Matt. 21:4-5; Mark 11:9-10; Luke 19:38; John 12:13-15	Triumphal entry into Jerusalem (public presentation of Messiah to the Jews at Jerusalem) or not. 1:2
Sin Offerings were burnt on top of the ashes of the Burnt Offering (in a clean place outside the camp).	Lev. 4:12; 6:11/ Matt. 27:33; Heb. 13:12; John 19:20, 41	Christ, as a sin offering, was crucified and buried (same location) outside city walls (symbolically apart from Judaism), but near the city. Judged in the city or outside the city. 1:2

Probability of chance fulfillment of geographic prophecies:
Total probability of fulfillment is one in 172,800,000 chances.

Time Prophecy	OT Reference	Probability of Fulfillment by Chance
Time of His death "Messiah cut off"	Dan. 9:24-27	Both the starting point and the ending point of Daniel's prophecy are fixed. There would be 69 groups of seven years or 173,880 days (69 years x 7 x 360 days/Jewish year = 173,880 days) from the command of Artaxerxes Longimanus to Nehemiah to rebuild the wall about Jerusalem (March 14, 445 BC) until Messiah's final presentation in Jerusalem (April 6, 32 AD) and subsequent death shortly after.[3] Note: this date will vary proportionally to the chronology used to date the rebuilding command.
The temple would still be standing at Christ's first coming to offer peace, and it would be the second temple built, not the first temple. (Solomon's temple was destroyed prior to the Haggai prophecy.)	Ps. 118:26; Hag. 2:6-9	Christ's presentation would happen after the second temple was built in 516 BC, but prior to its destruction in 70 AD. **The Jews are looking for a Messiah that cannot fulfill this prophecy.**
Sudden appearance in the temple during the time of the forerunner.	Mal. 3:1/ John 2:13-15	Christ to suddenly (unexpectedly) visit the temple during the ministry of John the Baptist or not. 1:2

Though the Jews are still looking for the Messiah, it seems pertinent to constrain the probability evaluation to a span of years from the building of the second temple until its destruction. Approximately 584 years x 365.25 days/year = 213,306 days possible as compared with the Daniel's exact prediction of Messiah's presentation.

Total probability of fulfillment is one in 426,612 chances.

Miscellaneous Prophecies	OT Reference	Probability of Fulfillment by Chance
Seed of the woman*	Gen. 3:15/ Gal. 4:4; Heb. 2:14.	Natural birth or sudden divine appearance in flesh. 1:2
Blessing to Gentiles also	Gen. 22:18, 26:4/ Acts 3:25-26; Gal. 3:8, 16; Heb. 6:14	Blessing (i.e. words, miracles, salvation) to Gentiles or Jews only. 1:2
No bone broken	Ex. 12:46; Num. 9:12; Ps. 34:20/ John 19:36	No bone broken or any number of bones broken. 1:2
Cursed on the tree	Deut. 21:23/ Gal. 3:13	Hung upon a tree, or put to death by stoning, the sword, or mob action. Note: The Jews stoned; they did not put criminals to death on trees. 1:4
Be plotted against by Jews and Gentiles together	Ps. 2:1-2/ Acts 4:25-28	Be plotted against by Jews and Gentiles together or Jews only or Gentiles only. 1:3
Adored by infants	Ps. 8:2/ Matt. 19:13-14; 21:15-16	Children adored Him or not. 1:2
His resurrection; body would not decay in the grave*	Ps. 16:8-10; 49:15; Isa. 25:6-12/ Mark 16:6; Acts 2:27; 13:35; 26:23; 1 Cor. 15:54	Raised from the dead or not. 1:2
Hands and feet pierced	Ps. 22:1-31/ Matt. 27:31, 35	Hands pierced, or feet, or both, or neither. 1:4
Would say from cross "My God, my God, why have You forsaken Me?"	Ps. 22:1/ Mark 15:34	Said the statement or not. 1:2
Time of darkness	Ps. 22:2; Amos 8:9/ Matt. 27:45	Though day, a time of darkness or not. 1:2
Mocked and insulted	Ps. 22:7-8/ Matt. 27:39-43, 45	Mocked or not mocked. 1:2
Scoffers to mock: "He trusted in God, let Him deliver Him"	Ps. 22:8; Ps. 31:14-15/ Matt. 27:43	Scoffers spoke these words or not. 1:2

Be thirsty during execution	Ps. 22:15/ John 19:28	Thirsty during His execution or not. 1:2
Stripped of clothes	Ps. 22:18/ Luke 23:34	Stripped naked before men or not. 1:2
Soldiers cast lots for outer coat	Ps. 22:18/ Matt. 27:35; Mark 15:24	Cast lots for, divide it, fight for it, or ranking soldier obtains it. 1:4
Soldiers divided inner garment	Ps. 22:18/ Matt. 27:35; Mark 15:24	Cast lots for, or divide garment. 1:2
Committed Himself to God before dying	Ps. 22:20-21/ Luke 23:46	Committed His spirit unto the Father before dying or not. 1:2
Accused by false witnesses	Ps. 27:12; 35:11/ Matt. 26:60-61; Mark 14:57-58	Accused by false witnesses or one witness or no witnesses. 1:3
Hated without a cause	Ps. 35:19, 69:4; Isa. 49:7/ John 15:24-25	Hated with or without cause. 1:2
Friends stand afar off	Ps. 38:11/ Matt. 27:55; Mark 15:40; Luke 23:49	Friends near, afar off, or complete desertion. 1:3
Betrayed by a friend	Ps. 41:9, 55:12-14/ Matt. 26:14-16, 47, 50; Mark 14:17-21; Luke 22:21-22; John 13:18-19	Betrayed by a friend (Judas), or a spy, or a Jewish zealot, or a random witness. 1:4
Betrayer would die without repenting to God	Ps. 55:13-15/ Matt. 27:3-5; Acts 1:16-19	Judas repents of his betrayal before dying or not. 1:2
His ascension into heaven	Ps. 68:18/ Acts 1:9; Eph. 4:8	Ascended to heaven or stayed on Earth. 1:2
Zeal in the house of God (sudden temple entrance)	Ps. 69:9; Mal. 3:1/ Matt. 21:12-13; John 2:17	Sudden and zealous action in temple or not. 1:2
Given gall (a narcotic – a pain killer) to taste	Ps. 69:21/ Matt. 27:34; Mark 15:23	Tasted (but did not internalize) the gall or not. 1:2
Given vinegar to drink	Ps. 69:21/ Matt. 27:48; John 19:29	Drank vinegar or not. 1:2
Spoke in parables	Ps. 78:2/ Matt. 13:34-35	Spoke in parables or not. 1:2

Prays for His enemies	Ps. 109:4/ Luke 23:34	Prayed for His enemies or not. 1:2
Repentance for the nations	Isa. 2:2-4/ Luke 24:47	Repentance for Jews only or offered to all. 1:2
Jews to have hardened hearts towards Christ	Isa. 6:9-10, 52:13-53:12/ Matt. 13:14-15; John 1:11, 12:39-40	Jews received Christ, or hardened their hearts and rejected Him. 1:2
Born of a virgin*	Isa. 7:14/ Matt. 1:22-23	Virgin birth or not. 1:2
To be sought by Gentiles	Isa. 11:10, 42:1/ Acts 10:45	Christ sought after by Gentiles or not. 1:2
The deaf shall hear*	Isa. 29:18/ Matt. 11:5; Mark 7:32, 37	Jesus healed the deaf or not. 1:2
The blind shall see*	Isa. 29:18/ Matt. 11:5; John 9:1-7	Jesus gave sight to blind or not. 1:2
Healing for the needy*	Isa. 35:4-10/ Matt. 9:30; 11:5; 12:22; 20:34; 21:14; Mark 7:30; John 5:9	Jesus healed those in need or not. 1:2
Would have a forerunner to make ready the way of the Lord	Isa. 40:3-5; Mal. 3:1/ Matt. 3:3; 11:10-14; Mark 1:2-3; Luke 3:4-5; 7:27; John 1:23	John the Baptist preceded Christ's coming to prepare the way or not. 1:2
The Redeemer to first come as a teacher, not a ruler	Isa. 48:17/ John 3:2	Christ came as a teacher or not. 1:2
Messiah was first to be a servant from the womb, not to be served.	Isa. 49:5/ Matt. 20:28	Messiah came as a servant of others or to be king over them. 1:2
The forerunner would have the spirit of Elijah.	Mal. 4:5-6/ Matt. 17:11-13	Did John the baptizer's ministry, as the forerunner of Messiah typify that of Elijah – did he preach national repentance? Yes or No. 1:2
Scourged	Isa. 50:6/ Matt. 27:26; Mark 15:15; John 19:1	Scourged or not. 1:2

Be beaten, struck in the face.	Isa. 50:6; Micah 5:1/ Matt. 26:67, 27:30	Beaten (buffeted) – struck in the face or not? 1:2
Spat upon	Isa. 50:6/ Matt. 26:67; 27:30; Mark 14:65; 15:19	Spat on or not. 1:2
Christ to be God's Servant	Isa. 52:13/ Matt. 12:11-18, 17:5; Phil. 2:5-8	Christ affirmed as God's Servant or not. 1:2
Silent when accused	Isa. 53:7/ Mark 14:61; John 19:9	Defended Himself at His trial or not. 1:2
Judged with those deserving death	Isa. 53:9, 12/ Matt. 27:38; Luke 23:33	Put to death alone, with one other, with more than one transgressor. 1:3
Buried with the rich	Isa. 53:9/ Matt. 27:57-60	Buried in a rich man's tomb, discarded the body, buried in potter's field, or just buried in family tomb. 1:4
No deceit in His mouth	Isa. 53:9/ John 18:33-38	He answered all questions truthfully at His trial or not. 1:2
Called those not His people	Isa. 55:4-5/ Rom. 9:25-26; Eph. 2:11-19	An offer of salvation to the Gentiles or not. 1:2
The Redeemer shall come to Zion to do His work	Isa. 59:16-20/ Rom. 11:26-27	Entered Jerusalem or not. 1:2
Massacre of infants	Jer. 31:15/ Matt. 2:17-18	Infants would be murdered at Christ's coming or not. 1:2
He would visit the second temple	Hag. 2:6-9/ Luke 2:27-32	Messiah would visit Solomon's temple or the second temple (which Herod refurbished). 1:2
Triumphal entry into Jerusalem on a colt the foal of a donkey	Zech. 9:9-10/ Matt. 21:4-5; Mark 11:2-10; Luke 19:35; John 12:13-15	Enter Jerusalem in a cart, while riding a horse, or a camel, or a donkey, or a colt of a donkey, or His disciples carried Him or He walked. 1:6
Jews would shout and rejoice at Messiah's entry into Jerusalem	Zech. 9:9-10/ Matt. 21:9; Mark 11:9-10; John 12:13-15	There was no crowd, or the crowds that gathered rejected Messiah, or the crowds rejoiced and shouted praises. 1:3

Sold for thirty pieces of silver	Zech. 11:12-13/ Matt. 26:14-15	Sold for 30 pieces of silver (a slave's price), or any amount of silver from 10 to 50 pieces, or any amount of gold pieces from 5 to 20 or Roman coinage from 10 to 30. 1:78
Betrayal money cast down in the temple	Zech. 11:12/ Matt. 27:3-5	Judas returned the betrayal money to the temple or he didn't. 1:2
Betrayal money used to buy potter's field	Zech. 11:12-13/ Matt. 27:9-10	Betrayal money used to buy a potter's field, or put back in temple treasury, or for private use by Pharisees, or given to poor. 1:4
Piercing of His body	Zech. 12:10/ John 19:34, 37	Body pierced or not. 1:2
Shepherd smitten, and sheep scattered	Zech. 13:1, 7/ Matt. 26:31; John 16:32	Messiah had to die or not, and disciples stayed near to Christ or scatter, if put to death. 1:4
Christ's forerunner would turn many to righteousness	Mal. 4:6/ Luke 1:16-17	Christ's forerunner's ministry turned many to righteousness or not. 1:2
Probability of chance fulfillment of miscellaneous prophecies: One chance in 6.56 x 10^{22}		

* The probability of these events, naturally speaking, is impossible – a extremely conservative probability of 1:2 (fulfilled by Christ or not) was ascribed. The reader is challenged to determine a fair likelihood of such events coming to pass by chance.

Other Fulfilled Prophecies	OT/NT Reference
Bruise Satan's Head	Gen. 3:15/ John 12:31-32; Heb. 2:14
Viewed as a serpent on a pole	Num. 21:9/ John 3:14-18
A great Prophet	Deut. 18:15-19/ John 6:14; 7:40; Acts 3:22-23, 7:37
Cursed on the tree	Deut. 21:23/ Gal. 3:13
Kinsman Redeemer	Ruth 4:4-9/ Eph. 1:3-7
A promised Redeemer	Job 19:25-27/ Gal. 4:4-5; Eph. 1:7, 11, 14
Declared to be the Son of God	Ps. 2:1-12; Prov. 30:4; Isa. 9:6/ Matt. 3:17; Mark 1:11; Luke 1:32, 13:33; Heb. 1:5, 5:5
Forsaken of God	Ps. 22:1/ Matt. 27:46
The Good Shepherd	Ps. 23; Ezek. 34:23-24/ John 10:11
Commends His spirit to the Father	Ps. 31:5/ Luke 23:46
"I come to do Thy will"	Ps. 40:6-8/ Heb. 10:5-9
Preached righteousness to Israel	Ps. 40:9/ Matt. 4:17; 5:20, 6:33
Known for righteousness	Ps. 45:2, 6-7/ Heb. 1:8-9
Eternal	Ps. 45:6-7/ Heb. 1:8-12; 13:8
Anointed by the Holy Spirit	Ps. 45:7/ Matt. 3:16; Heb. 1:9
The reproaches of men toward God fell on Christ	Ps. 69:9/ Rom. 15:3
Hated without a cause	Ps. 69:4/ John 15:25
"My soul is exceedingly sorrowful"	Ps. 69:20/ Matt. 26:38
Exalted by God	Ps. 72:1-19/ Matt. 2:2; Phil. 2:9-11; Heb. 1:8
A priest like Melchizedek	Ps. 110:1-7/ Heb. 5:6; 6:20; 7:21; 8:1; 10:11-13
Ascend to the right-hand of the Father	Ps. 110:1/ Mark 16:19; Heb. 1:3
The chief cornerstone rejected	Ps. 118:22-23/ Matt. 21:42; Mark 12:10-11; Luke 20:17; John 1:11; Acts 4:11; Eph. 2:20; 1 Pet. 2:4-8
The King comes in the name of the Lord	Ps. 118:26/ Matt. 21:9; 23:39; Mark 11:9; Luke 13:35; 19:38; John 12:13
A rock of offense to Jews	Isa. 8:14-15/ Rom. 9:33; 1 Pet. 2:8

A great Light to the nations	Isa. 9:1-2/ Matt. 4:14-16; Luke 2:32; John 8:12
God with us	Isa. 9:6-7/ Matt. 1:21, 23; John 10:30; 2 Cor. 5:19; Col. 2:9
Full of wisdom and power	Isa. 11:2/ Matt. 3:16; John 3:34; Rom. 15:12; Heb. 1:9
A meek Servant	Isa. 42:1-9/ Matt. 12:17-21; Luke 2:32
Vicarious sacrifice	Isa. 53:5/ Rom. 5:6, 8
Born a King	Jer. 30:9/ John 18:37; Rev. 1:5
Made a New Covenant with Israel (Gentiles are a second benefactor)	Jer. 31:31-34/ Matt. 26:27-29; Mark 14:22-24; Luke 22:15-20; 1 Cor. 11:25; Heb. 8:8-12; 10:15-17; 12:24; 13:20

Prophecy, uniformity and authenticity are unique facets of the Bible, but perhaps the most amazing mystery of all is its influence on those who read it (Heb. 4:12).

It is impossible to rightly govern the world without God and the Bible.

— George Washington

The New Testament is the very best book that ever was or ever will be known in the world.

— Charles Dickens

I believe the Bible is the best gift God has ever given to man. All the good from the Saviour of the world is communicated to us through this book.

— Abraham Lincoln

It is impossible to mentally or socially enslave a Bible-reading people. The principles of the Bible are the groundwork of human freedom.

— Horace Greeley

Appendix V - Christ's Miracles in Review

What is the value of Christ's miracles? Their testimony stands in strong contrast to the false miracles used to bolster support for false religions. The existence of these phony miracles does not cast doubt on the validity of Christ's miracles, rather they support the fact. Since false religions are deliberately propped up by false miracles, a pure religion (biblical Christianity) will not rely on false miracles. In evaluating the value of the testimony of Christ's miracles, remember that there is no counter testimony in any religion. Secular historians like Josephus acknowledged Christ's wonderful works. The unbelieving Jews admitted the same but attributed His miracles to Satan. What was the Lord Jesus' response to their accusations and disbelief? Satan would never effect the overthrowing of his own kingdom.

The word "miracle" is not found in Matthew's Gospel; rather, the miracles that the Lord performed are referred to as "signs." Signs of what? His miracles were *"signs of the times"* (Matt. 16:3) and were a direct fulfillment of Old Testament prophecy (Isa. 29:18-19; 35:4-6). The signs witnessed by Israel were irrefutable evidence proving that Christ was who He claimed to be – the Messiah. Both the Lord's preaching and His signs composed the kingdom message to the Jews. His miracles were not simply exhibitions of power or manifestations of God's grace, they were sermons in action; in this way, His miracles supplemented His preaching in an *evidential* manner. For this reason, Israel was the primary beneficiary of Christ's miracles, but on at least two occasions His miracles directly benefited Gentiles, while profiting on-looking Jews as well (Matt. 8:5-13).

The Lord often appealed to His teaching and miracles as credible evidence to the nation of Israel that He was the Christ. *"And Jesus went about all the cities and villages, teaching in their synagogues, preaching the gospel of the kingdom, and healing every sickness, and every disease among the people" (Matt. 9:35).* While in prison, John the Baptist's faith wavered concerning the Messiahship of Jesus. What was the Lord's response when John's disciples conveyed John's doubts about Him being the Messiah? *"Go and tell John the things which you hear and see: The blind see and the lame walk; the lepers are cleansed and the deaf hear; the dead are raised up and the poor have the gospel preached to them" (Matt. 11:4-5).* John was exhorted to examine the evidence – Jesus' miracles and message proved He was the Messiah.

Peter declared the following to the nation of Israel at the feast of Pentecost: *"Men of Israel, hear these words: Jesus of Nazareth, a Man attested by God to you by miracles, wonders, and signs which God did through Him in your midst, as you yourselves also know" (Acts 2:22).* Peter emphatically proclaimed that the miracles which Christ did were undeniably of God and a sign to Israel that Scripture had been fulfilled – Jesus Christ, whom they crucified was indeed their promised Messiah.

Only a fraction of Christ's performed miracles were written down for our appreciation (John 20:30-31; 21:25). Mark notes, *"For He healed many, so that as many as had afflictions pressed about Him to touch Him" (Mark 3:10).* The following is a summary of the miracles that were recorded:

Miracles of Physical Healing
Included are healings of fever (2), blindness (4), hemorrhage (1), dropsy (1), leprosy (2), paralysis (4), deaf-mute (1), and severed body parts (1).

Miracles of Resurrection

It is worthy to note that only three resurrections were recorded in the Old Testament; Elijah and Elisha accomplished these. The Lord raised three people from the dead during His ministry on earth, then effected His own resurrection also (John 10:17-18). The Lord Jesus was the seventh and, thus, the perfect resurrection of the Bible.

Miracles Related to Demon Possession

It is recorded seven different times that the Lord drove out demons from the host they possessed. In each case, being freed from demon possession brought emotional and physical healing.

Miracles Related to Earthly Physics

Besides miracles that brought personal healing, the Lord Jesus performed supernatural feats to demonstrate His power over creation. Twice, He calmed a raging storm by a simple command. Water became His sidewalk for crossing the Sea of Galilee and for Peter's brief excursion as well. Directly after this event, the Lord instantaneously moved their boat a great distance across the sea to arrive at Capernaum.

Miracles Related to Plant and Animal Life

Though the Lord had no tax liability, He graciously agreed to pay taxes so as to not stumble the unsaved. For this reason, and for this purpose only, Peter received the money via the mouth of a fish. On two different occasions, the Lord commanded fishermen to drop their nets for a great catch of fish. Near the end of the Lord's ministry, to demonstrate His disgust for fruitless Israel, He cursed a fig tree. The disciples noted the next day that it was completely withered.

Miracles Related to Food and Drink

On two different occasions, the Lord took a few fish and loaves of bread and multiplied them to feed thousands of people.

In so doing, He demonstrated that He was the Master of quantity. The Lord's first miracle, turning water into the best wine, confirmed Him to be the Master of quality. He is both willing and able to share all that He has and the best that He has with those who will trust Him.

God provided miracles ("signs") as a warning to the nation of Israel of forthcoming judgment if they did not repent (e.g. the hearing of strange tongues was God's warning sign: Deut. 28:49; Jer. 5:15; Isa. 28:11-12) and to affirm that Jesus Christ was the fulfillment of Old Testament prophecies – He was the promised divine Messiah.

Appendix VI – More Testimony of Divine Providence

As stated previously, I began a journal to record on an ongoing basis all the wonderful ways my wife and I have providentially seen the Lord's handywork. Here are two more accounts of God's providential care in the unusual circumstances involved in selling property.

The House on Lanterne Drive

In 1991, my wife and I were involved in starting a new local church. The location required us to drive a good distance from our home on Lanterne Drive; therefore, we made a decision to sell our house and move closer to where the believers regularly gathered. The house went on the market October 1, 1992. We committed the matter to the Lord in prayer and asked Him to sell our home for us without a realtor. Consecutive ads were placed in a local newspaper, and the Lord blessed us with a number of showings and a few second showings, but each opportunity fizzled out.

For months, we had been holding a Bible study in our home on Monday evenings. Several were in attendance, including one unsaved man named John, our neighbor across the street. In mid November, it became obvious that the timing for selling our house was not right; I told my wife Brenda, "I don't think the Lord wants us to move until John professes Christ as Savior." She agreed. We promptly took the house off the market and did no more advertising. Thankfully, John did profess Christ as Savior on December 14th.

On December 15th, we received a telephone call from a local woman, "I have an old newspaper which advertised that your house was for sale. Is your house still for sale? We really desire to move to your area." The answer was, "Yes, our house is for sale." The couple came over that very evening, looked over the house, and signed a contract shortly thereafter. The Lord graciously sold our home, for our asking price, without it being advertised, the day after John professed Christ as Savior.

The House on Kelley Road

After much prayer, it was determined in the spring of 2003 that we would work with another family to start another new church meeting in northwestern Wisconsin. We felt the timing of the move was imminent but knew the Lord's timing to be the best, so we committed the entire matter of selling our farmette to the Lord in prayer. To know the Lord's timing and will in this matter, we decided again not to use a realtor. Please understand, we are not opposed to using realtors, but wanted God to affirm our plans and the timing of them by controlling the sale of our home with minimal effort on our part. Consequently, we only listed the property on a single "for sale by owner" website for a short time.

Within a few days, we had a number of calls and emails inquiring about the property and also several showings. One young unmarried couple from Chicago made an appointment with us for a Tuesday afternoon showing, but they did not show up for it. We received a call from the man two days later apologizing for not coming or calling. He said "Sorry we didn't come; we had a baby Tuesday. But we really want to see the house – could we drive out on Saturday?" I said, "Will the new mother feel up to such an outing by Saturday?" He said, "No problem, she really wants to see the place, too." So the appointment was set.

I told Brenda not to even clean the house because this lead was going nowhere – a poor young couple living with two other families in an apartment on the south side of Chicago. What a long shot! The couple did arrive on Saturday, and after inspecting the farmette, the man said. "We want to buy it." Thinking I would just end the whole matter promptly and not waste anymore time, I inquired, "Have you been approved for financing?" The man offhandedly responded, "No, we will be paying cash for it." He must have seen my dumbfound expression, so he explained, "My fiancée just came into a legal settlement last week, and we will be using that to pay for the property." "Very well, cash is fine!" I said and continued, "We are asking $ _____ for the property." He said, "We will take it." I thought to myself – a cash deal and no negotiation, this sounds too good to be true.

"We are asking $ _____ for the tractor, implements, and feeders," I continued. He instantly responded, "We will take that, too." The man's mother had accompanied the couple to the showing. While we were talking about the details of the contract, she counseled the young couple, "You guys have no furniture. Maybe these good people would sell you some of theirs." This was another answer to prayer because the house we planned to move into in Wisconsin was a good bit smaller than the one for sale and we did not have enough room for all our stuff; we were purposely downsizing. In the end, we sold the young couple our china hutch, an end table, a coffee table, a couch, a loveseat, a padded chair, two lamps, a washer, a dryer, and a refrigerator. Not only did we not have room for these things, but I didn't have to move any of them, and my wife got all new appliances in the Wisconsin home.

There was only one other matter that the Lord needed to attend to, that was for our elderly dog Daisy. She had been on the farmette since she was a pup and had enjoyed free reign of the entire property. We didn't have the heart to move her to Wisconsin and constrain her final days of life in a kennel. After explaining this to the couple offering to buy our home, the young woman knelt down, kissed our dog on the nose and said, "Leave her here, I love her!" The other details of the contract were: immediate possession and no contingencies (besides well and septic inspections). After the young couple drove away, Brenda and I just looked at each other; we both found it hard to speak, but then in unison, we just smiled and said, "Praise the Lord." Only six weeks after listing our home, we were living in Wisconsin – the Lord's timing had been confirmed by His providential care!

Endnotes

Preface

1. Charles Darwin, *The Origin of Species* (Oxford University Press, Oxford, England; 1996, org. 1859), p. 5

Within Reason

1. Edythe Draper, *Draper's Quotations from the Christian World* (Tyndale House Publishers Inc., Wheaton, IL – electronic copy)
2. http://homepages.tcp.co.uk/%7Ecarling/god&bb1.html
3. Richard Dawkins, *Science and Christian Belief* (Vol. 7; 1994), p. 47
4. Todd, Scott C., "A View from Kansas on the Evolution Debates," *Nature* (Vol. 401, September 30, 1999), p. 423
5. Steven D. Schafersman, "Naturalism is an Essential Part of Science and Critical Inquiry" (Second revision, May, 1997, of the paper originally presented at the Conference on Naturalism, Theism and the Scientific Enterprise, sponsored by the Department of Philosophy, The University of Texas, Austin, TX (February 20-23, 1997)
6. Robert T. Pennock, "Naturalism, Theism and the Scientific Enterprise" (March 20-23, 1997 Conference at University of Texas at Austin)
7. Barbara Forrest, "Methodological Naturalism and Philosophical Naturalism: Clarifying the Connect" *Philo* (Vol. 3, No. 2; Fall-Winter 2000), pp.7-29
8. Guillermo Gonzalez and Jay Richards, *The Privileged Planet* (Regnery Publishing, Washington, DC; 2004), p. 337
9. *Philosophical Dictionary* (1764), quoted from Jonathon Green, *The Cassell Dictionary of Cynical Quotations.*
10. *Skeptical Essays* (1928)
11. http://www.philosophyofreligion.info/atheistquotes.html
12. Ibid.
13. Henry Morris, *Men of Science Men of God* (Master Books; 1988)
14. Bertrand Arthur Russell, *Why I Am Not a Christian* (Haideman-Julius Co. KS; 1929)
15. http://www.quotationspage.com/quotes/Bertrand_Russell

Within Reason (cont.)
16. P. L. Tan, *Encyclopedia of 7700 Illustrations* (Bible Communications, Garland, TX; 1996, 1979); "Atheism"
17. http://richarddawkins.net/quotes
18. http://www.tentmaker.org/Quotes/atheismqu-otes.html
19. *The Privileged Planet* DVD (Illustra Media; August 2004)
20. Duane Litfin, *The Bible Knowledge Commentary* (Victor Books, Wheaton, IL; 1983), p. 733
21. Edythe Draper, op. cit.; "reasoning"

Have You Lost Your Mind?
1. Edythe Draper, op. cit.; "Christianity"
2. Ibid.
3. John Hagerman, "Who Do You Want to Be Today?" (*Realty Times*; January 26, 2007):
   http://realtytimes.com/rtapages/20050302_whoyoube.htm
4. http://en.wikipedia.org/wiki/Universe
5. P. L. Tan, op. cit.
6. http://www.tentmaker.org/Quotes/atheismquotes.html

#1 The Uniqueness of the Earth
1. *The Privileged Planet* DVD, op. cit.
2. Guillermo Gonzalez and Jay Richards, op. cit., p. 147
3. "Astronomers Ponder Lack of Planets in Globular Cluster," *Space Telescope Science Institute;* http://oposite.stsci.edu/pubinfo/PR/2000/33/index.html
4. http://www.godandscience.org/apologetics/problifebad.html
5. Guillermo Gonzalez and Jay Richards, op. cit., p. 133
6. Ibid., p. 114
7. Ibid., p. 133
8. Ibid., p. 130
9. Ibid., p. 66
10. Ibid., p. 204
11. Ibid., p. 59
12. Ibid., p. 107
13. Ibid., p. 58
14. Ibid., p. 57
15. http://www.godandscience.org/apologetics/designs.html
16. Guillermo Gonzalez and Jay Richards, op. cit., p. 38
17 http://www.answersingenesis.org/home/Area/isd/boudreaux.asp
18. Guillermo Gonzalez and Jay Richards, op. cit., p. 137

#1 The Uniqueness of the Earth (cont.)

19. *The Privileged Planet* DVD, op. cit.
20. http://www.seds.org/messier/more/mw.html
21. S. W. Hawking, *A Brief History of Time* (Bantam Books, New York, NY; 1988), p. 123
22. Paul Davies, *Other Worlds* (Dent, London, England; 1980), pp. 160-161
23. Ibid., pp. 168-169
24. Hugh Ross, *Big Bang Refined by Fire* (Reasons To Believe, Pasadena, CA; 1998),
    http://www.godandscience.org/apologetics/probabilitieslife.html
25. J. Glanz, American Physical Society Meeting: "Hawking Blesses the Accelerating Universe" (*Science*; 1999), 284: pp. 34-35
26. R. Penrose, "An analysis of the structure of space-time." *Adams Prize Essay*, Cambridge University. Hawking, S.W. (1966). "Singularities and the Geometry of space-time." *Adams Prize Essay*, Cambridge University. S. W. Hawking and G.F.R. Ellis. (1968). The cosmic black-body radiation and the existence of singularities in our universe. *Astrophysical Journal* 152: 25-36
    Hawking, S.W. and R. Penrose. "The singularities of gravitational collapse and cosmology." *Proceedings of the Royal Society of London*. (1970); Series A: 529-548
27. P. L. Tan, op. cit.
28. Benjamin Wiker and Jonathan Witt, *A Meaningful World* (IVP Academic, Downers Grove, IL; 2006), pp. 179-180
29. Ibid., p. 180
30. Guillermo Gonzalez and Jay Richards, op. cit., p. 16
31. Ibid., p. 125
32. Edythe Draper, op. cit.; "creation"

#2 The Testimony of Nature

1. http://www.tentmaker.org/Quotes/atheismquotes.htm
2. Edythe Draper, op. cit.; "atheist"
3. C. S. Lewis, *God in the Dock* (Eerdmans Publishing Co., Grand Rapids, MI; 1970), pp. 52-53
4. G. A. Kerhut, *Implications of Evolution* (Pergamon, Oxford, UK; 1960), p. 157
5. http://news.nationalgeographic.com/news/2006/08/060810-evolution.html
6. http://news.bbc.co.uk/1/hi/sci/tech/4648598.stm
7. Jonathan Sarfati, *Refuting Evolution* (Master Books, Green Forest, AR, 1999), p. 127

Testimony of Physics and Chemistry

1. Dr. Walter Brown, *In the Beginning: Compelling Evidence for Creation and the Flood* - 7th edition (Online version at http://www.creationscience.com/onlinebook; 2006), First Law of Thermodynamics

2. David Hume to John Stewart (February, 1754), in *The Letters of David Hume*, 2 Vols., ed. J. Y. T. Greig (Oxford, England, Clarendon Press; 1932), I:187

3. Bertrand Arthur Russell, op. cit., "The First-Cause Argument"

4. W. J. Federer, *Great Quotations: A Collection of Passages, Phrases, and Quotations Influencing Early and Modern World History Referenced according to their Sources in Literature, Memoirs, Letters, Governmental Documents, Speeches, Charters, Court Decisions and Constitutions.* (AmeriSearch, St. Louis, MO; 2001), "Thomas Aquinas"

5. Dr. Jay. L. Wile, *Exploring Creation With Chemistry* (Apologia Educational Ministries, BookCrafters USA, inc., Chelsea, MI; 1998), p. 464

6. Ibid., p. 470

7. Neil Broom, *How Blind Is the Watchmaker?*, (InterVarsity Press; 2nd edition; 2001), p. 80

8. http://www.godandscience.org/evolution/index.html

9. Dr. Walter Brown, op. cit., *Chemical Elements of Life*

10. http://www.answersingenesis.org/home/area/isd/marcus.asp

11. Fred Hoyle and Chandra Wickramasinghe, "Where Microbes Boldly Went," (*New Scientist* 91; 1981), pp. 412-415

12. L. Orgel, "The Origin of Life on Earth" *Scientific American* (1994) 271 (4) p. 81. Note: Dr. L. Orgel is an atheist who has been working on origins of life research for over 30 years.

13. Rich Deem, http://www.godandscience.org/evolution/chemlife.html

14. L. Orgel, op. cit.

15. Ibid.

16. Ibid.

17. Ibid.

18. Ibid., p. 82

19. H. Bortman, "Life Under Bombardment" (NASA Astrobiology Institute; 2001 and H. Ohmoto, Y. Watanabe, H. Ikemi, S.R. Poulson, B.E. Taylor. 2006. "Sulphur Isotope Evidence for an Oxic Archaean Atmosphere" *Nature* (2006) 442:873-874

20. R. Shapiro, "The Prebiotic Role of Adenine: A Critical Analysis" *Origins of Life and Evolution of the Biosphere* (1995) 25:83-98

21. Rich Deem, http://www.godandscience.org/evolution/chemlife.html

Testimony of Physics and Chemistry (cont.)

22. R. Shapiro, "Prebiotic Cytosine Synthesis: A critical analysis and implications for the origin of life." (*Proc. Natl. Acad. Science USA*; 1999), 96:4396-4401

23. P. Monnard, C. L. Apel, A. Kanavarioti and D. W. Deamer, "Influence of ionic solutes on self-assembly and polymerization processes related to early forms of life: Implications for a prebiotic aqueous medium" (*Astrobiology*: 2002), 2:213-219

24. E. Szathmáry, 2000. "The Evolution of Replicators" *Philosophical Transactions: Biological Sciences* (2000) 355: pp. 1669-1676

25. L. P. Knauth, "Life on Land in the Precambrian and the Marine vs. Non-Marine Setting of Early Evolution" (*First Astrobiology Science Conference,* April 3-5, 2000, NASA Ames Research Center), 403 and L. P. Knauth, "Early Oceans: Cradles of Life or Death Traps?" (*Astrobiology Science Conference 2002*; April 7-11, 2002, NASA Ames Research Center), p. 9

26. C. Chyba, and C. Sagan, "Endogenous production, exogenous delivery and impact-shock synthesis of organic molecules: an inventory for the origins of life." *Nature* (1992), 355: pp. 125-132

27. http://www.godandscience.org/evolution/chemlife.html

28. G. Vogel, "A sulfurous start for protein synthesis?" *Science* (1998), 281: pp. 627-628

29. G. L. Schroeder, *Genesis And The Big Bang* (Bantam Books, NY; 1992), p. 25

30. L. Orgel, "The origin of life – a review of facts and speculations." *Trends in Biochemical Sciences* (1998), 23: pp. 494-495

31. S. A. Benner, "Old views of ancient events" (*Science*; 1999), 283:2026

32. Sir Fred Hoyle, "The Universe: Past and Present Reflections" *Review of Astronomy and Astrophysics* (1982), 20: p. 16

33. Frank Tipler, *Physics of Immortality* (Doubleday, New York, NY; 1994), Preface

34. Scott M. Huse, *The Collapse of Evolution* (Baker Bookhouse, Grand Rapids, MI; 1983), p. 94

35. P. L. Tan, op. cit., "Evolution"

36. Johnjoe McFadden *Quantum Evolution,* (W. W. Norton & Company; New York, NY; 2000), p. 85

The Testimony of Fossils

1. Charles Darwin, *The Origin of Species, Part Two* (1902), pp. 83, 88, 91, 92

The Testimony of Fossils (cont.)

2. Keith B. Miller, *Perspectives on an Evolving Creation* (Eerdmans Pub. Co., Grand Rapids, MI; 2003), p. 153
3. Jeffrey H. Schwartz, *Sudden Origins* (John Wiley, New York; 1999), p.89
4. http://evolution-facts.org/Evolution-handbook/E-H-12a.htm
5. David M. Raup, *Conflicts Between Darwin and Paleontology* (Field Museum of Natural History Bulletin, Vol. 50, No. 1, January 1979), pp. 23, 25
6. Stephen Jay Gould, "The Evolution of Life," chapter 1 in Evolution: Facts and Fallacies, ed. by J. William Schopf (San Diego, CA., Academic Press, 1999), p. 9
7. http://www.answersingenesis.org/creation/v23/i1/howold.asp
8. http://www.answersingenesis.org/home/area/feedback/2006/0303.asp
9. http://www.answersingenesis.org/creation/v23/i1/howold.asp
10. Jonathan Sarfati, op. cit., p. 112
11. Dr. Walter Brown, op. cit., *Shells on Mountains*
12. Rupke, N.A. "Prolegomena to a Study of Cataclysmal Sedimentation," *Why Not Creation?*, ed. Walter E. Lammerts (Baker, Grand Rapids, MI; 1973), p. 154
13. http://www.globalclassroom.org/antarct3.html
14. "Instant Petrified Wood," *Organic Geochemistry* (1984) 6: pp. 463-471
15. Austin, S. A. and J. D. Morris, *Proceedings of the First International Conference on Creationism*, vol. II, Creation Science Fellowship (1986), Pittsburgh, PA, pp. 3-15
16. http://www.answersingenesis.org/home/area/feedback/2006/0303.asp
17. H. Enoch, *Evolution or Creation*, (1966), p. 139

The Testimony of Astronomy, Biology, and Anthropology

1. Dr. Walter Brown, op. cit., *Strange Planets*
2. Ibid., *Faint Young Sun*
3. Ibid., *Missing Mass*
4. Ibid., *Hot Planets*
5. http://evolution-facts.org/Evolution-handbook/E-H-4a.htm
6. http://www.answersingenesis.org/creation/v26/i4/mercury.asp
7. S. R. Taylor, *Destiny or Chance: Our Solar System and Its Place in the Cosmos* (Cambridge University Press, Cambridge, England; 1998), p. 163
8. http://www.answersingenesis.org/Home/Area/bios/d_faulkner.asp

The Testimony of Astronomy and Biology (cont.)

9. http://www.answersingenesis.org/tj/v15/i2/oort.asp
10. C. Sagan, and A. Druyan, *Comets* (Random House, New York, NY; 1985), p 201
11. http://www.answersingenesis.org/docs/4005.asp
12. http://www.answersingenesis.org/creation/v25/i3/galaxies.asp
13. Hugh Ross, *The Creator and the Cosmos* (Nav. Press, Colorado Springs, CO; 2001)
14. http://www.answersingenesis.org/home/area/re2/chapter5.asp
15. Lee Spetner, *Not By Chance* (Judaica Press; Brooklyn, NY; 1997), pp. 131, 138
16. Ray Bohlin, *Creation, Evolution, and Modern Science* (Kregel Publications; Grand Rapids, MI; 2000), p. 41
17. Niles Eldredge, *Time Frames: The Rethinking of Darwinian Evolution and the Theory of Punctuated Equilibria,* (1985), p. 33
18. H. Enoch, *Evolution or Creation* (Evangelical Press; 1966; 1972), p. 139
19. *Charles Darwin, My Life and Letters – Origin of the Species* (#1/27 Origin of the Species Unknown / #2/13 The Experts Are Puzzled)
20. G.R. Taylor, *Great Evolution Mystery* (Secker & Warburg; 1983), p. 141
21. Jim Holt. "Science Resurrects God," *The Wall Street Journal* (Dow Jones & Co., Inc.; Dec. 24, 1997)
22. http://www.talkorigins.org/indexcc/CB/CB400.html
23. http://www.drdino.com/articles.php?spec=7
24. http://www.answersingenesis.org/creation/v23/i3/people.asp
25. Seth Borenstein, "Fossils Challenge Old Evolution Theory," (*Associated Press*, Washington, D.C.; August 9, 2007).
26. http://evolution-facts.org/Evolution-handbook/E-H-4b.html
27. Paul Davies, *The 5th Miracle: The Search for the Origin and Meaning of Life* (Simon & Schuster; 2000), p. 18
28. Michael Denton, *Evolution: A Theory in Crisis* (Adler & Adler, Chevy Case, MD; 1986), p. 77
29. Bertrand Russell, "WA?" *Look* (1953), p. 582
30. Cornelia Dean, "Scientists Speak Up on Mix of God and Science" *New York Times* (August 23, 2005)
31. Paul Davies, *The Edge of Infinity: Beyond the Black Hole* (Penguin, USA; 1995)

Nature Demands a Creator

1. Isaac Newton, *Optics* (1705); John Bartlett, *Bartlett's Familiar Quotations* (Little, Brown and Company, Boston, MA; 1855, 1980), p. 313
2. http://richarddawkins.net/quotes

Nature Demands a Creator (cont.)

3. Bertrand Arthur Russell, op. cit., "Defects in Christ's Teachings"
4. P. L. Tan, op. cit., "Evolution," quoting from *Christianity Today,* #1460,
5. Charles Singer, *A Short History of Science to the Nineteenth Century* (Clarendon Press; 1941).
6. P. L. Tan, op. cit., "No Body Made It," by W. G. Polack, #1467
7. http://www.talkorigins.org/indexcc/CA/CA602_2.html
8. http://www.talkorigins.org/indexcc/CA/CA602.html
9. John P. Koster, Jr., *The Atheist Syndrome* (Wolgemuth & Hyatt Pub., Brentwood TN; 1989), p. 87
10. Ibid., p. 63
11. Ibid., p. 82
12. Ibid., p. 83
13. Ibid., p. 91
14. Ibid., p. 100
15. Ibid., p. 107
16. Ibid., p. 110
17. Ibid., p. 118
18. Ibid., p. 12
19. http://www.aap.org/family/tv1.htm

#3 The Authenticity of the Bible

1. http://www.jesus-is-savior.com/False%20Religions/Atheism/famous_quotes_by_atheists.html
2. http://www.kids4truth.com/authBible_files/frame.html
3. Ibid.
4. Ibid.
5. Sharon Morad Leeds, summary of *The Origins of the Quran: Classic Essays on Islam's Holy Book,* Ibn Warraq, ed. (Prometheus Books, 1998) *http://www.angelfire.com/or/don9840/Quran.html*
6. *Documentary History of the Church* 4:461, June 11, 1843 quoted in Daniel Ludlow, ed. *Latter-day Prophets Speak* (Bookcraft, Logan, UT; 1988)
7. Norman L. Geisler and William E. Nix, *A General Introduction to the Bible* (Moody Press, Chicago, IL; 1968), p. 151
8. Ron Rhodes, *The Complete Book of Bible Answers* (Harvest House Publisher; 1997)
9. *The American Heritage Dictionary* (Houghton Mifflin Company, Boston, MA; 1978)
10. P. L. Tan, op. cit., "Bible and Archaeological Testings," #391
11. Ibid.

#4 The Uniformity of the Bible

1. C. I. Scofield, *Scofield Study Bible* (Oxford University Press, NY; 1967), p. 328, note 1
2. Bertrand Arthur Russell, op. cit., "Defects in Christ's Teachings"
3. Arthur Pink, *Why Four Gospels?* (Scripture Truth Book Co., Fincastle, VA; no date), pp. 109-110
4. P. L. Tan, op. cit., "How Ramsay Was Convinced," #392
5. http://www.tentmaker.org/Quotes/atheismquotes.htm

#5 The Prophecy of the Bible

1. http://www.thebereancall.org/Newsletter/html/1991/dec91.php
2. Bertrand Arthur Russell, op. cit., "Natural Law Argument"
3. *The World Book Encyclopedia*. Vol. 6. (Chicago: World Book Inc.; 2001), "Earth"
4. Smith, Peter J. *The Earth* (Macmillan Company, New York, NY: 1986)
5. http://pages.prodigy.net/jhonig/bignum/qauniver.html
6. http://en.wikipedia.org/wiki/Orders_of_magnitude_%28mass%29
7. Nigel Reynolds, "Tiny Tablet provides proof for Old Testament," (Telegraph.co.uk; July 13, 2007), http://www.telegraph.co.uk/news/main.jhtml?xml=/news/2007/07/11/ntablet111.xml
8. William MacDonald, *Believer's Bible Commentary* (Thomas Nelson Publishers, Nashville, TN; 1989), p. 2103

#6 The Human Conscience

1. Manuel Velasquez, Claire Andre, Thomas Shanks, S.J., and Michael J. Meyer, "Ethical Relativism" (*Issues in Ethics*, Vol. 5 No. 2; Summer 1992), http://www.scu.edu/ethics/practicing/decision/ethicalrelativism.html
2. C. S. Lewis, *Mere Christianity* (Macmillan Pub. Co., New York, NY; 1952), p. 5
3. Ayn Rand, *For the New Intellectual* (New American Library, NY; 1961), p. 17
4. http://quotes.zaadz.com
5. http://www.wacklepedia.com/e/et/ethics_1.html
6. Ibid.
7. http://drbeetle.homestead.com/sixth.html
8. Elizabeth Malone & Zina Deretsky (National Science Foundation; http://www.nsf.gov/news/special_reports/tsunami/index_low.jsp?id=preparing
9. Charles Darwin, *Origin of Species,* Encyclopedia Britannica Great Books ed; (Chp. 8), p. 119

#6 The Human Conscience (cont.)
10. Jerome Kagan, *Three Seductive Ideas* (Harvard University Press, Cambridge, MA; 1998)
11. R. A. Shweder, "Humans Really Are Different" *Science* (1999), 283: p. 798
12. Edythe Draper, op. cit.; "Conscience"
13. Ibid.
14. P. L. Tan, op. cit., "Pirate Confesses Hardening Conscience," #806
15. Bertrand Arthur Russell, op. cit., "The Moral Arguments for Deity"
16. http://www.tentmaker.org/Quotes/atheismquotes.htm
17. Ibid.
18. http://www.berith.org/essays/br/br04.html
19. http://en.wikipedia.org/wiki/Bertrand_Russell
20. http://www.berith.org/essays/br/br04.html
21. Bertrand Russell, *Conquest of Happiness* (1930), Chp. 9

#7 The Human Spirit's Need
1. http://www.philosophyofreligion.info/atheistquotes.html
2. Carl Sagan, *Cosmos* (Random House, New York, NY; 1980), p. 4
3. Ibid., p. 345

#8 The Inflammatory Name of Jesus
1. Franklin Graham, *The Name* (Thomas Nelson, Nashville, TN; 2002)
2. *The Works of Josephus – The Antiquities of the Jews* (Hendrickson Publishers, Peabody, MA; 1987), 18.3.3, p. 480
3. Ibid., 20.9.1, p. 538
4. John P. Koster, Jr., op. cit., p. 61
5. Tacitus, Annals 15.44, cited by Lee Strobel, *The Case for Christ*, (Zondervan Publishing House, Grand Rapids, MI; 1998), p. 82
6. Pliny, Letters, transl. by William Melmoth and W.M. Hutchinson (Harvard Univ. Press, Cambridge, MA; 1935), vol. II, X: 96, cited in Habermas, *The Historical Jesus*, p. 199
7. Lucian, "The Death of Peregrine," 11-13, in The *Works of Lucian of Samosata*, transl. by H.W. Fowler and F.G. Fowler, 4 vols. (Clarendon, Oxford, England; 1949), vol. 4., cited in Habermas, *The Historical Jesus*, p. 206
8. John P. Koster, Jr., op. cit., p. 61
9. David Bercot, *A Dictionary of Early Christian Beliefs* (Hendrickson Publishers, Peabody, MA; 1998), p. 558
10. Ibid.

#9 Miracles

1. W. E. Vine, *Vine's Expository Dictionary of Biblical Words* (Thomas Nelson Publishers; 1985)
2. Michael Levine, "Miracles" – *Stanford Encyclopedia of Philosophy* (Metaphysics Research Lab; 2005), http://plato.stanford.edu/entries/miracles/#Mir
3. Ibid.
4. W. J. Federer, op. cit., quoting Thomas Aquinas
5. Michael Levine, op. cit.
6. David Hume, *Enquiry Concerning Human Understanding*, edited by Tom L. Beauchamp (Oxford University Press, New York; 1999), p. 115
7. Ibid., p. 114
8. Michael Levine, op. cit.
9. A. R. Fausset, "Miracles" – *Fausset's Bible Dictionary* (Biblesoft, Electronic Database; 1998)
10. Ibid.
11. C. S. Lewis, "Miracles" op. cit. p. 216
12. Ibid.
13. Art Lindsley, "C. S. Lewis on Miracles" (*C. S. Lewis Institute*; 2004); http://www.cslewisinstitute.org/pages/resources/publications/knowingDo ing/2004/Miracles.pdf
14. Thomas Aquinas, quoted by Nancy Gibbs, "The Message of Miracles" *Time* (New York, NY; April 10, 1995), Vol. 145, No. 15, p. 68
15. http://www.thebereancall.org/Newsletter/html/1997/mar97.php
16. W. Grinton Berry ed., *Foxe's Book of Martyrs* (Power Books, Old Tappan, NJ; no date), Chp. II – "The Ten Primitive Persecutions"
17. Ibid., Chp. V – "An Account of the Inquisition"
18. Ibid., Chp. XIV – "An Account of the Persecutions in Great Britain and Ireland, Prior to the Reign of Queen Mary I"
19. http://www.bookrags.com/George_M%C3%BCller
20. P. L. Tan, op. cit., "Got to Be in Quebec," #1494
21. P. L. Tan, op. cit., "Setting the Sails," #1493
22. Stephen Abbott Northrop, D.D., *A Cloud of Witnesses* (American Heritage Ministries, Portland, OR; 1987), p. 287

#10 Changed Lives

1. Lee Strobel, *The Case for Christ*, (Zondervan Publishing House, Grand Rapids, MI; 1998), p. 16
2. E. Schuyler English, *H. A. Ironside – Ordained of the Lord* (Loizeaux Brothers, Neptune, NJ; 1976), pp. 99-101

#10 Changed Lives (cont.)

3. W. Grinton Berry ed., *Foxe's Book of Martyrs* (Power Books, Old Tappan, NJ; no date), p. 9
4. Warren Wiersbe, *The Bible Exposition Commentary, Vol. 1* (Victor Books, Wheaton, IL; 1989), p. 296
5. Charles Darwin, *The Voyage of the Beagle* (Harper & Row, New York, 1959), p. 141
6. P. L. Tan, op. cit., "Evolution," #1454
7. John P. Koster, Jr., op. cit., p. 50
8. http://www.bftw.org/index.cfm?page_id=147&expand=147
9. http://en.wikipedia.org/wiki/Huaorani
10. http://www.post-gazette.com/pg/06008/633940.stm
11. Warren Wiersbe, op. cit., p. 698

Is God Reason-able?

1. http://www.biblebb.com/files/MAC/sg2141.htm
2. P. L. Tan, op. cit.
3. Ibid.

Finding God and Being Found

1. Bertrand Russell, op. cit., "The Moral Argument"
2. Bertrand Russell, op. cit., "Fear, the Foundation of Religion"
3. Ibid.
4. W. J. Federer, op. cit., "Blaise Pascal"

Appendix I – Imprecise Logic

1. C. S. Lewis, *Miracles* (Harper Collins, London; 1947), p.166
2. http://en.wikipedia.org/wiki/David_Hume
3. http://plato.stanford.edu/entries/popper/#Life
4. Peter Singer, *Discovering Karl Popper* (The New York Review of Books, vol. 21, no. 7 (May 2, 1974)
5. Karl R. Popper, *The Logic of Scientific Discovery* (Routledge, 1st ed.; 2002), p. 31

Appendix IV – Prophecies of Christ's First Advent

1. http://www.bible-history.com/new_testament_cities_map/NTCITIESIsrael.htm
2. Alfred Edersheim, *The Life and Times of Jesus The Messiah* (Hendrickson Publishers, Peabody, MA; 1993), p. 42, 82
3. Sir Robert Anderson, *The Coming Prince*, (Hodder & Stoughton, London; 1881, reprinted by Kregel, Grand Rapids, MI; 1975)

Acknowledgements

The author is deeply indebted to all those who contributed to the publishing of *In Search of God*. Special thanks for the scientific and theological contributions of David Dunlap, Mark Kolchin, Steve Ratering, Ben Scripture, and Michael Windheuser. The editing work of Jane Biberstein and Larry Ondrejack is greatly appreciated. Thanks also to Jordan Henderson, Kathleen Henderson, David Lindstrom and David Miller for proofreading assistance, to Daveen Lidstone for cover picture selection, and to John Nicholson for cover design – I praise the Lord Jesus Christ for all of you!

Be Angry and Sin Not

If you mismanage anger, this book will guide you into better self-control. Be Angry And Sin Not tackles such questions as,

- *Why am I angry?
- *Should I be angry?
- *How do I control my angry feelings?
- *How can my anger benefit others and serve God?

Binding: Paper

Size: 5.5" X 8.0"

Page Count: 122 pages

Item #: B-7051

ISBN : 1897117051

Genre: Devotional/ Christian Living

Warren Henderson
Once an aerospace engineer, now serves the Lord with his wife Brenda in "full time" ministry. They are commended by Believers Bible Chapel in Rockford, Illinois. Warren is an itinerant Bible teacher and is involved in writing, evangelism, church planting and foreign missionary work.

GOSPEL FOLIO PRESS
I WILL PUBLISH THE NAME OF THE LORD

304 Killaly St. West | Port Colborne | ON | L3K 6A6 | Canada | 1 800 952 2382 | E-mail: info@gospelfolio.com | www.gospelfolio.com

BEHOLD THE SAVIOUR

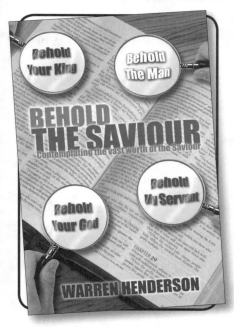

CONTEMPLATING THE VAST WORTH OF THE SAVIOUR

It was refreshing and encouraging to read a book, that did not focus on man's needs or a "how to" method for success. *Behold the Saviour* focuses on the Lord Jesus: His Godhood, human goodness and glories as revealed in the multi-faceted presentation of Holy Scriptures. For when we behold Him in His glory we are *"changed into the same image from glory to glory, even as by the Spirit of the Lord" (2 Cor. 3:18)*.
—Anonymous Pre-Publication Reviewer
(to Christ be the glory!)

Charles Haddon Spurgeon once said, "The more you know about Christ, the less you will be satisfied with superficial views of Him." The more we know of Christ, the more we will love and experience Him. This study has refreshed my soul. In the long hours of contemplating the vast worth that the Father attaches to every aspect of the Saviour's life, I have been encouraged to love Him more. If you're feeling a bit dry or spiritually despondent, *Behold the Saviour* afresh – and may the Holy Spirit ignite your passion for Christ and invigorate your ministry for Him. —Warren Henderson

Binding: **Paper**
Size: **5.5" X 8.5"**
Page Count: **208 pages**
Item #: **B-7272**
ISBN : **1-897117-27-2**
Genre: **Devotional**

Warren Henderson
An aerospace engineer, who now serves the Lord with his wife Brenda in "full time" ministry. They are commended by Believers Bible Chapel in Rockford, Illinois. Warren is an itinerant Bible teacher and is involved in writing, evangelism, and church planting.

GOSPEL FOLIO PRESS
I WILL PUBLISH THE NAME OF THE LORD

304 Killaly St. West | Port Colborne | ON | L3K 6A6 | Canada | 1 800 952 2382 | E-mail: info@gospelfolio.com | www.gospelfolio.com

HALLOWED BE THY NAME

WARREN HENDERSON

Revering CHRIST in a casual World

Is scriptural terminology important? Does wrong terminology tend to lead to erroneous Church practices? Do I ignorantly show disdain for the Lord's name by the way in which I address Him or speak of Him to others? What is the sin of blasphemy? Can a Christian blaspheme God today? These are some of the questions *Hallowed Be Thy Name* examines in detail. Our speech and behaviour reflect our heart's adoration for the Lord Jesus and, thus, directly affect our testimony of Him to the world. May God bestow us grace to *"buy the truth, and sell it not"* (Prov. 23:23), and may each one be subject to the *"good, and acceptable, and perfect, will of God"* (Rom. 12:2).

Binding: Paper

Size: 5.5" X 8.5"

Page Count: 160 pages

Item #: B-7450

ISBN : 1-897117-45-0

Genre: Christian Living

Warren Henderson
An aerospace engineer, who now serves the Lord with his wife Brenda in "full time" ministry. They are commended by Believers Bible Chapel in Rockford, Illinois. Warren is an itinerant Bible teacher and is involved in writing, evangelism, and church planting.

GOSPEL FOLIO PRESS
I WILL PUBLISH THE NAME OF THE LORD

304 Killaly St. West | Port Colborne | ON | L3K 6A6 | Canada | 1 800 952 2382 | E-mail: info@gospelfolio.com | www.gospelfolio.com